Together for the Common Good: Towards a National Conversation

Edited by
Peter McGrail and
Nicholas Sagovsky

scm press

© The editors and contributors 2015

Published in 2015 by SCM Press
Editorial office
3rd Floor
Invicta House
108–114 Golden Lane,
London
EC1Y OTG

SCM Press is an imprint of Hymns Ancient & Modern Ltd
(a registered charity)
13A Hellesdon Park Road
Norwich NR6 5DR, UK

www.scmpress.co.uk

Scripture quotations from the English Standard Version, Anglicized
Edition © Collins, London, 2003.

British Library Cataloguing in Publication data

A catalogue record for this book is available
from the British Library

978 0 334 05324 8

Typeset by Regent Typesetting, London
Printed and bound by
CPI Group (UK) Ltd, Croydon

Contents

Part 3: The Market and the Common Good

Acknowledgements

The editors of this volume are both members of the steering group of the Together for the Common Good Project (http://togetherforthecommon good.co.uk/). While not directly an activity of the project, this book would not have been written without the impetus provided by T4CG and the ongoing support of the steering group. The views expressed by the editors and the contributors do, nevertheless, remain entirely their own.

We must, first, acknowledge the consistent and generous support provided by Hymns Ancient & Modern and SCM Press for the T4CG Project and, specifically, for this book. We wish especially to thank Natalie Watson, Senior Commissioning Editor, for her encouragement and patience as we pursued our fascinating conversation with the contributors while keeping her waiting for action.

We also wish to thank CCLA Investment Management Ltd, and in particular Andrew Robinson, for hosting three study days at their extremely congenial office in the City of London. They provided an invaluable space in which the contributors to this volume could share ideas. It was remarkable that the things we were talking about related so closely to the ethical concerns of CCLA. Thank you, Andrew, for participating so fully in our discussions, making sure they were earthed in the realities of the financial and banking world which were all around us as we talked – just five minutes' walk from St Paul's Cathedral.

Finally, we must thank Liverpool Hope University, which also generously supported our meetings from their research budget.

Peter McGrail
Nicholas Sagovsky

Contributors

Philip Booth is Editorial and Programme Director of the Institute of Economic Affairs and Professor of Insurance and Risk Management at Cass Business School, City University, London. He is a fellow of the Institute of Actuaries and of the Royal Statistical Society. His publications include *Catholic Social Teaching and the Market Economy* (2nd edn, 2014, as editor and co-author), *Catholic Education in the West: Roots, Reality, and Revival* (2013, as co-author) and *Christian Perspectives on the Financial Crash* (2010, as editor). Philip was a school governor of a Catholic school for around 20 years.

Andrew Bradstock was during 2009–13 Howard Paterson Professor of Theology and Public Issues at the University of Otago, New Zealand. He is currently Secretary for Church and Society with the United Reformed Church and a member of the Joint Public Issues Team of the Baptist, Methodist and United Reformed Churches. He is a visiting professor at the University of Winchester and a member of the steering group of Together for the Common Good.

Malcolm Brown is Director of Mission and Public Affairs for the Archbishops' Council of the Church of England. He has been a parish priest and an industrial chaplain and has taught Christian Ethics and Practical Theology in a number of universities. He was Executive Secretary of the William Temple Foundation in Manchester from 1991–2000. He is the author of *Tensions in Christian Ethics* (SPCK, 2010) and editor of *Anglican Social Theology* (Church House Publishing, 2014).

Samuel Burgess is currently completing his DPhil at the University of Oxford. His thesis offers a theological defence of Burkean conservatism and argues for the continued relevance of Burke's thought to contemporary political questions. He was brought up in Bath and educated at Monkton Combe School before studying as an undergraduate at Durham and as an MPhil student at Cambridge.

Jonathan Chaplin is Director of the Kirby Laing Institute for Christian Ethics, Cambridge, a member of the Divinity Faculty of Cambridge University and Senior Fellow of Cardus, a Canadian Christian think-tank. He is a consultant researcher for the UK think-tank Theos and has written for *Guardian* CiF Belief. He has taught political theory and political theology in the UK, Canada and the Netherlands.

Maurice Glasman (Lord Glasman) is an English academic, social thinker and Labour life peer in the House of Lords. He is best known as the originator of Blue Labour, a term he coined in 2009. His research interests focus on the relationship between citizenship and faith and the limits of the state and the market. Author of *Unnecessary Suffering* (1996), he worked for ten years with London Citizens and through this developed an expertise in community organizing. He has a long-standing interest in Catholic Social Thought and was a speaker at the Together for the Common Good Conference in Liverpool.

Brian Griffiths (Lord Griffiths of Fforestfach) is a member of the boards of Goldman Sachs International and Goldman Sachs International Bank. He taught at the London School of Economics before becoming Professor of Banking and International Finance at the City University and Dean of the City University Business School. He was a director of the Bank of England from 1983–5. He left the Bank of England early to serve at 10 Downing Street as head of the Prime Minister's Policy Unit from 1985–1990. As special advisor to Margaret Thatcher, he was responsible for domestic policy-making and was a chief architect of the government's privatization and deregulation programmes. He is a member of the House of Lords Select Committee on Economic Affairs. Lord Griffiths was chairman of the Archbishop of Canterbury's Lambeth Fund and is chairman of Christian Responsibility in Public Affairs. He has written and lectured extensively on economic issues and the relationship of the Christian faith to economies and business and has published various books on monetary policy and Christian ethics.

Tehmina Kazi, Director of British Muslims for Secular Democracy since May 2009 and Executive Producer of the documentary film *Hidden Heart*, was also a freelance consultant for English PEN's 'Faith and Free Speech in Schools' project. She is a trustee of Hope Not Hate, an advisory board member of the Measuring Anti-Muslim Attacks project, an Inclusive Mosque Initiative committee member, and was a judge for the Accord Coalition's Inclusive Schools Award, 2014. She was named as one of the

BBC's 100 Women in October 2013 and 2014 and held the Eric Lane Fellowship at Clare College, Cambridge in January–March 2014. She is a Centenary Young Fellow of the RSA.

Clifford Longley is the author of *Just Money: How Catholic Social Teaching can Redeem Capitalism* published by the think-tank Theos and available at www.theosthinktank.co.uk, where a printed version can also be ordered. He formerly wrote about religious affairs for *The Times* and the *Daily Telegraph* and is now editorial consultant, leader writer and columnist at *The Tablet*, the international Catholic weekly. He has written a number of books and contributed regularly to the BBC Radio 4's *Thought for the Day* and *Moral Maze* programmes. He was the principal author of *The Common Good and the Catholic Church's Social Teaching* published by the Catholic Bishops' Conference of England and Wales in 1996. He was awarded a Lambeth Master of Letters in 2012.

Peter McGrail is a priest of Liverpool Roman Catholic Archdiocese and Associate Professor of Catholic Studies at Liverpool Hope University, where he is also head of the Department of Theology, Philosophy and Religious Studies. He has had several years' parish experience, and was director of the Department for Pastoral Formation (1996–2003) in Liverpool Archdiocese. He is the author of two books exploring the gaps between formal liturgy and life. He is a member of the Liturgy Committee of the Catholic Bishops Conference of England and Wales and chair of its Liturgical Formation subcommittee. He is the Roman Catholic observer on the Liturgical Commission of the Church of England. He is a member of the steering group of Together for the Common Good.

Esther D. Reed is Associate Professor in Theology and Religion at the University of Exeter, where she is also Director of the Network for Religion in Public Life. Her current research delves into questions of theology and international law, narrative theology in religious education and the theology of work. She has most recently published *Theology for International Law* (2013). She was also a co-author of the Christian Aid Report, *Tax for the Common Good: A Study of Tax and Morality* (October 2014).

Patrick Riordan SJ has taught political philosophy at Heythrop College, University of London, since 2002, having formerly worked at the Milltown Institute of Theology and Philosophy in Dublin. His current research interests are religion in public life, the philosophy of justice and the common good. His latest book, *Global Ethics and Global Common Goods*, is published by Bloomsbury. Other publications include *A Grammar of the Common Good: Speaking of Globalization* (2008) and *Philosophical Perspectives on People Power* (2001). He has also published articles on human dignity, natural law, business ethics and the just war theory in the context of terrorism.

Anna Rowlands is Lecturer in Contemporary Catholic Studies and Deputy Director of the Centre for Catholic Studies in the Department of Theology and Religion at Durham University. As a theologian she has worked closely with CAFOD, the Citizens Organising Foundation and the Caritas Social Action Network. She is founding Chair of a new UK network for academics and practitioners involved in the development of Catholic Social Thought and practice.

Nicholas Sagovsky holds professorial posts in theology at two ecumenical universities: Liverpool Hope and Roehampton. An Anglican, he has been a member of the Anglican Roman Catholic International Commission (ARCIC) since 1992. In 2008, he published a study entitled *Christian Tradition and the Practice of Justice*. He is on the steering group of Together for the Common Good.

Jon E. Wilson is a historian at King's College London, where his research and teaching focuses on politics and government in South Asia and Britain. His book on British power in India, *India Conquered. Britain's Raj and the Chaos of Empire*, will be published by Simon and Schuster in 2016. He is also a Labour activist and writes a weekly column for labourlist.net.

Foreword

As a young student rabbi in the 1970s, just over a year into my rabbinical studies, I was sent to Liverpool as student rabbi to its then Liberal (now Reform) congregation. It was a steep learning curve for someone raised in a politically left-wing but undeniably socially cosy northwest London Jewish home. It was before the riots of 1981. Tensions in the city were palpable. I loved Liverpool then and still do, with its civic pride and splendour, but also its sense of itself. It was a city fallen on hard times, with ethnic and sectarian tensions and real concern, often clumsily articulated if at all, about its future, and especially the future of its young. Into that somewhat fissile arena the two bishops, David Sheppard and (Archbishop) Derek Worlock, arrived in 1975 and 1976 respectively. They both, in different ways, felt a mission to work with the poor. They became friends, colleagues, fellow campaigners, but above all they became the leaders of a city in turmoil and distress, and through their efforts, across divides, they helped heal the wounds and inspired others to root out poverty, ethnic tensions, sectarianism and lack of aspiration. This volume is rooted in their lives and hopes, their work and inspiration. Their vision of the common good informs the writing of all the contributors, and speaks to us all, in all our traditions.

These days, when you walk from one cathedral to the other down the aptly named Hope Street, you can sense hope in the air, something brought by these two great men, gifted and inspired spiritual leaders, and passed on to thousands upon thousands of others. The memorial to David Sheppard, whose ashes are buried in 'his' cathedral, quotes Jeremiah 29.7: 'Seek the welfare of the city where I have sent you … and pray to the Lord on its behalf.' The full text is somewhat different:

Build houses and settle down; plant gardens and eat what they produce. Marry and have sons and daughters; find wives for your sons and give your daughters in marriage, so that they too may have sons and daughters. Increase in number there; do not decrease. Also, seek the peace and prosperity of the city to which I have carried you into exile. Pray to the Lord for it, because if it prospers, you too will prosper.

Jeremiah was not necessarily popular with the exiles for encouraging the peaceful activities of garden planting and house building: 'By the waters of Babylon we sat down and wept,' sings the Psalmist in Psalm 137. Weeping, gnashing of teeth, maybe rioting were nearer the mark, rather than the peaceful construction of houses (in an area of many slums and poorly maintained, though once magnificent houses) and planting of gardens in an area of few green spaces and even fewer *safe* green spaces. The two bishops were inspired by Jeremiah and encouraged activities that led to stability and a sense of ownership and pride in the area, while campaigning against the injustices and horrors of widespread unemployment, poor access to legal remedies, and a life of deprivation in an area of little hope.

Both believed in practical Christianity and, as a Jew from my practical tradition, I can only applaud them, since practical help was and is still needed, as well as healing sectarian divides. They led worship together publicly in a sectarian city. The theological divides were *de minimis* compared with the practical virtues of working, praying, fundraising and campaigning for the common good. They appeared together in pubs and on street corners. They appealed for calm, and together they promised to help rebuild and recreate with hope and opportunity. And they brought healing.

These fascinating chapters address what that means. They are the product of meetings and discussion, practical action and prayer. And they seek to restate the concept of the common good as just as relevant to us now as it was in Sheppard and Worlock's Liverpool. And there is much of great importance to learn from them. Yet we now need its contributors to work on Volume 2, with an account through faith eyes of the practical application of this idea. Liverpool is a happier, more thriving place than it was in the 1970s and 80s, in no small measure thanks to the work and sheer massive presence of Liverpool Hope University and the other Liverpool universities. But what will the students do when they are finished? How much can religious leaders, and indeed the tenets of faith more widely, contribute in reducing widespread youth unemployment, growing health inequalities, growing financial inequalities and the growing presence of food banks in the city and every city? My tradition is a uniquely practical one. As this volume debates the issues, I long for Volume 2 to focus on the practical role of religious organizations in righting some of these wrongs? Could it cite that great Jewish teacher Maimonides (1135–1204) in his description of charity as going from the lowest order of giving inadequate amounts, grumpily, to the highest of giving in such a way that the recipient never needs to ask for charity again? Can the faith communities focus on that concept of that charity, not the caritas of Christian understanding but the *tzedakah*, the social justice of Judaism, in evening up and resetting the balance? And can the faiths examine the duty of older, more senior people in supporting and encouraging the young? The common good, differently expressed, can be found in all our faiths. But the question remains of how it should be made real, who needs to take ownership of it, and how easy it is to make a difference when public attitudes seem to be shying away from any such concept. This book gives us brilliant insights into how faith and other leaders think of what can and should be done. Now we need Volume 2 to complete the story, with a practical toolkit, in the wake of David Sheppard and Derek Worlock, in whose memory this volume was put together, and who still have so many lessons for us all.

Rabbi Baroness Julia Neuberger DBE

Introduction

This book is the product of many conversations about the common good. It springs from the ministry of the Anglican Bishop David Sheppard and the Roman Catholic Archbishop Derek Worlock, working 'together for the common good' in Liverpool from the mid-1970s to the death of Worlock in 1996. In 2013, a conference was held at Liverpool Hope University, of which they were, in effect, joint founders, to celebrate their legacy and to discern how their hugely varied agenda can inspire those with similar hopes and concerns today. In that same year, Jorge Bergoglio had been elected as Pope (taking the name of Francis) and Justin Welby had been enthroned as Archbishop of Canterbury. Each brought to the life of the Church a new agenda (including a new commitment to the needs of the poor, especially migrants, and a recognition, after the financial crisis of 2007–08, of the need in all our communities for banks that can be trusted). Both speak frequently about reconciliation and the common good.

The conference left two key questions: 'What is the common good?' and 'How can we work for it together?' Both questions have been pursued by the steering group of the Together for the Common Good project, the participants at the conference, those, including parliamentarians, who have joined in 'common good' conversations, and the contributors to this book. Before beginning to write, most of the contributors were able to meet for three specially convened study days. The chapters we have produced reflect the discussion both at the conference and on the study days, but they are not a record of the conference, nor have the contributors read them formally to one another. They are the product of, and are intended to contribute to, a continuing conversation.

A word, first, about 'conversation': Karl Marx famously said, 'The philosophers have only interpreted the world in various ways; the point is to change it.'[1] The chapters here represent various attempts, from a UK perspective, to interpret the world in which we currently live. In doing so,

---

1 Eleventh thesis on Feuerbach, quoted, for example, in David McLellan, *The Thought of Karl Marx: An Introduction*, 2nd edn, London: Macmillan, 1984.

they draw on the riches of an interpretative tradition that goes back to the Greeks (Aristotle) and incorporates wisdom from the Scriptures of Jews, Christians and Muslims. This is, however, not intended to be an exercise in armchair interpretation. The word 'conversation' (meaning an exchange of views) has the same root as the verb to 'convert', to 'turn'. 'Turning' is what the Jewish Scriptures again and again call for from a people that has lost its way in a moral wilderness. 'See–judge–*act*' was the motto chosen by Cardinal Cardijn for the Young Christian Workers and then adopted more widely throughout the Catholic Church. If we accept the imperative of action, then we must look for the action to be based both on a clear-eyed, undeceived recognition of the reality by which we are confronted (something for which free media are vital), and on wise judgement about a good way forward (something for which democratic participation based on inclusive education is also essential). To say this is to say something about the quality of 'conversation' which must take place before there can be well-judged action which serves the common good. Conversation of this quality must be patient, attentive, well-informed and robust. It must be rooted in the needs and experience of local communities. It must be rooted in action and lead to action. Conversation of this quality is intended to change the world, in a transformative way to serve the common good.

Sheppard and Worlock

Sheppard and Worlock might not have put it quite like this. They tended to use other language in their published works, but their concerns were similar. They wanted change. They were both intelligent, educated, and gifted Christian leaders who set out to serve the people of Liverpool at what proved to be a time of crisis. This is why there is so much to be learned from studying the way they worked: understanding what they were able to achieve and acknowledging what they could not achieve.

The city to which they came was at a low point, as were other parts of Merseyside. Long-term economic problems stemmed primarily from the historic role of the port. Its success in the nineteenth century made Liverpool an imperial city; by the end of the twentieth its decline left major economic, political and social problems. The port had dominated the labour market, with long-term effects, because jobs were mainly semi- and unskilled, casual, irregular and poorly paid. Manufacturing never developed substantially so there was no core of skilled workers, which reduced the city's capacity to attract newer, higher-technology industries. The pattern of ownership was also a factor: it was a branch plant economy where much of the ownership and control was in the hands of a small number of largely absentee employers.

There was a history of sectarian tension between Catholics and Protestants, which had its roots in the only partial assimilation of the Irish Catholic immigrant community. Across the twentieth century, on the other hand, the city experienced a persistent loss of population: for a long period, on average, 10,000 people per year left the city. It was often the younger and more skilled who left to search for economic opportunities elsewhere. There was thus a growing imbalance between the large city infrastructure and a declining population base. Unemployment was consistently 50 per cent higher than the national average. The combination of selective migration and the level of worklessness clearly contributed to social exclusion, with high numbers living in poverty and suffering the attendant problems. There were notably vulnerable groups, including Liverpool's black community. Many black people were from families who had been in the city over several generations but the long-standing position of ethnic minorities had not increased their ability to enter the economic and social mainstream of the city. Their unemployment rate was disproportionately high and they were concentrated in a specific area of the city with very poor housing conditions.[2]

Local political forces also affected the city's capacity to respond to its problems. The 1970s and early 1980s saw a succession of minority and coalition administrations, so that while the council was the city's largest employer, the councillors could not give a clear political or strategic lead. By the time the Labour Party took majority control in 1983, it was dominated in the city by the Militant Tendency, which clashed dramatically with the Conservative-controlled national government about the level of financial resources being provided for services and especially the public housing programme. This confrontation attracted national headlines over a number of years, aggravating the city's existing structural social and economic problems, dragging down Liverpool's reputation and deterring external investors. This was the context in which Sheppard and Worlock had to work out their ministry.

David was the first to be appointed to Liverpool, in 1975. An avowed evangelical, Anglican Christian, he had captained England at cricket and developed his leadership skills further at the Mayflower Family Centre in London's Docklands. He then succeeded the probing New Testament

---

2 Michael Parkinson and Hilary Russell, 'Economic Attractiveness and Social Exclusion: the Case of Liverpool', paper prepared for the report *EUROPE 2000+* for the European Commission, Liverpool: European Institute for Urban Affairs, Liverpool John Moores University, 1994.

scholar, John Robinson, as Bishop of Woolwich. David's questions were not so much about how to *understand* the Christian gospel as about how to *communicate* it in and through appropriate social action. His aspirations for urban renewal had been evident since the publication of *Built as a City* in 1974.[3] In 1983, his Liverpool experience, which was rooted in the life of the city's diverse and often struggling communities, was reflected in his book *Bias to the Poor*.[4]

Derek was appointed Archbishop of Liverpool in 1976. The frequently quoted story that he came with a specific brief from Pope Paul VI 'to work with the poor and unemployed, and to prevent Liverpool becoming another Belfast'[5] may well be apocryphal, but it appropriately summarizes his personal sense of mission. For 20 years, he had served as secretary to successive Cardinal Archbishops of Westminster before himself becoming a bishop, late in 1965, in Portsmouth. He was deeply influenced by the Second Vatican Council (1962–5), attending every session, contributing to the drafting of the Decree on the Apostolate of the Laity (*Apostolicam actuositatem*, 1965) and to the schema that eventually became the Pastoral Constitution on the Church in the Modern World (*Gaudium et spes*, 1965). He was the first new English diocesan bishop to be ordained after the closure of Vatican II, and for 11 years sought faithfully to implement its teaching. When he moved north to Liverpool, he was regarded as a post-Conciliar progressive, and also as a safe pair of hands. It was in Liverpool that there took place in 1980, a National Pastoral Congress. This was an initiative by the Bishops' Conference, in which Derek played a leading role, to assess the implementation of Vatican II and to develop a strategy for the future in which the voice of the laity might better be heard. In 1991, the Bishops' Conference arranged another national event in Liverpool, once again with significant lay participation. This was a conference in celebration of the hundredth anniversary of Pope Leo XIII's encyclical *Rerum novarum*, 1891. The Pope had sought to steer a way between the capitalist, laissez-faire market economy of the industrial revolution and the largely atheist socialism of the workers' movement. His call for new forms of social solidarity is now regarded as the fountainhead of Catholic Social Teaching. From the 1950s, Derek had been sustained and influenced by that teaching, most concretely as it was lived out by the Young Christian Workers movement; to 'see–judge–act', and to give

---

3 David Sheppard, *Built as a City: God and the Urban World Today*, London: Hodder and Stoughton, 1974.

4 David Sheppard, *Bias to the Poor*, London: Hodder and Stoughton, 1983.

5 http://togetherforthecommongood.co.uk/background/articles/the-sheppard-worlock-years.html.

priority to care for the poor, was in his bloodstream. That the 1991 Conference took place in his adopted city – where it was hosted by the forerunner of Liverpool Hope University – must, as the Catholic press noted at the time, have been a cause of deep personal pleasure to Derek.[6]

As soon as Derek arrived in Liverpool, David reached out to him in friendship. The initiative was reciprocated in the spirit of Vatican II, which speaks of non-Catholic Christians as 'brethren', albeit 'separated'. For the two bishops, it quickly became a priority to make time for prayer and study together. Their best-known book, a reflection on what had become an iconic partnership, was entitled *Better Together: Christian Partnership in a Hurt City.*[7] From the time spent together, and also with David's wife Grace, in prayer and reflection, came strength to act at a moment's notice in situations of sometimes bitter conflict.

They arrived in a city where the churches had already formed an Ecumenical Council. In 1982, the leaders of the Merseyside churches recommitted themselves to working together while respecting one another's traditions, and in 1985 entered into a covenant to this effect. It was on this basis that Derek and David were able to work so closely with a single Free Church Moderator, first John Williamson of the United Reformed Church and then the Methodist John Newton. Behind the effective action of all the church leaders in the public arena lay bonds of friendship and regular communication.

The challenges of the Liverpool years have been well documented.[8] In 1981, severe rioting broke out in Toxteth. This was not the old sectarian violence, but a new expression of poverty, of tensions running high in the black community, of the human cost of unemployment and distrust of the police. For several days, Derek and David were present with local clergy on the streets, looking for ways to restore calm and broker understanding between the largely black community and the police. Out of the riots came the founding of the Liverpool 8 Law Centre. The rioting had been severe enough to be discussed in Cabinet. We now know that Mrs Thatcher wanted to cut government funding for Liverpool, but was dissuaded by Michael Heseltine, who had been approached behind the scenes by Derek and David. Heseltine subsequently became Minister for Liverpool and spent time in the city drawing up plans for urban redevelopment.

---

6 *The Tablet*, 22 April 1989, p. 3.

7 David Sheppard and Derek Worlock, *Better Together: Christian Partnership in a Hurt City*, London: Hodder and Stoughton, 1988.

8 For instance, in David Sheppard and Derek Worlock, *With Hope in our Hearts: God's Reconciling Love reflected in a unique Partnership*, London: Hodder and Stoughton, 1994; David Sheppard, *Steps Along Hope Street*, London: Hodder and Stoughton, 2002; and Clifford Longley, *The Worlock Archive*, London/New York: Geoffrey Chapman, 2000.

A happier landmark event was the visit to Liverpool by Pope John Paul II in 1982. It is a measure of how far the Catholics and the Anglicans in the city had moved from their sectarian past that the Pope was applauded all the way up the aisle of the Anglican cathedral and the entire length of Hope Street which links the Anglican and Catholic cathedrals (and after which Liverpool Hope University is named). Derek and David were not in the academic sense ecumenists, but they welcomed the affirmation of ecumenism at Vatican II. What they could do and what they could affirm together they did, but they remained loyal to their separated traditions. Publicly, and especially in times of crisis, they were seen as standing together, with leaders of other Christian traditions, in support of the people of their city.

In 1985, largely as a response to the rioting that broke out in a number of British cities in 1981, *Faith in the City* was published.[9] This was the report of the Archbishop of Canterbury's Commission on Urban Priority Areas (areas of urban deprivation), a commission of which David Sheppard was vice-chairman. It was addressed to 'Church and Nation', calling for action by both to address the multiple problems of urban deprivation. Chapters were devoted to precisely those issues with which David and Derek were so deeply engaged: first, to the renewal of the urban church ('developing the people of God') and then to the renewal of the nation, with chapters on urban policy (and governance); poverty, employment and work; housing; health; social care and community work; education and young people; order and law. The report was, as is well known, dismissed by an unnamed member of the Cabinet as 'pure Marxist theology', a remark which ensured its success. Derek's concern for the urban poor, those affected by the multiple dimensions of urban deprivation and disenfranchisement, was affirmed by *Sollicitudo rei socialis*, published in 1987. Pope John Paul II wrote:

> I wish to appeal with simplicity and humility to everyone, to all men and women without exception. I wish to ask them to be convinced of the seriousness of the present moment and of each one's individual responsibility, and to implement – by the way they live as individuals and as families, by the use of their resources, *by their civic activity*, by contributing to economic and political decisions and by personal commitment to national and international undertakings – the measures inspired by solidarity and love of preference for the poor.[10]

---

9 Archbishop of Canterbury's Commission on Urban Priority Areas, *Faith in the City: A Call for Action by Church and Nation*, London: Church House Publishing, 1985.

10 John Paul II, *Sollicitudo rei socialis*, 1987, 47 (our emphasis).

There were times during the Sheppard–Worlock years when the exercise of their shared spiritual leadership was explicitly called for. In 1985, 39 people were killed in a stampede at the Heysel Stadium in Belgium before a Liverpool–Juventus match. Most were Juventus fans from Turin. Derek and David were specifically invited by the leaders of the Liverpool city council to represent the city on a visit to Turin. Later, they led a noisy memorial service at Anfield, Liverpool FC's home ground, for those who had died in the tragedy. Four years later, 96 Liverpool fans were killed at the Hillsborough Stadium in Sheffield. The next day a Requiem Mass, to which Derek specifically invited David and other church leaders, was held at the Catholic Metropolitan Cathedral and a week later they jointly led a memorial service at Liverpool's Anglican Cathedral, both services packed with thousands of mourners.

Another strand in the work that Derek and David did together came from their engagement with issues affecting business and employment. During the Thatcher years, and especially after the bitter and destructive conflict of the miners' strike in 1984–5, there was very considerable concern about the levels of unemployment and distress generated as British industry was restructured to become more competitive and open to market forces. The bishops together founded the Michaelmas Group as a forum where senior decision-makers in the city, especially business leaders, could meet and talk about their common concerns for Merseyside. In 1995, the Council of Churches in Britain and Ireland undertook a major study, which was published in 1997 as *Unemployment and the Future of Work*.[11] It argued that the need was not just for work, but for 'good work', and that the aim of there being 'good work' for everyone was not to be written off as impossible. David was chair of the sponsoring body for the study, and Derek, until his death, was also a member of the committee.

Derek was diagnosed with cancer in 1992. He died in 1996 at the age of 75 and is buried in the Metropolitan Cathedral. David retired in 1997 and also died at the age of 75, in 2005. His ashes are buried in Liverpool Cathedral, under a memorial which quotes the book of Jeremiah: 'Seek the welfare of the city where I have sent you ... and pray to the Lord on its behalf' (Jer. 29.7).

---

11 Council of Churches for Britain and Ireland, *Unemployment and the Future of Work*, London: CCBI, 1997.

Claiming the legacy

The first aim of the conference at Liverpool Hope in September 2013 was to document and to reflect on the legacy of the Sheppard–Worlock years, while there are still people who remember them well. The second was to ask how that legacy can teach and inspire us today. In 1996, the Roman Catholic Bishops of England and Wales published a pre-election document on *The Common Good and the Catholic Church's Social Teaching*, which remains perhaps the best short statement on the common good available today.[12] It was addressed to Roman Catholics, but, as with the documents of Vatican II, it gave to many non-Catholics a phrase they had been looking for. With the collapse of Communism, and then the fall of the Berlin Wall in 1989, there had been a widespread free-market triumphalism with which many Christians were unhappy. Once the euphoria of the moment had subsided, many could see the growing inequality, the levels of unemployment, the dis-ease in communities that were ill-equipped to compete in a post-Communist world. It is this, the social cost of marketization, that Pope John Paul II addressed in *Centesimus annus* (1991), in which he embraced the new freedoms of the post-Communist world, albeit with considerable caution. Neither the state socialism of the left nor the market individualism of the right was held uncritically to offer a good way forward. In the British electoral moment of 1997, a clear and attractive presentation of Catholic Social Teaching, which emphasized both the dignity of the human person and the importance of the common good, proved extremely welcome. The tragedy was that it was offered in the name of the Catholic Church alone, and not in the name of all the churches.

Since that time, the phrase 'common good' has been current not only within but far beyond the Catholic Church. Pope Francis has made frequent reference to it in the context of Catholic Social Teaching, but, as Malcolm Brown notes, it had been made a specific priority by the Church of England for the five-year Synodical period from 2010 and then strongly endorsed by Justin Welby on taking up his role as Archbishop. It is because of this priority that the Church of England's commitment to the common good was debated and unanimously affirmed by the General Synod in July 2014.[13] It is now clear, as it was not in the time of Sheppard and Worlock,

---

12 Catholic Bishops' Conference of England and Wales, *The Common Good and the Catholic Church's Social Teaching*, Manchester: Gabriel Communications, 1996.

13 The motion passed by 299:0 (with two abstentions) was as follows: 'That this Synod: (a) affirm the theological imperative of serving the common good; (b) commend the practical activities which serve the common good, exemplified by our parishes, dioceses and the NCIs [National Church Institutions], and encourage their further development; and (c) call

that Anglicans as well as Catholics can use the language of the common good with confidence. What has been less clear is whether this applies to evangelical Christians, members of the Free Churches, Jews, Muslims and those of no religious faith. This is one question we set out to explore in this book, with the help of representatives of various faith traditions, such as Jonathan Chaplin and Esther Reed. All our contributors, from the resources of different traditions, affirm – and show why they affirm – the importance of the common good.

Since the time of Sheppard and Worlock much has changed. Market capitalism is here to stay and the welfare state is in an extended process of transformation into what has been called a 'market state'.[14] The extent and depth of that transformation are by no means fully clear. The shape of the future state depends upon the effective regulation of the market, levels of taxation and public spending, and the degree to which there will be pushback from those who are committed to developing new forms of democratic engagement, both at the national and the local level. It is also not clear how the green agenda will play out: whether the market can deliver the environmental safeguards and direction-setting, especially in the generation of power, that are necessary. In Part 3 of this book, Brian Griffiths and Maurice Glasman explore some of these questions.

New questions have arisen since the 1980s about the role of the state. The confidence in the state as a benign provider which led to the creation of the 'welfare state' has been severely dented. It no longer seems obvious, especially after 1989, that the state should be running the coal and steel industries, the generation of power, the transport system, the prisons or the Post Office. The one sector of national life (apart from the emergency services) which still to a large extent in the popular mind stands above this shift towards the private sector is the NHS. The paradox is that since the banking crisis of 2008 it seems obvious, as it did not before, that if there is to be confidence in the financial system, which is fundamental for social stability, for trade and so for human wellbeing, the state must be prepared to step in as lender of last resort. It is incumbent on the state, at a time when it has in so many ways been designedly losing power, to make sure there is enough 'good money' for all.

Perhaps the biggest change since the time of Sheppard and Worlock is the IT revolution, with its huge impact on the labour market, on levels

---

on churches at a local level, along with diocesan and national Church bodies, to ensure by word and action that the political parties are challenged to promote the common good when drawing up their manifestos for the 2015 General Election.' See www.churchofengland.org/media-centre/news/2014/07/general-synod-saturday-afternoon.aspx.

14 The phrase is Philip Bobbitt's. See *The Shield of Achilles*, New York: Knopf, 2002.

of inequality (inequality of access to communication and so inequality of wealth), on modes of solidarity (promoting simultaneously both individualism and networking) and, since the 'war on terror' and the rise of jihadist extremism, loss of freedom. The banking sector has been one in which IT-enhanced individualism has combined with frenetic market competition to produce noxiously irresponsible behaviour. The decline of participation in a whole range of activities which once promoted civic solidarity and conviviality continues apace. On the other hand, the incontrovertible evidence that we face an environmental crisis, and so a crisis of power-generation from non-renewable fuels, must draw us together as it is clear that everyone is affected by changing weather-patterns and there can be no immediate technical fix.

These are the sort of issues which we need to debate in terms of the common good. We dare not leave unchallenged political rhetoric which assumes that the populace cares for nothing but its own self-interest. Each of us is faced by questions about the trustworthiness of the institutions that make for a culture and communities in which all can flourish: when we speak about education, the countryside, transport, employment, policing, health or housing, it is not adequate to say, 'We're all customers and consumers now.' If we are not, what are we? It is the premise of the chapters in this book that we are all potentially participants in a national conversation (which of course must take local forms) about how we can and should live together. It is this, and not simply putting a cross on a piece of paper, which makes for a healthy and effective democracy.

What, then, is the common good?

The philosopher, W. B. Gallie, speaks about an 'essentially contested concept', by which he means a concept which contains, rather than brings to an end, a discussion.[15] Words such as freedom, democracy and justice set up a discussion around *what kind of* freedom, democracy or justice we have in mind. Only as we analyse these concepts can we discuss the merits of looking at them one way or the other. We suggest that 'the common good' is like this. We know broadly what it means – *a good that is shared, being the sole property of neither one party nor another* – but how we identify what such a good might be and how we speak about the 'sharing' is up for debate. The term comes from Aristotle, whose idea of 'the good' was formed by his experience of the Greek *polis* in which, as

---

15 W. B. Gallie, *Philosophy and the Historical Understanding*, London: Chatto and Windus, 1964, pp. 157–91.

Patrick Riordan reminds us, ideas of the good and the true and the beautiful were shared to a high degree. Aristotle's ideas of what makes a 'good' city, a 'good' society and a 'good' person are all interwoven and are based upon the premise that human beings are social animals. Aristotle speaks of human beings as made for social life ('social animals'), for life in the *polis* ('political animals'), for life in partnership ('animals made for life in common'). For Aristotle, it is incumbent upon human beings to recognize that this is what we are and, starting from this as a 'given', to work out how we best fulfil the demands and opportunities of being human: how we cultivate the life of virtue.[16] This Aristotelian approach is reflected in the thinking of Thomas Aquinas and, among modern philosophers, Alasdair MacIntyre.

John Rawls, author of *A Theory of Justice* and probably the most important political philosopher of the twentieth century, began from a position that was not dissimilar, though more indebted to post-Enlightenment individualism than what has been called 'Aristotelian social democracy'.[17] He aimed, by a thought experiment in the spirit of Kant, to work out ground rules for 'fairness' in society rather than for 'goodness', both individual and social. What he wanted to avoid was some form of utilitarian calculus, whereby the 'good' of 'fairness' was equated with the greatest happiness of the greatest number. For him, no human being could be regarded as expendable for the sake of the happiness of others. There can be no trade-offs of the good of the majority against the suffering of a minority (an ever-present danger for all forms of utilitarianism, which prioritizes 'the greatest good of the greatest number' and is often the form taken by state action, implemented by bureaucracies). However, he had to recognize that others would not agree with him and that many democrats would take a majoritarian view of the good. This debate goes to the heart of being human: on what basis can we say that *all* human beings are of such worth that none can be sacrificed against their will for reasons of state or for the good of the majority? For Rawls, who thought of himself as an unbeliever, the transcendent value of every individual was a matter of faith. He spoke about 'deliberative democracy' in which issues are discussed openly and fully by all until consensus is reached. His concern was for effective social and political structures that would sustain a 'fair' society: this was as far as he could go towards any idea of obviously

---

16 See, for example, S. Everson (ed.), *Aristotle, The Politics*, Cambridge: Cambridge University Press, 1988.

17 See John Rawls, *A Theory of Justice*, revd edn, Oxford/New York: Oxford University Press, 1999; Martha Nussbaum, 'Aristotelian Social Democracy', in R. Bruce Douglass et al. (eds), *Liberalism and the Good*, New York/London: Routledge, 1990, pp. 203–52.

shared political 'good'. For Rawls, as Tehmina Kazi notes, the common good refers to 'certain general conditions that are in an approximate sense equally to everyone's advantage'. One example would be the rule of law. Another, as discussed by Philip Booth, would be a robust and differentiated system of education that respects the consciences of all.

Aristotle begins somewhere else. Like Rawls, he is concerned with right human relations. He begins, however, not with society as a whole but with the intimate relations among family and friends. For him, friendship is a good in which human beings *share*: David and Derek spoke of a 'Christian partnership'. For each of the individuals who are friends there is simultaneously *both* the (subjective) good of the friendship *and* the (transcendent) good of the shared friendship in which each of the friends participates but which is the property of neither. The same would be true of a language, a culture or a project in which people share, but which is the property of no single individual. In this sense, a family, a village, a city or a nation could be seen as a project in which human beings share or participate, but which transcends the life and skills of any individual. The 'good' family or city or nation is robust enough to contain the conflicts that inevitably arise, so that the members find a way through the conflict to an agreement which all can accept. Where there is true consensus, that consensus is indeed a *common* good. Where there is a history of conflict-and-resolution we can speak of a 'tradition', like that of the common law. For a thinker such as Burke, as Sam Burgess argues, this is how the good society is constituted. Shared tradition is in itself a common good. For others, though, shared tradition can all too easily become oppressive. For the sake of a renewed and more inclusive common good it must, as Jon Wilson argues, be challenged and remade through vigorous argument. This is the essence of the feminist critique against the patriarchal nature of the traditions received in the West. We live in a post-revolutionary age, when the bonds of tradition have been loosed for the sake of a greater common good, but we are not yet comfortable with what that post-post-revolutionary common good might be.

If we cannot *define* 'the common good', is the concept so general in its scope as to be useless when we need to discern a way forward through specific action? We think not. We think it is possible to point to instances of the common good – even if we cannot say what they all have in common. We have already mentioned a number: a robust banking system, the rule of law, stable weather patterns (to which we might add clean water), opportunities for good work, the universal health care provided by the National Health Service (not forgetting competent and trustworthy public health provision), education which includes training in critical thinking. To these we must add a market which enables people to buy and sell in a way that satisfies all parties. We can see how the examples from banking, the rule of law, the weather, employment, the NHS and education all make for human flourishing. What we cannot always see is how that good end can best be achieved. The same is true of the market: there is huge disagreement about the extent to which, say, international trade is actually free, and to what extent it should be regulated by states 'to ensure its freedom' (for such regulation may be the very means of its being skewed towards particular interests, such as those of the nation-state or multinational cartels). To take the example of banking: should the 'banks that are too big to fail' be broken up so that there is more competition both in investment banking and on the high street? Is that the best way for government to serve the common good of its citizens? Or would that be to put UK banking at such a disadvantage internationally that it would not be in a position to survive? The dilemmas at the heart of these questions are easy to see, but it is far harder to judge what may be the best way forward.

This is why, as Anna Rowlands and Andrew Bradstock argue, a searching and inclusive conversation needs to take place before action is attempted prematurely. In the absence of such a conversation, it is virtually certain that any action would serve those who have the dominant interests in the conversation: in a conflicted situation the interests of the powerful would prevail and the interests of the poor would be overlooked. Who will listen to the poor and who will speak for the common good? This is the question addressed to all people of goodwill, with or without religious faith, by Catholic Social Teaching. In his book, *Mammon's Kingdom: An Essay on Britain, Now*, David Marquand writes:

> For centuries, the nations of the British archipelago have been part of what Edward Gibbon called the 'great republic' of Europe. The legacies of ancient Athens and republican Rome can still be detected in our political culture. Those of ancient Jerusalem, medieval Christendom and early modern Europe still colour our moral imaginations. The teaching of the Hebrew prophets and of Aristotle, Augustine and Aquinas, to mention only a few, are part of our inheritance. We won't rediscover the language of the common good or resolve the crisis of the moral economy that broke in 2007–8 if we close our minds to their legacy – or to that of the Muslim scholars whose commentaries on Aristotle left an enduring impression on Christian thought.[18]

---

18 David Marquand, *Mammon's Kingdom: An Essay on Britain, Now*, London: Allen Lane, 2014, p. 184.

This more or less describes the shape of the discussion in Part 2 of this book. Marquand goes on:

> We need a wide-ranging national conversation, across the boundaries of party, doctrine and tradition, about the economic, political and moral crisis that has engulfed us: a twenty-first-century equivalent of the nineteenth-century debate on 'the Condition of England Question' ... The conversation should not be an end in itself. The ultimate objective is change, change not talk. But there can be no worthwhile change without a new public philosophy; and the last, best hope for discovering such a philosophy lies in talking together and learning from one another.[19]

Which precisely expresses what the Together for the Common Good project as a whole seeks to do, and what the writers have tried to do in this volume. We want to give impetus to a 'wide-ranging conversation' in which 'the ultimate objective is change, change not talk'.

Where the editors would differ from Marquand is that we approach this task in the spirit of Sheppard and Worlock. We see them as constantly, untiringly working for the common good, both nationally and, even more, at the level of the city. We see them cultivating strong bonds of friendship and conversation which extended to include church leaders and members of other traditions, together with all people of goodwill. For us, it would now be inconceivable not to include those of non-Christian faiths, and those of no explicit faith at all, in such a conversation. It would also be inconceivable not to look for ways of promoting such a conversation at the local, as well as the national level. This is only to promote what Catholic Social Teaching, as Clifford Longley reminds us, calls subsidiarity and solidarity.

Sheppard and Worlock, to our knowledge, when they spoke out together, did not talk explicitly about the common good. They talked, in concrete terms about the good of the community, the good of the city. The common good is not 'something' which can be added, as top-dressing, over and above the sum of individual goods. It is that without which (call it, in concrete terms, family, community, city, nation or the body of humanity itself) there can be no individual flourishing and through which the individual discovers himself or herself anew: a person-in relation, unique, engaged, of infinite worth.

Peter McGrail
Nicholas Sagovsky
Liverpool Hope University

---

19 Marquand, *Mammon's Kingdom*, p. 187.

PART I

The Language of the Common Good

I

The Language of the Common Good[1]

ANNA ROWLANDS

Together for the common good?

Several years ago I was involved in running a conference for London schools which are members of the broad-based community organization Citizens UK. While many schools share in joint action through Citizens UK's campaigns promoting payment of a 'living wage', immigration regularization, safer bus routes, community land trusts and local 'city safe' initiatives, opportunities to reflect on the deeper relationship between community organizing and school life are rare.

Citizens UK is one of a small number of civil society groups to make explicit use of the language of the common good as part of its public work.[2] Strong emphasis is placed on translating a politics of the common good into the development of new community leaders and building strong, enduring community relationships, or 'public friendships', within and between established civic institutions in a given locality. Relationship building, leadership development and action on matters of common, public concern are seen, in that order, as the way to renew a politics of the common good, and in so doing to resist the perceived twin dominance of market and state. Saul Alinksy, founding father of community organizing, argued that the hollowing out of the 'thick' civil space between the individual and the market, the individual and the state, has devastated the modern political landscape.[3] An agnostic Jewish sociologist, Alinsky saw in cultural forms

---

1 This is an edited version of the keynote address given by Anna Rowlands at the Liverpool Hope Conference, Together for the Common Good, in September 2013.

2 On the connections between Community Organizing and Catholic Social Teaching see Austen Ivereigh, *Faithful Citizens*, London: Darton, Longman and Todd, 2010. For a more formal academic discussion and an evangelical perspective see Luke Bretherton, *Christianity and Contemporary Politics*, Oxford: Blackwell, 2010 or Jeffrey Stout, *Blessed Are the Organized: Grassroots Democracy in America*, Princeton NJ: Princeton, 2010.

3 See Saul Alinsky, *Reveille for Radicals*, New York: Vintage, 1969 and *Rules for Radicals*, New York: Vintage, 1971.

as diverse as street gangs and religious communities the vestiges of older forms of solidarity which have held out against such social evisceration. His hunch was that religious groups in particular (but not alone) held the key to reawakening a shared, multi-institutional politics of the common good. While the community organizing that takes place in the UK now still draws from Alinsky's 1950s critique of the democratic crisis and his vision for a renewed civil society, it has also out-performed Alinksy, refining, developing and challenging his narrative and practice. Nonetheless, a relationship with faith communities and a consistent ownership of the language of the common good remains at the core.

During our London conference – largely led by the pupils themselves – I was particularly struck that, rather than starting our conversations about the common good with either a deductive common good 'theory' or an inductive articulation of a set of shared concrete 'problems', we were asked to start by each writing a poem. We were asked to begin each line of our poem with the phrase 'I am ...' Reflective prompts – serious and humorous – were given to inspire each line. Awkwardly, we adults composed and read aloud our poems, unsure as to where the task would lead us. The pupils were rerunning for us the lesson that had been their entry into community organizing and thinking about the common good. Writing poetry may sound a curious way to motivate politically disengaged students from an economically deprived secular school community in north London to engage in shaping their communities. Nor is it generally where we (academics and many community activists) begin our thinking or practice in relation to the common good.

At the end of the workshop the teacher shared with us her belief that the first step towards motivating her students to increase their desire to participate in new and deeper ways in their school and local community had been to stimulate their imaginations, to awaken a deeper sense of who they were; to discover something of their own mystery, dignity and humour. Beginning with poems shaped and read together was intended to stimulate the restoration of something vital that had been beaten down, stripped away or simply unawakened by her pupils' life experience. The core pedagogical point was that the politics and practice of the common good begins with recognition of personhood, with imagination, with the delicate building of trust, through humour, and with an exchange of gifts. I am, of course, formalizing the language very slightly as I share the story. Yet, underneath the teacher's analysis lay a deep echo of Rowan Williams' argument that the two great non-secular forms of life remain art and religion: non-secular in the sense that they have the capacity to challenge both the limits and the excesses of the secular, rather than oppose the secular outright.[4] This session was a refreshing reminder that a non-instrumentalist vision of the common good – although entirely practical, material and social – does not start with either a list of problems or a perfected theory of the common good simply in need of application.

Having spent a number of years attempting to help reintroduce notions of the common good into the discourse of organizations, I find that this process can quickly run into the ground in two ways. First, such attempts can produce the impatient, flat and sceptical question: so, this sounds OK, but can you just tell me how it delivers worked-out solutions to my current problem? It's not that this question is entirely wrong, but it is perhaps a question that starts in the wrong place, and therefore ends up seeking therapeutic, ready-packaged and instrumentalist answers. Difficult though it can be to communicate, the temporal practice of the common good needs to be recognized as an open-ended process of reflection and action that requires us to do some reasonably demanding (but not impossibly hard) thinking about both our dominant cultural notions of what it means to be human and our ultimate social vision. Second, any attempt to talk about the common good as a helpful concept and practice can tend to feel too generalized and abstract. This isn't a problem of theory or metaphysics per se, but with the fact that Christian (and specifically Catholic) reflection on the common good too often leaves out the more phenomenological matter of how it *feels* to *inhabit* such a metaphysics as an embodied social practice. We are often so busy making a case for the reasonableness of thinking in terms of the common good that we fail to share and communicate the contours of this pursuit as a formative moral journey. Do we major on the metaphysics or/and the highly concrete practice and underplay the need for a more phenomenological accompanying account of the common good?

A focus solely on the metaphysics or on particular concrete common good practices often also fails to take account of the context for our current conversations about the common good. It seems that we are currently caught in the difficult tension between our pull towards the absolute necessity of some kind of notion of the common good, and its seeming impossibility. To address the kinds of social, political, economic, technological and environmental challenges we face seems to require some fundamental conversation and agreement about the goods we hold and experience as 'common'. However, the obstacles and opposition to such kinds of conversation and such fundamental visions of civil communion

---

4 Rowan Williams, *Grace and Necessity: Reflections on Art and Love*, London: Continuum, 2005.

are overwhelming.[5] Our ethical and political life is situated painfully at the heart of this tension. In concrete terms, this is the fault-line experienced by any mainstream politician attempting to engage the language of the common good to frame their politics, or someone in business deploying this vision to ground their contribution to a firm. To respond to this challenge by rushing to proclaim the impossibility of speaking about 'the common good' is to despair too quickly. To assert only the absolute necessity of common good talk and ignore the struggle to negotiate the good in the context of endlessly inventive forms of abusive power, violence and loss is to ignore the struggle to be fully human in a community of others. It is also to ignore the less than innocent history of the idea of the common good, which has often been deployed in ways that are patriarchal, racist and imperialist by turn.

Engaging with a Christian understanding of the common good

In this light, I want to suggest three very basic contextual reasons why, despite (and because of) these many challenges, we need to continue to engage with the difficult truths present in a Christian understanding of the common good. A far more developed account is possible and necessary; but this is merely to state the obvious. First, to seek the common good is to seek a way of speaking and acting that unites rather than divides. This does not mean that all conflict is avoided – a point to which I will return below. However, the concept and practice of the common good does represent an indispensable language and practice of relationship. Charles Taylor names the tendency towards a moral and social atomism in the way we conceive of the good in public life and public policy.[6] This is evident in the assumption that our common welfare is always reducible to the benefits enjoyed by individuals. Any public or common good on this account is in the end no more than the sum of its parts, the benefit felt by the individuals concerned. In contrast, Taylor argues, the Christian conception of the common good rests on the notion that there are at least two kinds of goods which are irreducibly common, goods that are more than the sum of their parts. These are, first, the goods of a shared culture that form the background to our practices and social institutions. He talks

5 See David Hollenbach, *The Common Good and Christian Ethics*, Cambridge: Cambridge University Press, 2002, pp. 9–22, 56–61.

6 See dialogue between Alasdair MacIntyre and Charles Taylor in the collected essays: John Horton and Susan Mendus (eds), *After MacIntyre: Critical Perspectives on the Work of Alasdair MacIntyre*, Cambridge: Polity Press, 1994.

of the irreducibly common good of a shared language or a shared culture. And then, there are goods that incorporate essentially shared understandings of their intrinsic value, for example friendship. These are forms of relational goods, rooted in deeper truths about human nature that cannot be reduced only to the enjoyment of the individual.

Some fundamental notion of irreducibly common goods, which produce the experience of a good that is more than the sum of their parts, seems vital in contesting the atomistic and divisive social language that permeates our social spaces. Lest this sound overly esoteric, it is worth noting the extent to which we are currently surrounded by divisive social language. Much of the political language that has been shaping our public conversations about austerity has been highly divisive. In fact, it has seemed at times as if the notion of virtue itself required a willingness to speak in such terms: the deserving versus undeserving poor, strivers versus skivers. This kind of language comes to dominate our public spaces and fails to recognize the irreducibly common goods that ground a peaceable social order.

The second reason we need the language and practice of the common good is connected to the first: because a Christian conception of the common good maintains a focus on the whole which is greater than the sum of parts it continues to speak of human value rooted in an account of *being*, rather than merely human function. That's precisely what the teacher and pupils from north London understood implicitly. It therefore provides a necessary challenge to all forms of public and private action seeking to reduce the human body and human relations to functions and interests, to costs and benefits. The danger is that an account of private and public goods alone is too thin, morally speaking, to prevent the instrumentalizing of human life and the endless invention of new forms of exclusion. As Hannah Arendt noted so clearly, the language of function and interest quickly gives way to a legitimated practice of human superfluity; to a notion that some people are not essential, can be discarded, expelled or even exterminated.[7] In contrast to the language of function and interest, forms of common good language (when handled well) contain humanizing words that help us speak publicly not only of hope but of the unacceptable and difficult: suffering, failure, pain and tragedy. We are given a response to difficulty that is more than silence, suppression, distraction or consumption.

The third reason we need to maintain an engagement with the language and practices of the common good concerns the paradoxical challenge

---

7 See Hannah Arendt, *The Human Condition*, Chicago: University of Chicago Press, 1958.

of learning to live with a vision of life in communion, but in the context of a generation experiencing the challenges and opportunities of radical plurality. While we rightly talk about isolation, atomization and hyper-individualism as challenges to the common good, this captures only one dimension of a more complex social story. Arguably, what we face is not a simple decline of socialization but the simultaneous eclipse and rebirth of new forms of socialization. Catholic Social Teaching began to discuss this reality in its handling of the common good from the 1980s onwards. John Paul II described forms of increasingly intense social interdependence, which he carefully and very deliberately distinguished from forms of social solidarity.[8] He argued that increased use of all forms of technology, rapidly intensifying forms of human migration, the increased experience of bureaucracy in everyday life, are all social facts which speak of newly intensified forms of socialization. However, such forms of interdependence and socialization are not necessarily expressions of solidarity or civil communion. Each has the potential to be so, when rightly engaged. John Paul II argued that solidarity is the solid social practice and moral virtue that moves us from intensity of socialization towards a community of *caritas*, justice and peace.

Echoing and deepening this analysis, David Hollenbach SJ suggests that these forms of contemporary interdependence simultaneously shape and limit our engagement with the common good.[9] Intensified plurality of this kind makes conceiving of the common good more difficult, yet our only real ethical possibility. Hollenbach raises a series of questions for advocates and critics of the common good alike. Without some shared sense of the Real and the Good, it seems increasingly difficult to address any of the really complex questions we face. Finding ways to reflect on challenges as varied and significant as the crises in political authority, the challenges brought by human migration, the fallout from the economic crisis, intensified forms of global conflict and displacement, ecological change and the future of social care, requires some kind of concept of common good. However, he asks: given the evisceration of our common good practices and the layers of ethnic, religious and economic difference to be negotiated, can a commitment to the common good be revitalized without, at least in the short term, simultaneously increasing social conflict?

It seems clear that any properly metaphysical account of the common good we seek to pursue in response to these stark challenges needs to be more open to handling paradox and conflict, more *aporetic* and more

---

8 See John Paul II's social encyclical: *Sollicitudo rei socialis*, 1987.
9 See Hollenbach, *The Common Good and Christian Ethics*, especially Chapter 4.

phenomenological by turn. Both John Paul II and Francis have suggested that an account of conflict needs to be brought within a Catholic Social Teaching of the common good. While this is hinted at as a necessary development, it is not yet a sustained theological reflection.[10]

A further (not unrelated) point concerns the need to prize the idea of a shared sense of the good apart from a narrow notion that this implies only the search for a rational intellectual consensus or a search for cultural homogeneity. This is to recall that the Christian understanding of the truly good is rooted first and last in forms of *communion* rather than in *agreement* per se. In Christian tradition, communion and plurality are, at least in theory, interconnected rather than opposing notions. This is not to suggest a dualism between practices of communion and rational discussion. The co-belonging and interrelation of these elements is crucial to a Catholic social vision. Rather, it is to resist any attempt to reduce 'communion' to rational agreement, and to recognize that sometimes even those with the best intentions tend to focus in a reductive way on the discursive element of the common good. Alasdair MacIntyre is surely right that we still lack spaces for handling the properly deliberative element of the common good – but given the more spacious and imaginative teleological contours of the Thomist account of the common good, we need to talk about more than *just* the deliberative element. Christian reflection on the common good needs to serve genuinely *plural* Christian forms and practices of the common good, of communion and gift exchange.

Thomas Aquinas offers resources for an account of the common good that attempts to hold together communion and plurality. In his writings on the common good and political rule Aquinas suggests that within creation multiple forms of practical 'care' exist so that we may be guided towards the end already purchased for us by Christ.[11] He notes that if we were destined only for an end that lies within ourselves, then the care of the doctor, teacher, banker, or tutor would be sufficient for us to live the good life. However, in faith we are destined for an end outside ourselves and therefore need a wider form of spiritual 'care' from our political leaders to guide us beyond ourselves to communion with God and with each other. Aquinas argues that we see here an analogy between the care for the 'one' and the care for the 'whole' or the 'multitude'. If the highest good of the one person is to be found in seeking education, physical health and material goods to sustain life, then it follows that these are the goods that the virtuous ruler needs to seek and protect for society as a whole:

---

10 See Francis' Apostolic Exhortation, *Evangelii gaudium*, 2013.

11 This section refers to Aquinas' 1267 letter to the King of Cyprus, *On Kingship* (*De Regimine Principum*).

health, knowledge, and wealth maximization. But here, Aquinas says, Christian faith makes all the difference. The Christian believes the good life to consist of other, truer ends: to live well together in peace, rendering mutual assistance and in so doing learning to participate in something of the life of God. This requires a capacity for a future-oriented reading of moral relationships and neighbour love. My neighbour is not just the person with whom I find myself in proximity now, but also the person with whom I might be destined to share the life of communion in God eternally. This is a radically inclusive, future-oriented vision of neighbour love.

For Aquinas, this vision connects to the creaturely need to form communities and live as 'a people'. Writing before the modern era, Aquinas does not presuppose an ethnic and linguistic concept of nationhood. Instead, echoing and developing Cicero, what for him constitutes 'a people' is an acceptance of being gathered (in difference) under one ordering and limiting set of laws and one government so as to live well, rendering mutual assistance. We are called to render mutual assistance to each other according to the principles of contributive justice: I render assistance both according to the skills and capacities I have as a unique person and according to the real needs of my neighbour. Through living, exploring, persevering in and continually discovering this created social nature in absolutely concrete and social ways, we also (providentially ...) enjoy, discover and participate in something of God. Living the creaturely life well draws us into the life of God. Seeking the temporal common good folds us into the eternal common good.

At root, the practices of politics and faith are shared responses to the question: what life do we wish – or in our case are we called – to live together? In the Catholic social vision what 'non-secular' faith gives to 'secular' politics is a vision of the very purpose of politics in the life of the common good. The beginning and end of politics then, is the common good. What makes a Catholic account of the common good distinct from the idea of the greatest good for the greatest number is its teleological account of civil communion as an immanent participation in the communion that we receive in salvation. This faith-based vision is also characterized by its orientation towards the biblical preferential option for the poor, and its understanding of solidarity as an ongoing act of accompaniment and social justice. The common good is therefore measured less according to the greatest good for the greatest number and more against the wellbeing and participation of the least. It seeks to render the existence and social experience of the most marginalized and superfluous visible in the mathematics of our political calculations.

Immigration and the common good

Immigration is a hot political topic. For the last decade it has continued to poll in the top three political issues voters tell the government they care about. In some (but not all) areas of the country tensions between migrants and established communities are high. All of the main political parties have been told by the pollsters that they must do something to show that they are willing to deal with labour market pressures, to reduce pressure on public services, to deal with the perceived failures of multi-culturalism and to show that they can deter people from seeking a life in the UK. It is a very complicated situation to make sense of, and one of the most challenging common good issues we face. Right now, we have an awkward public non-conversation about immigration which lacks any real sense of being held within the moral framework of common good thinking and practice. This is where the competing and colliding realities of the global, national and local meet with profound intensity.

I want to point out some basic things about the way that the common good or common welfare tends to be thought of in current public debate about immigration. Then I want to say something briefly about the ways in which a Christian account of the common good turns those categories on their heads. To begin with, I hope you will recognize how often we hear statements such as these: 'The fair, or moral purpose of immigration policy is to ensure that only migration which is in the British national interest [i.e. economic interest] should be allowed or encouraged.' 'We need clear policies that offer a preferential option for British workers and which bring in the most highly qualified that we can recruit from abroad.' 'We should take *some* refugees – but nothing we do for current refugees should offer any encouragement to others to think about coming here.'

Standing up for appropriate national self-interest is taken to mean that public policy should be such that it largely deters migration to the UK, especially among unskilled and low-skilled economic workers, together with those seeking refugee status, and that we should also quickly enforce removal on those without leave to remain. We need practical policies, we are told, that enact this deterrence. It was little surprise to discover that the Coalition government had set up a group inside the policy-making process called the 'hostile environment' working group, nor that the government has recently decided to withdraw its financial support from the 'Mare Nostrum' Mediterranean migrant rescue operation, lest it encourage more migrants to cross between Africa and Europe.

Christian 'common good' thinking about immigration does not begin or end with the category of 'national interest'. It does not inherently dismiss the idea of a national community, but it begins with questions of human value and it sets immigration within a wider Christian imagination and story. That story begins with recognition of some basic parts of the biblical tradition: a biblical command to honour the dignity of each person, to offer particular hospitality and care for the stranger, and to recognize our universal kinship through Christ beyond national borders. We should note the privileged role for migrants in the sacred narratives of faith communities: God sometimes instructs his faithful to *become* migrants – Abraham being our classic example; God often calls migrants to be prophets and truth tellers (like Ruth); and Christ himself is seen, especially in the Fourth Gospel, as one who comes among us from elsewhere. In the Bible migration is not viewed in pathological terms, first and foremost as a problem (although for many it brings great suffering). Rather, migration is seen as a basic feature of the human condition and indeed a metaphor for the life of faith itself. However, we should note that the Church's own practice has often failed to live up to such a vision, with Christian religion supporting displacement and stigma as well as hospitality.

Such a Christian imagination might set the tone and it might give some hints about appropriate and inappropriate language to use, but it doesn't tell us how we resolve the very painful modern policy dilemmas through which we must resolve the conflict between different, finite goods. At one level, answering that question is a task that belongs to the whole community, but to help us think more practically about the common good and immigration, Catholic Social Teaching has built on that biblical background to propose some principles which can help build a bridge between our Scripture and our context.[12] They are rather different to the principles that seem to guide the policy conversation at the moment.

First, the purpose of immigration policy must have the dignity of the human person at its heart. In a world of nation-states, we all require the protection of some form of state, and we can't survive for long without this. Political membership is a basic necessity, not a secondary luxury.[13] For persons to be stateless is not, therefore, morally acceptable.

---

12 I have summarized, analysed, critiqued and referenced these principles in much greater depth in my article 'On the Temptations of Sovereignty: The Task of Catholic Social Teaching and the Challenge of UK Asylum Seeking', *Political Theology* 12:6 (2011), pp. 843–69. These principles are gathered from across a range of official Vatican texts, including the papal social encyclicals and the publications of the Pontifical Dicastery for the Care of Migrants and Itinerant Peoples.

13 See Pontifical Dicastery for the Pastoral Care of Migrants and Itinerant Peoples, *Erga migrantes caritas Christi* (*The Love of Christ Towards Migrants*), Vatican City, 2004.

Second, where people are displaced from the state to which they belong by conflict, persecution, violence or hunger, they have an absolute right to seek sanctuary elsewhere.[14] Because political membership is so basic to all forms of economic and physical wellbeing, when deciding whom to let in and whom to refuse, states should offer priority to refugees over voluntary economic migrants. However, migration for economic purposes is not rejected by the Catholic Social Tradition. Nor is there any suggestion in an economy of communion that low-skilled economic migration has less value than high-skilled economic migration.

Third, Catholic Social Thought believes that the common good is best served by placing a strong moral obligation on the most materially prosperous states to receive, protect and integrate the migrant – whether economic or refugee. The state may set some limits as to how many people it receives, but it must have a fair process for making its decisions, balancing the resources that the receiving community has available to its own established population and the needs of newly arriving migrants. This also means being aware of those places most affected by the burden of providing hospitality and the dynamics of competition. Unjust laws are those that fail to distribute burdens equally, thus threatening the conditions necessary for social virtue. If those required to act as a de facto host community for newly arrived migrants are among the most socially deprived themselves, this raises real questions about the distributive failures of government and civil society.

Fourth, national borders and identities, while important, are a good only when they provide both an ordered and peaceful way of life and when they make possible hospitality to others, facilitating the building of friendships between cultures and persons. Borders are a good insofar as they provide the context for enriched forms of internal and external friendship and community. And here government has an important mediating role, as do the institutions of church and society. Maximizing the provision we can offer without causing unnecessary suffering to others requires governments and communities to establish just measures for the integration of those who arrive and to notice and mitigate any unfair burden to communities or individuals.

Fifth, while Catholic Social Teaching frames its engagement with migration issues in terms of human dignity and the common good, it does have things to say about rights and responsibilities. Migrants have a duty to seek ways to participate in the 'host' society and, in return, migrants must be recognized as bearers of cultural and social, as well as political,

---

14 See Vatican II, *Gaudium et spes* (*The Pastoral Constitution on the Church in the Modern World*), 1965, 65.

rights. This means a right to work where work is available and a right to some form of meaningful civic participation. As with the thinking that undergirds support for the living wage, the minimum conditions for survival must include ways to participate in an established community and not merely to survive.

In entirely practical ways, these kinds of common good principles have led the churches of all denominations to be at the forefront of challenges to the detention of children for immigration purposes, the principle of *any* immigration detention itself (especially indefinite detention) for purely administrative purposes, the brutality of enforced removals, the withdrawal of welfare from destitute asylees; as well as campaigning for the right to work for those who wait years for decisions on their immigration status, the regularization of undocumented migrants.

Yet, we reduce our vision of the common good to strongly statist conceptions of justice if we fail also to note the practices of communion that are internal to the worshipping life of faith communities. Perhaps even more significant for migrants than advocacy, has been the recognition, companionship and human contact provided by churches – something which runs against the logic that dominates our cultural moment. This happens when churches offer a context of participation not only in prayer and worship but also in the social, cultural and political life of a congregation. Churches, mosques, temples and synagogues have become an alternative kind of civil society for many migrants, offering a form of faith-citizenship to those denied, either temporarily or permanently, such privileges by the nation-state. In truth, migrants report very mixed experiences of welcome and rejection in religious settings, so again common good triumphalism must not be allowed to gloss over complex realities. However, the positive experience of migrants who have sought and found an alternative society within the churches is a reminder that the common good is first and foremost something we witness and incarnate through the vibrant, creative lives of our own communities.

Conclusion: thinking with the imagination of the common good

My example for this chapter needn't have been about immigration: I could have undertaken a similar analysis based on penal policy, or a living wage, on how we relate labour to capital, the role of money, youth unemployment, homelessness, food poverty or the environment. All these are common good questions that challenge our faith life, our politics and our economy at its core. All of them connect the local, national and global in challenging ways. All of them reveal the ways in which Christian kinship language changes things. What a difference it makes to think not of market or nation alone, but first with the imagination of the common good.

A Catholic – and therefore a more broadly Christian – view of the common good cannot be contained only in talk of Christians relating to each other. It implies endless creative partnerships between individuals, institutions and associations who share something of this vision of a common life. No faith, no political party, no campaigning association can *be* or *do* the common good alone. The politics of the common good is plural and spacious. As faith communities, we should be proud that we have kept alive a language and institutional practice of the common good through a period of very significant challenge to much implied in that vision of human society. But surely part of the challenge to the Churches and faith communities is to look towards each other and outwards in new ways. The next level of challenge is to move from the goods of our multiple civil societies, on which there has been so much focus for the last few decades, towards quite new ways in which we can *together* practise plurality and communion, reciprocity and friendship.

2

The Unexamined Society:
Public Reasoning, Social Justice
and the Common Good

ANDREW BRADSTOCK[1]

The current revival of interest in the common good is exciting, and not just because it has the potential to change the way we do politics. It also provokes us to reflect upon the sort of society we have and the kind of society we would like.

We are not in the habit of reflecting in this way. There have been moments when we have endorsed new political platforms at the ballot box, but we do not routinely engage in reflection upon the purpose of our corporate life together and the values and principles upon which that life is built.[2] Perhaps in this we fall foul, collectively, of the judgement Socrates made about individuals who leave their lives 'unexamined'.

The process leading to the referendum on independence in Scotland in 2014, however, demonstrated that, when people do have the opportunity to decide the kind of country they wish to live in, they have both the inclination and capacity to engage in robust and informed debate. Participation in that referendum was, at 85 per cent, higher than for any UK election in living memory,[3] suggesting that, when profound political change, beyond an agenda set by mainstream political parties, is at stake, people have an appetite for democratic engagement in its fullest sense.

Embracing the common good also impels us to move beyond the party political agenda to consider the kind of society we wish to live in. Placing both human dignity and human community at the centre of political and economic decision-making, the common good challenges us to consider

1 I would like to acknowledge the help of Jenny Sinclair, Jonathan Chaplin and Maria Power, who read and commented on drafts of this chapter.

2 Perhaps the last example of a 'national conversation' about how our polity operates, and in whose interests, was the so-called Putney Debates in 1647.

3 www.theguardian.com/news/datablog/2012/nov/16/uk-election-turnouts-historic.

the extent to which we live in solidarity with each other, recognize our interdependence, and seek the wellbeing of all.

More positively, it dares us to come together to find ways in which we can forge a fairer and more equal society, one in which all can enjoy fulfilment in the economic, political and cultural life of that society. As Catholic Social Teaching, one of its main wellsprings, asserts, 'the common good is the reason that the political authority exists'.[4] Thus it pushes us to think beyond our traditional understanding of democracy, with its emphasis on periodic elections involving parties promoting sectional interests, towards the question of what 'politics' is for and how it can fulfil its *raison d'être*, the welfare of the people for whom it has been created. It also takes us beyond a 'right/left' polarization of politics, seeing neither greater power for the state, nor greater freedom for the market, as necessarily the key to improving human wellbeing: factors such as a renewing and reinvigorating of civil society will also be involved. Pursuing the common good is about recovering hope, vision and purpose, or, in Christian terms, discovering how all can know the 'life in all its fullness' which Jesus placed at the heart of his mission (John 10.10).

Public reasoning

Both Amartya Sen[5] and Michael Sandel[6] have argued that public reasoning, more than elections, defines what democracy is about. South African theologian John de Gruchy sees democracy both 'as a *vision* of what society should become and ... as a *system* of government that seeks to enable the realization of that vision within particular contexts'.[7] We need to encourage and embrace the public reasoning and envisioning of which these writers speak if we wish to forge an alternative to our current politics, in which sections of society, divided by competing interests, press their disparate concerns on a state which has no core of shared values to draw upon in order to adjudicate on these disputes.[8] But how, concretely,

---

4 Pontifical Council for Justice and Peace, *Compendium of the Social Doctrine of the Church*, Vatican City: *Liberia Editrice Vaticana*, 2004, 168, p. 95.

5 Amartya Sen, *The Idea of Justice*, London: Penguin, 2010, pp. 321–37.

6 Michael Sandel, *Justice: What's the right thing to do?*, New York: Farrar, Straus and Giroux, 2009, Ch. 10.

7 Cited in Richard Harries, *Faith in Politics? Rediscovering the Christian Roots of Our Political Values*, London: Darton, Longman and Todd, 2010, p. 64 (emphasis in original).

8 See Paul Vallely, 'Towards a New Politics: Catholic Social Teaching in a Pluralist Society', in Paul Vallely (ed.), *The New Politics: Catholic Social Teaching for the Twenty-First Century*, London: SCM Press, 1998, p. 154.

might we develop a public conversation about the 'good life' in a society characterized by ideological, religious and moral plurality?

On the one hand it will be argued that, in a pluralist society, no one particular set of beliefs should be allowed to prevail over others, nor should the state be seen to endorse one conception of the good society over others. Yet, the very point about the common good is that it is *not* imposed from outside (or above) but emerges from open, inclusive discussion committed to exploring competing convictions regarding in what it might consist. It serves precisely, as Michael Sandel says, to generate 'a more robust public engagement with our moral disagreements'.[9] To seek the common good is to take pluralism and social difference *more* seriously than does conventional politics since, as Anna Rowlands asserts, it involves addressing these challenges by promoting a more deliberative and participatory politics.[10] No society will ever agree conclusively regarding in what 'the good life' fully consists but, as Alain de Botton has argued, this 'should not in itself be enough to disqualify us from investigating and promoting the theoretical notion of such a life'.[11]

Social justice

I want to pursue a way forward suggested by Raymond Plant in his essay *Politics, Theology and History*. Recognizing the potential pitfalls in promoting discussion specifically about 'the common good', Plant proposes a focus on 'social justice', a search for those 'common needs or basic goods which people have to have in order to ... pursue any conception of the good whatever it might be'.[12]

Such an approach, Plant suggests, addresses the question of how a shared vision of society – such as is implied by the common good – might be pursued in a pluralist society. Plant is clear that

> to argue that the common good can consist in a rich, deep and elaborated form of substantive agreement on values and human purposes ... looks both implausible and potentially dangerous in a society marked by moral diversity in which individuals believe strongly that judgments

---

9 Michael Sandel, *Justice*, p. 268. Cf. Pontifical Council for Justice and Peace, *Compendium of the Social Doctrine of the Church*, 170, p. 96.

10 Anna Rowlands, 'Faith in the Common Good', unpublished briefing paper, 9 June 2014.

11 Alain de Botton, *Religion for Atheists: A Non-believer's Guide to the Uses of Religion*, London: Hamish Hamilton, 2012, p. 83.

12 Raymond Plant, *Politics, Theology and History*, Cambridge: Cambridge University Press, 2001, p. 198.

about substantive and, indeed, ultimate values are for them to make by exercising their own judgment.[13]

Promoting debate on 'social justice', however, renders the task of pursuing the common good less a search for some kind of 'substantive common purpose' or 'transcendent moral order' than an attempt to identify, 'the range of goods and services, benefits and opportunities which all citizens need to have in order to pursue their conception of the good, whatever it might turn out to be'.[14]

There will still be groundwork to do, given liberalism's antipathy to the merits of social justice. For Friedrich Hayek and the neo-liberal economic school, it is fundamentally not the responsibility of the state to tinker with the outcomes of a market system in which everyone is freely allowed the opportunity to buy and sell. If some people find themselves without the essentials of life, that is simply a consequence of the various transactions that take place within the market and cannot be considered unjust unless such transactions are coerced. Thus, for neo-liberals, even if the state responds to this by redistributing income, it does not do so in the name of 'justice'. Hayek famously dismissed social justice as a 'mirage'.[15]

At the other end of the liberal spectrum will be those for whom responsibility for the administration of social justice must lie with the state. But while the state could have a role in the quest to satisfy basic needs, over-reliance on it can serve to weaken, deskill and disempower communities as well as generate dependency. 'Redistribution without reciprocity', as Maurice Glasman has written, can 'leave its recipients untransformed': 'the state can undermine responsibility, agency and participation'.[16]

The idea that even a minimal shared understanding of 'social justice' may be attainable is also rejected by the philosophically liberal view, articulated most cogently by John Rawls.[17] For Rawls, it is essential that governments in liberal democratic societies do not espouse one normative concept of 'the good', only that they provide adequate procedures to enable each member to choose from a range of 'goods' and debate their relative value. A government promoting one particular notion of 'the good

---

13 Plant, *Politics*, pp. 196–7.

14 Plant, *Politics*, p. 198.

15 F. A. Hayek, *The Mirage of Social Justice*, London: Routledge and Kegan Paul, 1976. See also Plant, *Politics*, p. 203.

16 Maurice Glasman, 'The Good Society and the Politics of the Common Good', lecture given at the Centre for Social Justice, 11 February 2014, http://centreforsocialjustice.org.uk/UserStorage/pdf/Events/Glasman-speech.pdf.

17 See for example, *Political Liberalism*, New York: Columbia University Press, 1993.

life' risks imposing on everyone values espoused only by some. It fails to respect people's ability and right to choose their ends for themselves.

Yet as we have already noted, by definition the common good is not something 'imposed' from above: rather it emerges from open, mature discussion. In any case, as Sandel argues, an individual's deliberation about their own 'good' cannot but involve reflection on the good of the community to which he or she is bound. It is mistaken to think that one can remain neutral regarding the values upon which a society is grounded, or the ends to which it should be directed: 'it may not be possible, or even desirable, to deliberate about justice without deliberating about the good life'.[18]

For Sandel, achieving a just society involves more than securing individual 'freedom of choice': we have also 'to reason together about the meaning of the good life, and to create a public culture hospitable to the disagreements that will inevitably arise'.[19] John Finnis also wants to go beyond Rawls in arguing that the pursuit of the common good and justice requires more than the establishment of certain procedural rules which ensure individual liberty or fair play. For Finnis the community needs to operate together to, 'secure the whole ensemble of material and other conditions, including forms of collaboration, that tend to favour, facilitate and foster the realization by each individual of his or her personal development'.[20]

In the light of this I want to suggest that it is possible to conceive of a debate about the merit and meaning of social justice, addressing the question:

> *Do we, as a society, agree that we have a responsibility towards those among us who lack the means to pursue their conception of the good life, and commit ourselves, with the practical support of government, to work to ensure that that lack is remedied; or do we consider that, both in principle and practice, pursuing social justice is wrong and that, so long as individuals are free to pursue their own lifestyle and subjective preferences, government has no responsibility other than to ensure that that freedom is maintained?*

Such a debate would not only deepen our political discourse, moving us from a focus on individual material wellbeing toward what best serves the

---

18 Sandel, *Justice*, p. 242.
19 Sandel, *Justice*, p. 261.
20 Cited in Nicholas Sagovsky, *Christian Tradition and the Practice of Justice*, London: SPCK, 2008, p. 173.

'common weal', it would provoke critical thinking about the operation of the market and the question whether it should work to promote the wellbeing of all. I want to consider each in turn.

Politics

Pat Logan has highlighted the potential of the common good to change the nature of political discourse within democratic societies. He writes,

> A notion of the common good gives us a language which can take us beyond the notion of politics as simple *bargaining*, where one group's rights and interests are played off against another's, to mature political *argument*, where communication and a common search for good can be pursued.[21]

Michael Sandel also wants a renewing of political discourse towards 'a politics of moral engagement',[22] noting that in order for this to happen there needs to be a reorientation among citizens, away from a focus on purely individual concerns towards the importance of building a common life together. He writes,

> If a just society requires a strong sense of community it must find a way to cultivate in citizens a concern for the whole, a dedication to the common good. It can't be indifferent to the attitudes and dispositions, the 'habits of the heart', that citizens bring to public life. It must find a way to lean against purely privatized notions of the good life, and cultivate civic virtue.[23]

Oliver O'Donovan is also worried that what inspires people to political action is less a concern about wider social issues than the defence of their private or sectional interests;[24] and if, like Sandel, he does not explicitly use the language of 'conversion' when considering how a shift to concern for the common interest might be achieved, Clifford Longley does refer to the involvement of the conscience in embracing the common good and the

---

21 Pat Logan, *A World Transformed; When Hopes Collapse and Faiths Collide*, London: CTBI, 2007, p. 125.

22 Sandel, *Justice*, p. 269.

23 Sandel, *Justice*, pp. 263–4.

24 Oliver O'Donovan, *The Desire of the Nations: Rediscovering the Roots of Political Theology*, Cambridge: Cambridge University Press, 1996, p. 271; cf. Vallely, *Towards a New Politics*, p. 151.

need for a 'moment of *metanoia* when the truth really strikes home that "we are all responsible for all"'.[25]

What this *metanoia* involves, as the papal encyclical *Sollicitudo rei socialis* implies, is a shift, when confronting social issues, from harbouring feelings of pity or a concern to make a practical response, to a recognition of our 'solidarity' and 'interdependence' one with another. The response to social problems should not be 'a feeling of vague compassion or shallow distress' at others' misfortunes, rather 'a firm and persevering determination to commit oneself to the common good; that is to say, to the good of all and of each individual because we are all really responsible for all'.[26]

As the US activist and writer Jim Wallis likes to put it, the change we need is that which moves us beyond wanting to keep up with the Joneses to making sure the Joneses are OK![27] I shall return to how this change might be encouraged later.

The economy

A debate on the common good will provoke reflection about the operation of the market and the role of government, challenging those who hold polarized positions with respect to both to think in new paradigms. It will prompt us to move beyond wanting to see excessive power invested in either the market or the state, recognizing that both should work together to promote the wellbeing of all. While the market will need maximum freedom if it is to enable, in the words of the Vatican II document *Gaudium et spes*, 'people, either as groups or as individuals, to reach their fulfilment more fully and more easily',[28] common good considerations bring us back to the question of social justice by asking whether it is meaningful to talk about people having the 'freedom' to pursue their conception of 'the good' if they lack the basic necessities to be able to do it.

Engaging with the common good, then, prompts questions about the very purpose and end of market activity. As the Catholic Bishops' Conference of England and Wales noted in their document on the common good issued prior to the 1997 general election, 'market forces, when properly regulated in the name of the common good, can be an efficient mechanism

---

25 Clifford Longley, 'Government and the common good', in Nick Spencer and Jonathan Chaplin (eds), *God and Government*, London: SPCK, 2009, p. 163.

26 John Paul II, *Sollicitudo rei socialis*, 1987, 38.

27 Jim Wallis, *Rediscovering Values: On Wall Street, Main Street, and Your Street*, New York: Howard Books, 2010, flyleaf.

28 Vatican II, *Gaudium et spes* (*Pastoral Constitution on the Church in the Modern World*), 1965, 26.

for matching resources to needs in a developed society'. No other system is superior in terms of encouraging wealth creation, advancing prosperity and enabling poverty to be relieved. But when the economy itself becomes the end rather than the means, when the distinction between the market as a 'technical economic method' and 'a total ideology or world view' is blurred, individual rather than common interest may prevail. As the bishops put it,

> An economic creed that insists the greater good of society is best served by each individual pursuing his or her own self-interest is likely to find itself encouraging individual selfishness, for the sake of the economy ... A wealthy society, if it is a greedy society, is not a good society.[29]

Other commentators on the common good reflect the bishops' concerns regarding the potential of free market economic theory to claim more for itself than is warranted. For Nick Townsend,

> business activity should never be subjected to an *overriding* imperative of maximizing profit. Rather, it can and should be a hard-headed form of love of neighbour, in which the *end* is to supply goods and services – things that are good for and of service to people – and the wholly necessary *means* is making a profit.

He concludes, 'In neoliberal capitalism ends and means have been mistaken for each other.'[30] John Gray also notes how market freedoms should only be a means to an end, that end being individual wellbeing.[31] Indeed, for Clifford Longley it is on account of its identifying a distinction between the market as a tool and as an ideology 'that Catholic Social Teaching has an important contribution to make to current thinking on how to make contemporary capitalism a gentler beast'.[32]

Here we return to the suggestion that 'social justice' serve as a starting point for a conversation about the common good. If the minimum demand of a social justice agenda is that all citizens have the basic goods, services and opportunities they need in order to pursue their conception of the good, this challenges us explicitly to confront the question of the

---

29 Catholic Bishops' Conference of England and Wales, *The Common Good and the Catholic Church's Social Teaching*, London: 1996, 78–80, p. 19.

30 Nicholas Townsend, 'Government and social infrastructure', in Spencer and Chaplin (eds), *God and Government*, p. 126.

31 Cited in Vallely, 'Towards a new Politics', p. 151.

32 Clifford Longley, 'Structures of Sin and the Free Market: John Paul II on Capitalism', in Vallely (ed.), *The New Politics*, p. 107.

'means' and 'ends' of market activity. Is our concept of 'justice' one which demands that no one should be excluded from having a stake in society, including those who are most marginalized, regardless of how they came to be in that situation? And does that lead us to want to argue that the market should be open to that degree of regulation necessary in order for it to meet that end? Or do we consider the goal of the market simply to be its freedom to operate in a wholly unfettered manner, viewing its outcomes not as matters of justice or injustice but the necessary consequences of a morally neutral process?

At present we take it to be the duty of government to create and sustain the conditions under which we, as citizens, are free to produce and consume as we wish. Our notion of the 'good society', albeit that it may be implicit, is one in which maximum individual freedom is guaranteed and government, taking note of the demands we citizens express, enables those demands to be satisfied with minimal interference. Recovering the common good brings into view another vision of society, one in which we also take into account those shared moral obligations which make up the bonds of community and which government must also protect.

To the liberal economist, the unfettered operation of the market is precisely the way to satisfy the demands of the common good, to enable each person to reach their fulfilment more fully and more easily. Yet we still have the issue of those who, for whatever reason, do not or cannot reach their fulfilment. Can we meaningfully talk about people being 'free' to pursue their conception of the 'good life' if they lack the basic necessities needed in order to be able to do it? As Plant has argued,

> If the state is seen as a guarantor of freedom for individuals, then it would be part of the responsibility of the state to secure to individuals the resources and opportunities they need to be *able* to do what they are *free* to do.[33]

Among these might be health, education and a degree of financial security.

For Michael Sandel the growing gap between rich and poor is a further theme which 'a new politics of the common good' should address, undermining as it does the 'solidarity that democratic citizenship requires'.[34] Richard Wilkinson and Kate Pickett have identified the adverse social outcomes found in societies characterized by a high degree of inequality,[35]

---

33 Plant, *Politics, Theology and History*, p. 206.

34 Sandel, *Justice*, pp. 263, 266.

35 See in particular Richard Wilkinson and Kate Pickett, *The Spirit Level: Why More Equal Societies Almost Always Do Better*, London: Penguin, 2009, and the website of the Equality Trust: www.equalitytrust.org.uk.

and Sandel also notes what he calls the 'fiscal' and 'civic' social effects of deepening inequality: 'fiscal' in the sense that, as the rich live ever more separate lives and withdraw from public places and services, so they become unwilling to support them through their taxes, and their quality deteriorates; and 'civic' in the sense that what were once public spaces cease to be places where citizens from different walks of life encounter one another. 'The hollowing out of the public realm', Sandel concludes, 'makes it difficult to cultivate the solidarity and sense of community on which democratic community depends.'[36] A common good approach would seek to engage all sections of society in debating this issue, exploring questions such as the extent to which narrowing the inequality gap would be in the interest of all, and whether public institutions and services might be rebuilt so that rich and poor alike would want to take advantage of them.

Government

Economic reforms of this kind raise the question of the role of government in promoting the common good. Clearly government would play a part in any drive to reduce inequality, but common good teaching challenges more broadly the notion that (in Catholic Social Teaching terminology), 'the right ordering of economic life' can 'be left to a free competition of forces'.[37] Indeed, Catholic teaching argues that, while all members of society have a role, according to their capacity, in attaining and developing the common good, 'the State' has the *responsibility* for attaining it 'since the common good is the reason that the political authority exists'.[38]

Catholic teaching thus poses a challenge to the current orthodoxy that, left to its own operations, the market can meet the needs and wants of individuals and society. In a document issued following the demise of Communism in 1989, John Paul II warned against embracing a free-market capitalism 'not circumscribed within a strong juridical framework which places it at the service of human freedom in its totality'. For the Pope, neither unrestricted capitalism nor 'the socialist system' was compatible with a 'society of free work, of enterprise and of participation'; for while such a society would not be 'directed against the market', it would demand 'that the market be appropriately controlled by the forces

36 See Sandel, *Justice*, pp. 266–7.
37 Pius XI, *Quadragesimo anno*, 1931, 88.
38 Pontifical Council for Justice and Peace, *Compendium of the Social Doctrine of the Church*, 2004, 167–8.

of society and by the state, so as to guarantee that the basic needs of the whole of society are satisfied'.[39]

A 'common good' perspective on the market prompts a number of questions for us today, including whether policy decisions must always be considered *first* in terms of their economic implications, or whether factors such as the extent to which they are 'right' or 'just' be given more consideration; might, in other words, seeking the common good lead us at times to agree on a course of action *because it is for the good of all* before agreeing how it will be realized?

A common good orientation would also challenge us to ask whether growth in GDP is necessarily the best indicator of our collective health and wellbeing, or whether that might be dependent upon other factors; to think afresh about our responsibility to those beyond our immediate community, including those not yet born, in the light of what we know about climate change and the imperative to adopt more sustainable lifestyles and business practices; and to reflect upon whether the marketization of services is always the right course, or whether some should still remain 'services', paid for from the public purse? Importantly, it would also challenge the fundamental liberal assumption that our motive for engaging in market activity is primarily to acquire personal wealth and comfort, and that we do not also have the capacity to be concerned for 'the other' and the wellbeing of wider society.

Subsidiarity

If pursuing the common good requires that governments be open to the possibility of acting, on our behalf, to ensure that the market works for specific ends which we agree are socially desirable, this is not to say that it envisages the return of big government: as noted earlier, it is the responsibility of *all* members of society to promote and work for the common good, not simply politicians and government officials. The common good flourishes primarily at the grassroots. Often spoken of in the same breath as the common good is the concept of 'subsidiarity', another core feature of Catholic Social Teaching, which specifically rejects the notion that governments arrogate power to themselves: indeed, stressing the importance of community initiative, mutual cooperation and decentralization, subsidiarity asks of the state that it only undertake those activities which exceed the capacity of individuals or private groups acting independently. 'As much freedom as possible, as much intervention as necessary' describes

39 John Paul II, *Centesimus annus*, 1991, 35.

the ideal relationship between government and local communities in the search for the common good.[40]

Subsidiarity and the common good should be seen as complementary rather than standing in isolation to one another. Thus for example, while subsidiarity requires schools, hospitals and the police to be administered as low-down the chain of decision-making as possible, it does not require such services to be privatized. As Clifford Longley has put it,

> To insist on the withdrawal of 'the state' from health, education or welfare provision, as some of the more extreme proponents of subsidiarity advocate, is not a true application of the principle because it could easily undermine, rather than promote, the common good.[41]

Conclusion

The common good challenges us to address the fundamental, and essentially religious, question of what it means to be human. It asks whether we primarily see ourselves as autonomous individuals, whose goal as a society extends only as far as realizing individual potential, individual goals and individual freedom, free from any responsibility to seek a common purpose or care for those unable to realize these individual goals? Or whether we believe that our humanity is constituted most profoundly by our relationships, such that our personal wellbeing includes reference to the fact of our sharing a common life together.

These are questions we need to discuss in order to encounter the central truth to which the common good attests, that we only fully flourish *as individuals* when those around us flourish too. Of course, the conversation is alive in many quarters, but the challenges involved in developing it are great, which is why the language of 'conversion' is appropriate. We noted earlier Sandel's assertion that creating a just society involves changing 'the habits of the heart' and 'leaning against purely privatized notions of the good life', albeit that self-interest (in the sense that my individual flourishing depends on the flourishing of all) may inspire action for the common good no less than pure altruism.

Participation in projects seeking to *actualize* the common good is one way in which its benefits can be realized by all. If the common good is rooted in 'the local', then it is through experiencing the difference it can

---

40 New Zealand Church Leaders, *Social Justice Statement*, 1993, 28: www.justice.net.nz/justwiki/social-justice-statement-1993.

41 Longley, 'Government and the common good', pp. 167–8.

make at grassroots that we can begin to embrace it as a mode of politics. From schoolchildren identifying issues of concern in their local neighbour-hood and preparing cost-effective and creative solutions for submission to their local authority,[42] to people with divergent perspectives and interests on specific topics coming together to listen, dialogue and generate new and mutually beneficial ideas for action,[43] the common good can prove its value as a new kind of conversation that goes beyond old divisions – left and right, business and unions, secular and faith, local and national – to create new and hopeful possibilities.

An important catalyst for common good activity can be the Church, which has nurtured the concept of the common good and is at the centre of many communities promoting civic action and building relationships across divides. The Christian faith can also provide, for some, a 'foun-dational narrative' or 'reason' for a society ordered around mutuality rather than individualism, that of human beings made in the image of a Trinitarian God whose very essence is relational and interdependent.[44]

If the Catholic catechism is right that,

> a society that wishes and intends to remain at the service of the human being at every level is a society that has the common good – the good of all people and of the whole person – as its primary goal,[45]

we need urgently to develop a public conversation about how such a society might be achieved.

---

42 Lyn Campbell QSM, 'Where does social justice start?', in Ruth Porter (ed.), *Pursuing Social Justice in New Zealand*, Auckland: Maxim Institute, 2007, p. 16.

43 Such dialogues have been promoted by 'Together for the Common Good' – www.togetherforthecommongood.co.uk.

44 Cf. Tim Gibson, 'Spirituality and the countryside: a rural perspective on Christian formation and the Big Society', in Alan Smith and Jill Hopkinson (eds), *Faith and the Future of the Countryside: Pastoral and Theological Perspectives on Rural Sustainability*, London: Canterbury Press, 2012, pp. 204–6; Anna Rowlands, keynote lecture at the Together for the Common Good conference, Liverpool, September 2013, http://togetherforthecommongood.co.uk/viewpoints/opinion-pieces/articles/anna-rowlands.html.

45 *Compendium of the Social Doctrine of the Church*, 165.

PART 2

Traditions of the Common Good

3

Aristotle and the Politics of the Common Good Today

PATRICK RIORDAN SJ

Introduction

What is a politician within a modern democratic system to make of appeals to the common good? The usual context of democratic politics is polarization between government and opposition parties. In this situation the basic attitude of a party politician is that her party's policies are better on the whole that those of her opponents' parties. Whether or not she uses the language of common goods, she will normally defend the view that her programme better serves the interests of the country, the welfare of all, as indicated in measures of employment and unemployment, social welfare, health care and education provision, along with justice and security concerns. Any appeals to the common good will be filtered through this framework, and will be tested whether the presented appeal supports her party's policies, or those of the opponents. Reactions will follow accordingly, either of endorsement or rejection. Anyone appealing to common goods in public discourse will have to anticipate this reality and a possible defensive or aggressive reaction.

There is another level on which politicians of opposing parties actually agree in endorsing the democratic system for handling conflict. It is a system which recognizes the pervasiveness of conflict, but is committed to handling that conflict by non-violent and non-coercive means.[1] So parties in conflict, competing with one another to achieve and hold onto power, to implement policies and attain political objectives of change, nonetheless accept as their common goods the democratic system and the rule of law as the political and legal framework within which they must carry out their conflict.

As well as anticipating the partisan reactions of democratic politicians, advocates on behalf of common goods will have to reflect whether

---

1 Bernard Crick, *In Defence of Politics*, new edn, London: Continuum, 2005.

their account of the common good is sufficiently attuned to the reality of conflict. Failure to accept the givenness of conflict and to recognize that the adversarial political manner of managing conflict is a great good, a significant achievement of our common history, will undermine appeals to common goods, making them appear implausible or idealistic.

Anticipation of politicians' reactions should not stifle the challenge when the advocate for common goods wishes to point to elements of discrimination or neglect, when policies are unjustifiably harmful to some persons or their goods. The relevant criteria operative in such challenges are two-fold: first, any policy which excludes specific individuals or groups from sharing appropriately in the benefits of social and economic cooperation is evidently not for the common good; and second, any policy which is detrimental to any dimension of human good, for instance privileging wealth at the expense of health, is not for the common good.[2] Such challenges, however, can usually also be formulated in terms of values such as equality and non-discrimination, liberty and autonomy, to which parties' political programmes as well as the political system in general may already be committed. The fear of seeming partisan should not deter critics from voicing their complaints about failures to achieve common goods. The reality of political conflict is the background context motivating participants either to meet genuine challenges or find that their support is lost to opponents.

What is a democratic politician to make of appeals to common goods when they are presented from a faith-based position? The spontaneous defensiveness in the context of adversarial politics is reinforced by anxieties not to appear to be functioning at the behest of some church or embracing a sectarian doctrine likely to alienate other members of the electorate. At the same time, the religious perspective may function to signal concern about the total context, the common horizon within which conflicts are carried out in political contest and in debates in civil society. The concerns of the faith communities to safeguard common human and moral values at a level removed from the cut and thrust of daily politics can be beneficial, reminding those engaged in conflict about the fundamental values at stake beyond party advantage, or swings in power or support.

In this chapter I will attempt to show how the Catholic tradition on the common good, by relying on concepts borrowed from Aristotle, avoids the dangers rightly worrying to democratic politicians. Aristotle might seem irrelevant for politics today. His view of politics may appear to be too

---

2 I elaborate these criteria and ground them in a reading of Aristotle in my *A Grammar of the Common Good*, London: Continuum, 2008.

moral, too idealistic, relying on presuppositions of harmony and agreement. The modern situation characterized by conflict, pluralism and an insistence on rights and entitlements requires a different account. But the modern descriptions of politics are unable to provide a coherent account of the common goods of politics, something which Aristotelian political thought is able to do. Revisiting Aristotle's core ideas we find his analysis can be reworked to apply to modern conditions, and at the same time provide an overview of the common goods of politics and other forms of cooperation. I will first recall some key elements from Catholic Social Thought, then I will identify elements from Aristotle's thought which can be relevant to the common good of politics, and I rework these to show their continuing relevance. The resulting account of common goods, I argue, is free from the dangers of sectarianism or theocracy.

The Catholic Church on the common good

When the Catholic Church offers her thought on common goods to citizens and politicians she does not intend that those ideas should be identified as somehow her exclusive property. The Second Vatican Council's Pastoral Constitution on the Church in the world of today, *Gaudium et spes*, is addressed not only to believers but to the whole of humanity (2). The pastoral constitution (26) follows Pope John XXIII's letter *Mater et magistra*, in describing the common good in terms of the set of conditions which enable people, both as individuals and as groups, to achieve fulfilment.[3] This statement lists the conditions as economic, social, cultural, and political. Implicit in this is a recognition that there is a form of development and fulfilment which is appropriate to humankind to which human striving is oriented. Also it is clear that this fulfilment is not simply a matter for individuals. There is a fulfilment of community without which human development would be incomplete. But most notably, the Council does not insist at this point what would comprise complete human fulfilment. This is left open, while the sets of conditions are considered.

The complexity of this position is important. The Church and the Council have a very definite view that human fulfilment consists in 'communion with God' (*GS* 27). All humans are said to have the same end, as designated by their Creator, namely, God himself (*GS* 24). However, the Council recognizes that others such as atheists will not be able to

---

3 Vatican II, *Gaudium et spes* (*The Pastoral Constitution on the Church in the Modern World*), 1965. Hereafter *GS*.

accept this teaching, and yet the Church expects that cooperation can be achieved in those elements which are conditions for human fulfilment, however it is understood. A fundamental disagreement is acknowledged, but not such that it would rule out all cooperation.

This was a startling innovation for the Church, which traditionally focused, not on the conditions or the means, but primarily on the ends. Heavenly glory, the vision of God in Christ, the communion of the saints in the resurrection, these are ways of speaking of the ultimate end of human life and of the Christian pilgrimage. Given this understanding of human fulfilment, the Church traditionally presented her guidance and her sacraments as the means to enable believers to achieve their salvation. However, in the Council's Pastoral Constitution the Church addresses not only believers, but all humankind in a spirit of cooperation and willingness to dialogue. Noticeable in this and other documents is the declared willingness to cooperate with everyone, including those of other faiths and atheists, in the acknowledgement that all people of goodwill strive for human fulfilment as they understand it. And given the reality of our world that many of these visions of fulfilment will not be compatible with one another, the hope is that people will be able to cooperate on the things on which they can agree. In all probability those things on which people can readily agree will not include the comprehensive vision of the ultimate good of fulfilment, but may include the ordinary means which everyone will have to rely upon to strive towards their ultimate ends. Hence the Church's emphasis on the common good in the social political context as the set of conditions which will enable each one and every group to achieve its fulfilment.

This radical change is part of a bigger pattern, in which the recognition of the centrality of religious liberty is paramount. No one ought to be coerced in their conscience.[4] Even those who are mistaken or misguided deserve respect, since they exercise their core freedom of identifying and pursuing the truth as they see it. There we find their dignity, their entitlement to respect. Along with this goes the declaration of respect for the secular nature of the state. The Church in Council acknowledges the autonomy of the secular and the distinctive purposes which belong to the state. This is far from earlier forms of teaching, surviving even into the twentieth century, which obliged the state to serve the mission of the Church. On that earlier view only an avowed Catholic state could be a

---

4 See the Council's Declaration on Religious Liberty, *Dignitatis humanae personae*, www.vatican.va/archive/hist_councils/ii_vatican_council/documents/vat-ii_decl_19651207_dignitatis-humanae_en.html.

good state. While the Vatican Council acknowledges the distinctiveness of the two institutions and their corresponding ends, the Council nonetheless sees the possibility of cooperation, but without one party encroaching on the domain of the other. In addition, the Church undertakes not to attempt to use the power of the state in order to achieve its own ends.[5]

The hope is that by concentrating on the conditions necessary for human flourishing, all groups in civil society will be able to find ways of collaborating for the sake of securing the conditions which will benefit all. There can be discussion of details of course, and there will be plenty of disagreement, but in general the relevant conditions will include the peace and security assured by the existence of a stable political order, the civil and political rights assured by a sound legal order, and the material supports for life and action assured by an economic and cultural order. There can be considerable variety in the forms exhibited in states and societies: that these orders are common goods of their respective societies does not entail that they are all uniform in their structures and procedures. It is important to recognize that these reflections are expressly situated in the second half of the twentieth century. The Church addresses the world of its time, not propounding a doctrine for all times and for every place, but in the consciousness of the distinctiveness of its time and place. So the respect for the dignity of humans, which in some formulation or other will always have been and always will be part of the Christian vision, now relies on the languages of individual freedoms and of rights.[6] Respect for human dignity animates this concern with securing the conditions for the wellbeing of individuals and of groups.

Care must be taken, then, when using the singular expression with the definite article: *the* common good. Consistent with the Church's usage, and depending on the context, the term common good may refer to the ultimate end of human striving as known in faith, it may refer to the ultimate end of human life as something as yet unknown, but subject to debate between representatives of different faiths and none, or it may refer to some set of conditions or other, economic, social or political, which a particular community deems appropriate for its circumstances: full employment, a comprehensive health care system, education, social welfare. Another way of putting this is to say that the term is to be applied analogically. Its meaning can shift, not arbitrarily, but systematically, from context to context. In every case it will refer to some objective of human cooperation, whether striven for explicitly or implicitly. It does

---

5 GS, 76.
6 Jack Mahoney, *The Challenge of Human Rights*, London: Blackwell, 2007.

not always have a religious meaning. To understand this analogical nature of common goods I explore the thought of Aristotle, whose political ideas as received in the Christian tradition by Albert the Great and Thomas Aquinas have informed the Catholic discourse on common goods. This ancestry underlines the point that the notion of common good is not distinctively Christian, even if it is the case that the Catholic Church has long relied on the concept for the presentation of her social thought.

Learning from Aristotle

Will a democratic politician who is wary of sectarian elements in a faith-based appeal to common goods be reassured in being told that the language is borrowed from Aristotle? Even if he is pre-Christian, does Aristotle not have his own commitment to a comprehensive doctrine of human fulfilment? And besides, isn't his comprehensive vision irrelevant to modern circumstances, in which conflict and difference instead of harmony and unity characterize political existence? Are not the differences such as to make Aristotle's thought irrelevant for our twenty-first-century concerns? Since these are valid questions, Aristotle might not be the philosopher of choice to guide a citizen or politician who must engage in an explicitly secular public arena.

There is no denying the major differences between the *polis* as Aristotle understood it, and a modern liberal democratic state. Three in particular are significant. First, Aristotle thought that it was a shared view of the good understood as a vision of fulfilment which constituted political community.[7] Our modern states don't think that, but something quite different if not opposed to it, namely, that the state's rationale is to manage conflict between adherents of different visions of the good life. So it is expected that conflict and diversity characterize our modern states, and not harmony and shared moral vision.

Second, Aristotle thought that the primary concern of the lawmakers in the *polis* would be the moral excellence of the citizens, because it is precisely the concern for the goodness and moral wellbeing of the citizens which makes a community political in the full sense, and not simply a commercial or military undertaking.[8] Our modern states abjure any such

---

7 Aristotle, *Politics*, Bk I c. 1: 'Our own observation tells us that every state is an association of persons formed with a view to some good purpose. I say "good" because in their actions all men do in fact aim at what they think good.' Trans. T. A. Sinclair, Harmondsworth: Penguin, 1972.

8 *Politics* Bk III c. 9: 'all who are concerned with lawful behaviour must make it their business to have an eye to the goodness or badness of the citizens'. Compare Bk VII c. 8.

moral task, and confine themselves to the enforcement of a minimum, as required to ensure order and security. Modern lawmakers would reject any suggestion that their concern should be to make people good. They would more likely follow John Stuart Mill's 'harm principle' and insist that state power should not be used to restrict human liberty except where the exercise of that liberty involves harm to others.[9]

Third, Aristotle's language was normative and teleological, in contrast to the contemporary reliance on the language of rights. Aristotle understood human nature as oriented to a completion or fulfilment.[10] It followed from this that he took as a standard of action the best that could be done or achieved, in much the same way as an athlete today would measure her performance against the established records, or at least against her personal best. The language of contemporary politics is based on rights, as limits on what states may do to citizens, and not on the good or the best achieved so far.

What should follow from this consideration of the three major differences: conflict as opposed to harmony, avoidance of harm and not promotion of moral excellence, and securing rights instead of facilitating fulfilment? One conclusion is to withdraw all Aristotelian endorsement from the modern state, and deny that it could ever be the locus of rational approval or loyalty in Aristotelian terms. So on such an account, the modern state cannot possibly be the agent of the Aristotelian common good as the highest good embracing all other goods. Alternatively, I suggest that the three points of contrast can be reworked to allow for an Aristotelian style reading of our current situation, without abandoning the sources of critique. But first it is necessary to consider what Aristotle actually says.

Aristotle: key ideas

Some preliminary remarks about Aristotle will help to situate the discussion. I want to take him at his word in what he says in a number of key passages. The first is the remark early in the *Politics* that it is the sharing of a view of what is good and evil, right and wrong, just and unjust, that makes a household or a political community (*Politics* Bk I c. 2). Aristotle insists that shared meaning is essential to the existence of a political entity.

---

9 John Stuart Mill, *Utilitarianism, On Liberty and Considerations on Representative Government*, H. B. Acton (ed.), London: Dent, 1972, p. 79.

10 *Politics* Bk I c. 2: 'whatever is the end-product of the perfecting process of any object, that we call its nature, that which man, house, household, or anything else aims at being'.

And because shared meaning is so essential to political existence, Aristotle also remarks on the capacity for reasoned speech as the distinctive human capacity equipping the human for politics.[11] That capacity is exercised by participation in any manner of deliberation about what is beneficial or harmful, just or unjust. Deliberation may be ongoing, but it is oriented to getting some answers, and adequate answers would be part of the common good of those engaged in the deliberation, the members of the polity. This is also implied, in part, by a second remark from Aristotle which I want to take seriously, which is that as all action is for the sake of some good, so too all action in common, all cooperation, is for the sake of some good (*Politics* Bk I c. 1). This needs to be qualified slightly by Aristotle's own remark, allowing for the possibility of error, that people act and cooperate for the sake of something which is thought to be good. And third, we should take Aristotle at his word when he reminds us that it is not always the same good which is pursued in these forms of cooperation. 'Since there are many actions, arts and sciences, it follows that their ends are many too – the end of medical science is health; of military science, victory; of economic science, wealth' (*Ethics* Bk I, c. 1).[12]

We are familiar from our experience with the myriad forms of co-operation including political cooperation: what are the goods that are pursued in common? What are the shared views of those goods, the shared meaning which sustains the collaboration? And how might we engage in the reflection on that meaning along with the other participants, so that we pursue only truly valuable goods? Considering Aristotle's point about sharing a view of the good, is talk of the common good to be confined to communities of such a scale that all the participants can deliberate about their own goods in common? In other words, can a liberal democratic state with a market economy have a common good? Is it only the small scale community such as the Greek city state with its restrictions on citizenship which is able to realize the ideal?[13] Aristotle can be read as saying as much, but his texts provide resources for considering the common

---

11 *Politics* Bk I c. 2: 'Nature, as we say, does nothing without some purpose; and for the purpose of making man a political animal she has endowed him alone among the animals with the power of reasoned speech ... Speech ... serves to indicate what is useful and what is harmful, and so also what is right and what is wrong. For the real difference between man and other animals is that humans alone have perception of good and evil, right and wrong, just and unjust. And it is the sharing of a common view in these matters that makes a household or a city.'

12 *The Ethics of Aristotle: the Nicomachean Ethics*, trans. J. A. K. Thomson, Harmondsworth: Penguin, 1976.

13 Alasdair MacIntyre in various publications raises such concerns. See his 'Politics, Philosophy and the Common Good', *Studi Perugini* 3 (1997), reprinted in *The MacIntyre Reader*, ed. Kelvin Knight, Cambridge: Polity Press, 1998.

good of polities which fail to measure up to the highest standards. The non-ideal cases do not appear in his examination *only* as examples of defect, or deviance from the best case scenario, although they are definitely that. They also can be analysed as instances of cooperation in the pursuit of a good in common. I will take Aristotle at his word, when he says that '*every polis* is an association of persons formed with a view to some good purpose' (*Politics*, Bk I c. 1). Among the good purposes which Aristotle identified we can recognize themes which today figure in the analyses of political scientists. Security, the freedom from danger hoped for from mutual non-aggression pacts, prosperity, as achieved by treaties ensuring trade in goods and services, were as familiar to Aristotle as they are to us. But he thought that politics in the fullest sense would comprise something more. Aristotle in his analysis of any matter takes his standard from the best case, whether an object of botany or zoology, or of ethics or politics. He explains that the nature of any kind of thing is to be read from its perfection, that stage of its existence when it has achieved what it is capable of being. So the seed or the sprouting plant are to be understood in terms of what they are on the way to becoming. Similarly with forms of cooperation in the social and political arena. The political is understood as that which can be the end of a process, a stage of self-sufficiency, at which nothing is lacking which might yet complete the development.[14] The good life is the notion he uses for that form of cooperation in which 'nothing is lacking'. The good life, realized in politics, is introduced in contrast to life itself, which is secured in the household.

In considering the relationship between the household and the city, Aristotle maintains that there is a common good appropriate to each of them. In his short genealogy at the beginning of the *Politics* he describes a process of development of forms of human collaboration for common advantage, from the partnership of pairs (male and female, master and slave) to the formation of households, the emergence of villages, and associations of villages. The city/*polis* emerges when the collaboration is sufficiently sophisticated to provide the association with everything it needs to achieve the good life (*Politics* Bk I c. 2). However, the household is not presented here as merely a stage in the evolution of the polis, as the caterpillar is a stage in the life cycle of the butterfly. The household relates to the *polis*, not as a deficient or immature city, but as an essential element within the city which provides important preconditions for

---

14 '[W]hatever is the end-product of the perfecting process of any object, that we call its nature, that which man, house, household, or anything else aims at being. Moreover the aim and the end can only be that which is best, perfection; and self-sufficiency is both end and perfection.' Aristotle, *Politics* Bk I c. 2.

the polity. Aristotle makes this point in terms of the distinction between life itself, and the good life.[15] The household nurtures life on a daily and generational basis. The city pursues the good life.

Even if we accept that the modern state is very different from the *polis* envisaged by Aristotle, it does not follow that we must abandon any investigation of the goods in common which are pursued and ought to be pursued in the forms of cooperation we now label political. In line with Aristotle's own usage, we should not confine talk of common goods to the best case. His generalization in the opening words of the *Politics* applies to all instances of cooperation and community, that all pursue some good, or something which appears to them to be good (*Politics* Bk I c. 1). We should be able to identify goods in common even in deficient and restricted instances of cooperation. The tools of common good analysis can remain available for the critique of the relevant restrictions and deficiencies, but also facilitate appreciation of the real good to be found in the cooperation.

Reconstructing Aristotle's propositions

Returning to the three major differences noted above, I will show that far from being irrelevant to modern politics Aristotle's thought illuminates what is actually going on in terms of the common goods of cooperation among the participants, citizens and officials, within democratic states. The first difference contrasted the reality of conflict with the harmony of agreement on what is good and just. However, even if we accept that government in liberal democracies is predicated on conflict, it does not follow that an Aristotelian analysis is irrelevant. To the extent that the conflict we encounter is managed politically, that is, by means which rely on talking and reasoning, the process of politics can be understood as oriented to attaining agreement on what is good, just and lawful, even though that agreement and harmony is still a long way off.[16] To the extent that majorities and powerful interests accept the obligation to allow minorities to have their say, to provide reasons to the defeated why the chosen policy is not unjust, and to respect constitutionally protected rights, their position in power is not purely coercive domination. The acceptance of certain limits – the rule of law, constitutional constraints on power, and the myriad requirements concerning transparency and accountability –

15 *Politics* Bk I c. 2: 'The final association, formed of several villages, is the city or state. For all practical purposes the process is now complete; self-sufficiency has been reached and so, while it started as a means of securing life itself, it is now in a position to secure the good life.'

16 Bernard Crick, *In Defence of Politics*. See n. 1 above.

reflects a considerable degree of agreement about the manner in which conflict is to be handled. The extent of the good on which we already agree is not as broad as Aristotle would have envisaged, but it is nonetheless a considerable achievement arising from a history of trial and error, of crises and problems. The historical development of the elements of the rule of law shows how solutions were developed to prevent the recurrence of problems already encountered.[17] Operative in this history is a vision of what is just, and what is good, which is vague and never fully articulated, but finds concrete expression in the answers given to the actual problems faced. So an Aristotelian can appreciate the forging of piecemeal and fragmentary agreement about the good and the just which sustains modern politics, even if it falls far short of the Aristotelian ideal.

The second difference highlighted above was that the modern lawmaker does not have an eye to the character formation of citizens, and so does not conform to the measure Aristotle set for a *polis*. Once again I take it as read that this is the case. Once again I suggest that an Aristotelian analysis is not therefore obsolete in this situation. One medieval Aristotelian provides a way forward. Aquinas remarks that the good is predicated in different senses, either simply, or qualified in some way.[18] A qualified sense of goodness is the goodness of conformity with the law's requirements, and a more complete goodness is realized when a virtuous character acts spontaneously in accordance with the law from a direct willing of the comprehended good.[19] So Aquinas following Aristotle can confirm that the law's purpose is to make people good, and he qualifies Aristotle by noting that the attainable goodness is the minimal sense of conformity with the civil law.[20] If they conform their behaviour to what the law commands, avoiding those actions which are prohibited, and performing whatever actions are required, people are *in this sense* good. This meaning

---

17 Tom Bingham, *The Rule of Law*, London: Allen Lane, 2010.

18 Thomas Aquinas declares that 'leading its subjects into the virtue appropriate to their condition is a proper function of law. Now since virtue is that which makes its possessor good, the consequence is that the proper effect of law on those to whom it is given is to make them good, either good simply speaking or good in a certain respect.' *Summa Theologiae* 1a2ae q.92 a.1, ed. and trans. Thomas Gilby OP, London: Blackfriars, 1966.

19 Joseph Raz draws a similar distinction between compliance and conformity: conformity is doing what the law requires while compliance is doing what the law requires because the law requires it. Cf. J. Raz, *Practical Reason and Norms*, 2nd edn, Oxford: Oxford University Press, 1999, pp. 178–9; also Scott Hershovitz, 'The Authority of Law', in Andrei Marmor, *The Routledge Companion to Philosophy of Law*, New York and London: Routledge, 2012, pp. 65–75 at p. 67. Note the difference to Aquinas' distinction, which doesn't pick out the fact of the law's command, but the reasons for the sake of which the law is enacted.

20 Aquinas, *Summa* 1a2ae q.92 a.1 ad3m: 'the political commonwealth cannot flourish unless its citizens are virtuous, at least those in leading positions: it is enough for the good of the community if others are so far virtuous that they obey the commands of the ruling authorities'.

of goodness is the only one which human law with its instruments can attempt to guarantee, or at least address. The coercive force of law can succeed in effecting conformity, but has no proper instrument for ensuring that the conformity springs spontaneously from virtuous character. The lawmaker can hope that habituation through the discipline of laws can lead to the formation of character, but she cannot make it happen.[21] Implicit in Aquinas' remarks that at least the lawmakers must be virtuous is the thought that no society which relied *solely* on the enforcement of law ensuring conformity could survive. The complete police-state, regulating and monitoring everything, is doomed.

From an Aristotelian perspective it is noticeable that the law-making of our modern democratic states is oriented to the regulation of behaviour in the greatest detail. The law specifies where one may and may not smoke, how fast one may drive, how one may or may not redesign or paint the house façade, who and under what conditions may become employers of other people, and so forth. All of these regulations are introduced for some purpose, deemed good and worthwhile by their proponents, but those who advocate and introduce the laws are motivated by something more than simply effecting material obedience. They have a vision of the good which they hope to realize via the instruments of the law, for instance protecting the health of workers by prohibiting smoking in the workplace, protecting lives jeopardized by speeding traffic. This becomes articulated to some extent in the debates for and against some bill. The good indeed is what is at stake in the making and enforcing of the law, although it is important to bear in mind Aristotle's caveat that people can be mistaken about their good. So while in the previous point I suggested that our modern political societies do operate with a shared view of the good, namely, a minimum of agreement on how conflict is to be managed, here I draw attention to the way in which our various efforts to legislate result in setting standards to which citizens are expected to conform in exercising their responsibility towards others. The law does attempt to make people good, in the qualified sense sketched by Aquinas.

While for Aristotle the capacity for reasoned discourse is the feature which equips humans for politics, he would have expected the relevant language to be that of the good, while in modern politics the language

---

21 Considering the need for human law, Aquinas writes: 'some are bumptious, headlong in vice, not amenable to advice, and these have to be held back from evil by fear and force, so that they at least stop doing mischief and leave others in peace. Becoming so habituated they may come to do of their own accord what earlier they did from fear, and grow virtuous. This schooling through the pressure exerted through the fear of punishment is the discipline of human law.' *Summa* 1a2ae q.95 a.1.

of rights predominates. This was the third major divergence from the Aristotelian standard highlighted above. But again there is a possibility of revision. Alasdair MacIntyre has shown convincingly that Alan Gewirth's attempt to provide a philosophical grounding for rights has failed.[22] He has also remarked how liberal political systems continue unfazed by such failure. How can this be? I suggest that the dilemma evaporates once we realize that the language of rights is not what it claims to be. Introduced to deal with the lack of a shared language of the good, it pretends to be an alternative, rooted in something incontrovertible and agreed, but in fact it functions as it does to the extent that it is a way of expressing and protecting human goods.

For instance, consider John Stuart Mill's rejection of any account of rights as rooted in human nature or natural law, and his utilitarian account of rights as grounded in utility in the broadest sense, as the interests of the human as a progressive being.[23] On Mill's view, rights are instituted in society to facilitate the development of the human individual and human society. The law creates rights for the sake of some purpose. Those holding the opposite view insist that the law does not create rights as such, but recognizes existing moral rights and institutionalizes them. With MacIntyre we can see that this debate is interminable, but perhaps we can also see that it is irrelevant. Neither position must prevail for the members of a liberal democratic state to continue successfully to use the language of rights. All it requires is that the rights identified and defended are sufficiently linked to genuine goods: human life, freedom of conscience, freedom of speech, religious liberty. The debate then is about the good, in the context of disagreement on the good, but seeking to construct agreement. Note that I am not appealing to goods to justify rights claims, but arguing that the meaning of the content of rights claims is rooted in the corresponding goods.

Aristotle rescued?

I have been attempting to offer an Aristotelian version of what we find in modern democratic states, to provide a context for understanding the common goods of politics in a secular sense. Although the modern state does not exemplify the Aristotelian *polis*, it nonetheless can be appreciated

---

22 Alasdair MacIntyre, *After Virtue. A Study in Moral Theory*, 2nd edn, Notre Dame, Indiana: University of Notre Dame Press, 1984, pp. 66–71.

23 J. S. Mill, *Utilitarianism, On Liberty and Considerations on Representative Government*, ed. H. B. Acton, London: Dent, 1972, p. 79.

in Aristotelian terms for what it does achieve. Despite its fundamental divergences from the Greek *polis*, the modern state exemplifies certain key ideas: the sharing of meaning which sustains political cooperation; the development of qualities of character which are demonstrated when participants in political cooperation abide by minimal standards as laid down by law; and cooperation itself as a mode of participation in the good life, elements of which are itemized in the many goods to which people are said to have rights. Although diverging from Aristotle's own application of these ideas and his conclusions, my reworking of his analysis allows us to see the essential core of the modern state. At the same time, this use of Aristotle's ideas allows us to recapture an essentially modern concern which is to limit the power of the state. Aristotle's ideas when applied to the modern liberal state allow us to recognize certain limits to the state's competence. Although based on shared meaning, the content of that meaning is inevitably limited to what can be achieved in public deliberation among persons and groups whose comprehensive doctrines are diverse. Although aspiring to equip people for a life in freedom, the goodness of character it can effect by its own instruments is confined to conformity to the minimal requirements of the civil law. And although avoiding the danger of imposing a particular conception of human fulfilment on its citizens the state nonetheless requires acceptance of a set of limited standards for human behaviour as formulated in the sets of human, civil and political rights. The limits implicit in these positions allow the state to remain free from domination by any sectarian doctrine, even one of a non-religious nature such as atheistic humanism.[24] While ensuring the independence and freedom of the liberal state, these limits also allow for the criticism of the state and its officers whenever they would attempt to overstep the limits and take on an inappropriate role, for which they are not competent, in specifying the ultimate good of humans and their societies, and in specifying the standards of moral fulfilment and goodness.

Contrary to what Aristotle considered as the point of politics, namely, the good life as the achievement of excellence in performance of distinctive human activities, both theoretical and practical, my argument points to the necessity of confining the purposes of modern politics. Explicitly religious concerns and theological content are to be excluded from the liberal democratic state's understanding of its nature and purpose. Of course,

---

24 Note Rawls' identification of secularism as a comprehensive doctrine, along with those of a religious nature, from which the overlapping consensus at the heart of a liberal polity should be independent: cf. John Rawls, 'The Idea of Public Reason Revisited', in *The Law of Peoples*, Cambridge, MA: Harvard University Press, 1999, pp. 143, 149.

this does not preclude citizens and indeed theologians having a faith-based perspective on the state. It is simply that the state cannot include such a perspective in its own self-understanding and in its understanding of its own common good. However, the state is not compromised by allowing for the maintenance of other *fora* for the debate about the highest good and the pursuit of the unrestricted common good, even if these are not its proper business.

Faith-based, but not theocratic

I suggest that the above reworking of Aristotle's thought is compatible with what the Catholic Church has formulated as its view of the modern state committed to protecting human liberty, and its own relationship with such a state. This involves a recognition of the autonomy of the secular, as well as a commitment to renounce the use of state power to achieve religious objectives. That this development in the mid-twentieth century involved a radical turnaround in the Church's political understanding cannot be denied. It should be emphasized that the Church's position is rooted in a theological stance, and so it does not amount to an acceptance of a relegation of religion to a purely private sphere. The acceptance of the possibility of cooperation for establishing and maintaining the conditions for the flourishing of human persons and their communities is compatible with tolerance for diverse comprehensive doctrines. It does not insist on agreement on ultimate goods in order to engage in cooperation on more instrumental and conditional goods.

Some theocratic positions take the opposite view. Taking Aristotle's assertion that the good life pursued in the *polis* is the highest good which embraces all the rest, they fill their notion of the highest good with content from their religious faith. They conclude that the political authorities have responsibility to pursue that highest good so understood. Then the authorities are understood to be obligated to bring about harmony and unity in society in the shared acceptance of this good, and to legislate so as to make people good and equip them for salvation. Not every religiously grounded position on politics is theocratic in that sense. There are other theologically grounded positions which can support the exclusion of concern with God as the highest good from the agenda of the state. Early in the Christian tradition Augustine realized that the instruments available to civil authorities, typically coercive force, were inappropriate and inadequate to the task of making people good. In fact, he generalized his view that only God could make people good according to the divine standard of goodness, and hence that it could not be the responsibility of political authorities to make people good.[25]

This position receives a more nuanced reworking by Aquinas, who is reluctant to abandon so much of Aristotle. And so Aquinas can retain the insights of both his mentors, Aristotle and Augustine, by relying on distinctions such as that invoked above between the different senses of 'good'. John Finnis has worked through some of this material, and so I rely on his conclusions at this point.[26] He draws on Aquinas to show that there is a perspective on the good relative to the state which does not exhaust the human good and leaves scope for other agents and authorities. In particular, since the interior attitude and intention (virtue) of agents is a major dimension of their goodness or holiness, and this is not accessible to the instruments of the human lawmaker and enforcer, it follows that the human authorities cannot have the unrestricted common good as their appropriate goal. Their object is the domain of means and conditions, facilitating the pursuit of the good by persons and groups. The delineation of religious liberty helps to mark this distinction, since it specifies limits to what the state may do in interfering, either positively or negatively, with the freedoms of people to follow their religious conscience.[27]

Drawing on this account of goodness and of the limited capacities of the modern state I argue against theocrats that the instruments of the state are unsuitable for making people good and getting them to conform to the requirements of their religious world view. Without wishing to consider the validity of the ends proposed, I concentrate on the inherent limitations of the modern state which, both in Aristotelian terms and in terms of its own self-understanding, is not designed to deliver the kinds of effects which Aristotle and the theocrat hope for.

Conclusion

Many people in the United Kingdom, including its politicians, might be reluctant to adopt the language of common goods for fear of endorsing some religious position or being tricked into approving some proposition

25 Augustine, *The City of God*, ed. D. Knowles, trans. H. Bettenson, Harmondsworth: Penguin, 1972; R. A. Markus, *Saeculum: History and Society in the Theology of St Augustine*, Cambridge: Cambridge University Press, 1970.

26 John Finnis, 'Public good: the specifically political common good in Aquinas', in R. P. George (ed.), *Natural Law and Moral Inquiry: Ethics Metaphysics and Politics in the Work of Germain Grisez*, Washington, DC: Georgetown University Press, 1998, pp. 174–209.

27 Martha Nussbaum, *Liberty of Conscience: In Defense of America's Tradition of Religious Equality*, New York: Basic Books, 2008, offers a very helpful reworking of the value of religious liberty as safeguarding the liberal polity.

contrary to their convictions. It is to be hoped that the foregoing discussion of Aristotle and of the Catholic Church's development of his ideas are sufficient to remove those fears. This discussion shows that a religious vision of the *summum bonum* or unrestricted common good is not an appropriate common good of the modern liberal democratic state.[28] While a liberal democratic state can have an appropriate common good of its own, this will be understood, not in terms of policies designed to bring about human flourishing, but in terms of policies securing the means and conditions for people and groups to pursue their own flourishing. The processes of liberal democratic politics can be understood as the search for and facilitation or provision of those conditions, ever changing as elements of human flourishing are discovered and clarified. For instance, the invention and development of the language of human rights can be understood in terms of this dynamic. In that context current debates about the relative weights of equality and liberty exemplify the search for the appropriate conditions to allow individuals and groups to pursue their own visions of the good life.[29]

Will the debates within a pluralist society in a liberal democratic state never address questions of the ultimate human good? Of course, there are such further debates, aesthetic, cultural, anthropological, philosophical and theological, about what constitutes human wellbeing and human flourishing, and these need to be fostered and facilitated in the broader political culture of civil society, in institutions of education, academia, publishing and churches. The availability of the language of common goods will prove useful for communicating a faith-based vision of human fulfilment but such a vision will be offered for consideration and free acceptance or rejection. But as argued above, the business of the liberal democratic state in providing conditions for flourishing does not have to await the resolution of such debates. Its business can be carried on while allowing the debates to continue, leaving open the determination of what would constitute human flourishing. A liberal democratic state which attempted to fix policies according to one preferred answer to the questions about the highest good would be exceeding its proper limits and violating liberties.

In practice, however, it is more likely to be the case that appeals to the common good do not invoke some ultimate good but are holding public authorities to account for their failure to provide the conditions for the

---

28 It is worth recalling that the common good is understood here in a practical as distinct from an ontological sense, as that good in common for the sake of which people knowingly cooperate.

29 Roger Trigg, *Equality, Freedom, and Religion*, Oxford: Oxford University Press, 2012.

flourishing of everyone and every group. That failure can be due to a deliberate or unintended exclusion of some from a share in the benefits of social cooperation, as when some groups suffer disproportionately from austerity policies, or it can be due to an imbalanced emphasis on some aspects of human good to the detriment of others, as when economic efficiency trumps educational values. In such cases the appeal to common goods holds the authorities to account for their responsibility in providing for everyone and every group the conditions for their wellbeing. Responsible politicians will not hesitate to accept the validity of the concept of common good and its criteria, even if they might wish to enter into reasoned discourse about the goodness of the disputed measures.

4

Wealth and Common Good

ESTHER D. REED

Wealth is about more than money. It's about assets (property, goods, valuables, money, equity funds and other economic resources) that can be manipulated without the hindrance of debt. Thomas Piketty made precisely this point recently when his surprise bestseller *Capital in the 21st Century* described the historical evolution of income and wealth distribution in advanced economies.[1] Piketty's central observation was that the return on capital outstrips economic growth such that wealth rises and inequality increases. Wealth, inherited wealth especially, affects money flows and slows economic growth in societies where inequality is highest because fewer people have money to spend. Free market economics does not spread riches fairly or 'lift all boats' because wealth inequality typically hinders growth and leads to the control of political processes by a tiny high-income and high-wealth elite. This chapter argues that Christianity is not always anti-wealth per se but has much to say about the use of wealth not merely for personal advantage but for common good.

Through the eye of a needle

It's funny how humour works. The routine interaction between father and son in the cartoon overleaf is expected to concern life-attitude, the virtues and education more generally, not the brute fact of the boy's inheritance. To the sardonically minded, it is the inheritance that will really bring success not high moral standards or education. Hence the raised eyebrow or twitch of the lips because we don't expect this dark truth to be faced so openly.

---

1 Thomas Piketty, *Capital in the 21st Century*, Cambridge, MA: Harvard University Press, 2014.

"Son, I'm leaving you with the 3 vital elements of success — self confidence, sound education, and inherited wealth."

Jesus used humour in one of the most famous New Testament passages about wealth:

And a ruler asked him, 'Good Teacher, what must I do to inherit eternal life?' And Jesus said to him, 'Why do you call me good? No one is good except God alone. You know the commandments: "Do not commit adultery, Do not murder, Do not steal, Do not bear false witness, Honour your father and mother."' And he said, 'All these I have kept from my youth.' When Jesus heard this, he said to him, 'One thing you still lack. Sell all that you have and distribute to the poor, and you will have treasure in heaven; and come, follow me.' But when he heard these things, he became very sad, for he was extremely rich. Jesus, seeing that he had become sad, said, 'How difficult it is for those who have wealth to enter the kingdom of God! For it is easier for a camel to go through the eye of a needle than for a rich person to enter the kingdom of God.' Those who heard it said, 'Then who can be saved?' But he said, 'What is impossible with man is possible with God.' (Luke 18.20–27; see also Mark 10.25; Matt. 19.24)[2]

---

2 All biblical citations from the *English Standard Version* Anglicized edn, London: Collins, 2002.

It's not quite 'Hey, did you hear the one about the camel?', but Jesus uses exaggeration to the point of folly or ridicule. Like the saying, 'If your right eye causes you to sin, tear it out and throw it away' (Matt. 5.29) or 'Why do you see the speck that is in your brother's eye, but do not notice the log that is in your own eye?' (Matt. 7.3), the idea of a camel going through the eye of a needle stretches the idea beyond normal proportions thus making the point effectively.[3] Exaggeration draws attention to difficulties facing the extremely rich wanting to enter the kingdom of heaven, both to encourage a change in behaviour and raise awareness.

So, how exaggerated is the point being made? Can one who fails to distribute all their goods to the poor remain a disciple of Jesus Christ? In the ancient Church only a small number of committed ascetics applied Jesus' instruction to the rich ruler, 'Sell all that you have and distribute to the poor' to their own lives. So Peter Brown observed recently in his magnum opus *Through the Eye of a Needle: Wealth, the Fall of Rome and the Making of Christianity in the West*. Relatively few took Jesus' teaching literally while most lived humdrum lives serving God amid earning a living, running a business, trading honourably and honestly, giving alms to the poor, and suchlike: 'To treat the renouncers of wealth as the heroes and heroines of a "true" Christianity and to view all other forms of religious giving as somehow a betrayal of the essential radicalism of the Christian movement is to merely echo the high-minded language of the ascetic movement.'[4]

Yet the choice in Luke's Gospel for the rich man addressed by Jesus is stark. He may either enter the Kingdom of God or keep his wealth. And the question of whether the renunciation of wealth is the only route for the disciple of Christ who hopes to enter the Kingdom of God echoes down the centuries. Other New Testament passages suggest that Jesus did not disallow private property. Jesus told the parable of the talents to chastise laziness and the lack of due diligence with respect to God-given resources (Matt. 25.14–30). He ate with rich as well as poor (Mark 15.43; Luke 19.1–10), did not exclude anyone from the Kingdom of God solely on the grounds of wealth but required all to be faithful stewards of the gifts God has given. Like early Church believers, present-day readers might draw a

---

3 Some have suggested that the eye of a needle (Gk *belone*) was the name of a small gate in the wall of the city of Jerusalem, or that the Greek word *kamelos* could have been pronounced *kamilos* which was the word for a ship's cable or rope, which would be impossibly difficult to thread through the eye of a domestic needle. See Darrell L. Bock, *Luke 9:51–24:53*, Ada, MI: Baker Academic, 1996, p. 1485.

4 Peter Brown, *Through the Eye of a Needle: Wealth, the Fall of Rome and the Making of Christianity in the West, 350–550AD*, Princeton and Oxford: Princeton University Press, 2012, p. xxv.

distinction at this point between 'literal' and 'direct' interpretations of the text and suggest that, while Jesus' words apply to all disciples 'directly', they might not apply 'literally'.[5] Such a reading would be convenient but runs the obvious risk of blunting the challenge of the passage to seek first the Kingdom of God and its righteousness.

"Don't fret about that Kingdom of Heaven stuff – you would obviously liquidise the camel first."

The issue for our purposes remains the extent of Jesus' exaggeration in conversation with the rich man. Can we ease the discomfort we feel from the sharp-pointed needle of literalism, and the application of his words to all believers, without compromising the nub of the parable that concerns the all-inclusive and absolute claim of God upon all earthly wealth? Studies have shown that regular exercise may alter how a person experiences physical pain. The longer we continue to work out the greater our tolerance for discomfort can become.[6] In a similar way, the longer we practise living in unquestioning prosperity (however modest), the greater our tolerance for the discomfort of Jesus' words may become.

---

5 Augustine made this distinction in *On Christian Doctrine* Bk III, Ch. 5.
6 M. D. Jones, J. Booth, J. L. Taylor, B. K. Barry, 'Aerobic training increases pain tolerance in healthy individuals', *Medicine and Science in Sports and Exercise* 46:8, 2012, pp. 1640–7.

Building bigger barns

The various literary genres of the Gospels deploy a range of modes of communication. Some parables employ types of satire to illustrate, expose and denounce tendencies in human nature. One such parable is about building bigger barns in which the foolishness of seeing wealth merely as means for the accumulation of yet more wealth is parodied to draw attention to its ultimate futility.

> Someone in the crowd said to him, 'Teacher, tell my brother to divide the inheritance with me.' But he said to him, 'Man, who made me a judge or arbitrator over you?' And he said to them, 'Take care, and be on your guard against all covetousness, for one's life does not consist in the abundance of his possessions.' And he told them a parable, saying, 'The land of a rich man produced plentifully, and he thought to himself, "What shall I do, for I have nowhere to store my crops?" And he said, "I will do this: I will tear down my barns and build larger ones, and there I will store all my grain and my goods. And I will say to my soul, 'Soul, you have ample goods laid up for many years; relax, eat, drink, be merry.'" But God said to him, "Fool! This night your soul is required of you, and the things you have prepared, whose will they be?" So is the one who lays up treasure for himself and is not rich toward God.' (Luke 12.13–21)

According to the law and custom of the time, an older son would have received twice the inheritance of other sons but would have been obliged to support his mother and any unmarried sisters. It would have been commonplace for brothers to leave the inheritance intact and farm it together although the law provided for the possibility of brothers asking for their share. The point at issue appears to be an elder brother's dilatoriness in handing over the younger brother's material share in the inheritance, and the younger brother approaches Jesus for a judgement. Jesus declines to pronounce (though had been addressed as a 'Rabbi' authorized to arbitrate) but tells the parable that, according to Luke's comment, shifts the conversation to the eternal inheritance of those 'rich toward God'.[7]

The parable is characteristically brief but, for those of us sympathetic to the enquirer's situation, the humour is discomfortingly sharp. The man in the crowd who asked the question was seeking resolution in customary manner of a long-standing grievance when Jesus replies with his account of the 'fool' whose covetousness is made a lesson for all who have ears to hear. It would have been accepted practice to take a legal grievance to a

---

7 François Bovon, *Luke 2: A Commentary on the Gospel of Luke 9:51–19:27*, trans. Donald S. Deer, Minneapolis MN: Fortress Press, 2013, p. 206.

Rabbi. Instead of a decision on his case, however, the man got a stinging message preached to the whole crowd about the dangers of wealth and desire for possessions. Anger and embarrassment perhaps rose in his face and we can imagine him wince as Jesus makes no concession to his difficulties but cuts to the quick where money and wealth are concerned.

The literary context is a conversation between Jesus and the crowds during which Jesus railed against the hypocrisy of the Pharisees, saying: 'Nothing is covered up that will not be revealed, or hidden that will not be known' (Luke 12.2). What has been said in the dark shall be heard in the light and what has been whispered in private rooms shall be proclaimed from the rooftops! Jesus' transparency agenda is cosmic. 'Beware', he says (Gk προσέχω, *prosechō*), in a combination of both warning and threat, because anything unworthy will be made public. Hypocrisy will be exposed. 'Do not fear those who kill the body, and after that have nothing more that they can do ... [F]ear him who, after he has killed, has authority to cast into hell. Yes, I tell you, fear him' (Luke 12.5). Wealth brings protection against some of life's ills but God is more to be feared than any earthly ambition or power. 'Luke's God', says commentator François Bovon, who is 'stronger than death, is also more dangerous than death.'[8]

That the rich man's land produced plentifully is not morally problematic. The man is not reprehended for being rich, for farming well, storing his grain sensibly or planning for the future. His profits were not ill-gained. The problem seems to lie in his attitude to profit and his desire to hoard wealth rather than use it with and for others. In a conversation with a Pharisee which comes just before this text, Jesus lambasted his practice of tithing mint and cumin and other herbs but neglecting true love and justice, that is, attending to the letter of the law but not its spirit (Luke 11.37–44). 'Woe to you! For you are like unmarked graves, and people walk over them without knowing it' (Luke 11.44). This dark saying associates modes of social acceptability that mask greed with spiritual death; the venom of Jesus' reply is not directed at the practice of tithing per se but at the deceptions of the heart. Similarly in the parable, the problem is not with storing the corn safely or the farmer's stewardship of his wealth but with the point at which his attitude to wealth crossed into vice:

> Carried away by the logic of profit, he wanted to cap the success of his enterprise by the enlargement of his warehouses ... There is no question about there being goods, therefore something positive. But on the land-owner's lips, the emphasis is on property, '*my* goods', '*my* crops'.[9]

8 Bovon, *Luke* 2, p. 180.
9 Bovon, *Luke* 2, p. 200.

" I don't ask for much, all I want is more. "

The moral problem in the parable lies not with the wealth that accrues to hard work and the blessings of the harvest but the fool's becoming ensnared in the allure of yet more reserves and failing to use his wealth well. Peter Brown writes about wealth in the fourth and fifth centuries, but his basic points are relevant here:

> Wealth came mainly from labour on the land. This means that, every year, over 60 percent of the wealth of the Roman empire was gathered at harvest-time ... For everyone, the harvest was a time of finality. The piles of grain gathered on the threshing floor were all that there was. And only a small portion of these piles would remain in the hands of the farmers ... [T]he rich had privileged access to wider and more lucrative markets ... The rich alone could also defeat time.[10]

---

10 Brown, *Through the Eye*, pp. 11–14.

The rich man in the parable could store the abundance of the harvest and wait to sell when the prices were high, that is when grain was scarce and people hungry. Those who could store the surplus of the harvest by gathering it into their granaries, says Brown, were the ones who could take advantage, every year, of the rise in prices. They could 'make a killing' in times of shortage. 'Not surprisingly, therefore, granaries emerge as the economic villains of the ancient world.'[11]

For the ancient church, interpreting Jesus' teaching, the cost of wealth is both social and spiritual. Life brings trials of two kinds, writes Basil the Great, Archbishop of Cappadocia, Asia Minor (d. 329), in a sermon preached on this text. Either the afflictions of poverty test our souls as gold is tried in a furnace, he said, or the very prosperity of our lives is an occasion for trial and temptation.[12] Those for whom the fields bring forth plenty and the vines hang heavy with grapes but are hard-hearted and indifferent to the poor, those who are immovable and implacable, should be more fearful of the morrow than the hungry.

> *If riches abound, set not your heart upon them* (Ps. 62.11) ... And just as a wide stream is distributed through the fruitful earth by many channels, so let your riches flow, that by many means they may reach the homes of the poor. Wells, when they are drawn from, flow forth in a purer and more abundant stream. Where they are in disuse they grow foul. And so do riches grow useless, left idle and unused in any place; but moved about, passing from one person to another, they serve the common advantage and bear fruit.[13]

If one is fortunate enough to have 'riches abound', the expectation is that this wealth is put to common advantage so that it bears fruit for more than the immediate recipient. The rich man had failed to think and act proactively about how others might benefit from his wealth and opted instead for an investment plan that built walls around his profits. His only consideration was his personal security and comfort. He had omitted to think of others and, says Basil, thereby turned his wealth into a stagnant pond of fetid water likely to do more harm than good. This man who enjoyed physical comforts and prosperity was more truly wretched in his abundance and miserable in his good fortune.

---

11 Brown, *Through the Eye*, p. 14.

12 Basil the Great, Eighth Sunday after Pentecost, 'I will pull down my barns', in M. F. Toal (ed. and trans.), *The Sunday Sermons of the Great Fathers*, Vol. 3, London: Longmans, Green, 1959, p. 325.

13 Basil, 'I will pull down my barns', p. 329.

Thomas Piketty and Basil seem to agree that there is no general tendency towards greater economic equality. The wealthy can build bigger barns to ensure that their capital will grow but the poor cannot, and so social inequality tends to increase across the generations. 'For you wheat becomes gold, wine grows into gold, wool is woven into gold. All that is brought and sold, every human activity, brings you gold. Gold itself brings forth gold, when you multiply it at interest,' writes Basil.[14] While conducting business profitably is not morally reprehensible, the temptation for those with assets is to look to a famine to make more money and become a dealer in human misery. Avarice ('your eyes ever on money' but never taking a look at one's fellow human being, so that inequality increases) becomes a way of life.[15] Poverty is the lack of a thousand things, writes Basil, and can be defined in many ways, but the critical point is the following:

> That bread you hold in your clutches: that belongs to the starving; that cloak you keep locked away in your wardrobe, that belongs to the naked; those shoes that are going to waste with you, they belong to the barefooted; the silver you buried away, that belongs to the needy.[16]

Early teachers of the Church understood poverty with reference to physical impact on the body and in relation to debt.[17] When a person is cold, hungry or sick due to poverty it's time for others to get serious about relieving their situation. If this poverty is due in any way to exploitation by the rich, including low wages or debt bondage, there should be moral outrage. Christ himself suffers in the bodies of those people without adequate nutrition or stiff with cold:

> For when you the servant are drunk with wine, while he the Master suffers hunger, and has not even the food His body needs, what meaning has the name of servant for you? And will it trouble you the more that you live in a three-storied house, while He is without shelter?[18]

The responsibility of wealth is to ensure that these impacts on the body do not happen.

---

14 Basil, 'I will pull down my barns', p. 329.

15 Basil, 'I will pull down my barns', p. 328.

16 Basil, 'I will pull down my barns', p. 332.

17 Susan R. Holman, *The Hungry are Dying: Beggars and Bishops in Roman Cappadocia*, Oxford: Oxford University Press, 2001, Ch. 3, pp. 99–134.

18 St John Chrysostom in M. F. Toal, *The Sunday Sermons of the Great Fathers*, Vol. 3, p. 318. Sermon for Seventh Sunday after Pentecost (2 Cor. 8.15).

Common good as shared project

It's important to be clear at this juncture that common good is *not* an idea or thing whose substance may be defined but a set of responsibilities pertaining to a shared project of which all are part. Contrary to what some neoliberals have claimed, the common good neither has nor requires clearly defined substantive content that may be specified a priori because common good is more like an activity, a set of responsibilities or a common project, which is inconceivable when individuals are thought about as isolated one from another. F. A. Hayek talked about,

> the constitutional limitation of man's knowledge and interests, the fact that he *cannot* know more than a tiny part of the whole of society and that therefore all that can enter into his motives are the immediate effects which his actions will have in the sphere he knows.[19]

His concern was that no one possesses a fuller comprehension of the good of society as a whole than anyone else. Christian tradition, he says, urges following one's conscience 'for the particular things of which *he* knows and ... cares',[20] the implication being that talk of common good is non-sensical and dangerous.

Hayek's mistake was to suppose that responsible talk of the common good entails the idea that the elite few know what's good for everyone else. Aristotle said that children are the good common (*koinon agathon*) to parents – a shared task or responsibility oriented towards building a common life, a family.[21] The common good is humanity's shared project of living together, not an idea or thing whose substance may be defined but a set of responsibilities pertaining to a shared project of which all are part. It takes different form(s) at different times and places. Thomas Aquinas' related theology of natural law is more like a set of requirements and responsibilities than something to which reference can be made in a fixed way. Consider his answer to the question whether there is natural law in us:

> [I]t is evident that all things partake somewhat of the eternal law, in so far as, namely, from its being imprinted on them, they derive their

---

19 F. A. Hayek, *Individualism and the Economic Order*, Chicago: University of Chicago Press, 1996, p. 14.

20 Hayek, *Individualism and the Economic Order*, p. 14.

21 Aristotle, *Nicomachean Ethics* (Loeb Classical Library. trans. H. Rackham, Cambridge, Mass.: Harvard University Press, revd edn, 1934), VIII, 1162a, 28–9, p. 502.

respective inclinations to their proper acts and ends. Now among all others, the rational creature is subject to Divine providence in the most excellent way, in so far as it partakes of a share of providence, by being provident both for itself and for others. Wherefore it has a share of the Eternal Reason, whereby it has a natural inclination to its proper act and end: and this participation of the eternal law in the rational creature is called the natural law.[22]

For Aquinas, the essence of law is something pertaining to reason; law has a necessary reference or relation to reason. As Jean Porter observes, Aquinas' concession to contingency is substantive. Discernment of God's will is not satisfied by formulaic obedience to a set of precepts but requires thoughtful, prayerful deliberation on the needs and issues of given contexts. Moral responsibility might look different in different times and places. Like his fellow scholastics, he 'leaves room for considerable flexibility with respect to specific ways of understanding God's creative activity' both in nature and politics.[23] The common good is not predetermined, but is about the conditions necessary for the flourishing of all. Moral reasoning is always contextual and embedded, requiring an element of improvisation because every agent is somehow confronted with novel circumstances and dilemmas. Within divine providence, however, a family thrives in its relation to a wider community, local communities are part of a larger people or nation-state, a nation-state prospers through relations (for example, trading relations) with other nation-states, and so on. The common good is more verb than noun, that is, a collaborative project that might look vastly different in one community or culture as compared to another.

Wealth as responsibility

Today, in our own context, the debate about wealth and common good is *inter alia* about economic inequality. Piketty's *Capital in the 21st Century* caused a stir and demonstrates helpfully that free-market and patrimonial capitalism built on inherited wealth produces terrifying inequalities. He says less, however, than does Christian tradition about any possible connection between wealth and common good. His point is that the seriously

---

22 Thomas Aquinas, *Summa Theologia*, Blackfriars edn, London: Eyre & Spottiswoode, 1963, Ia2ae q.95 a.2.

23 Jean Porter, *Nature as Reason: A Thomistic Theory of the Natural Law*, Grand Rapids, MI: Eerdmans, 2004, p. 85.

wealthy are likely to enjoy the highest returns because capital tends to grow faster than economies, especially those with significant inequality. Where there are no other forces pushing against the accumulation of wealth by a few, inequality will increase ineluctably.

Richard Wilkinson and Kate Pickett's *The Spirit Level: Why Equality is Better for Everyone*, far more than Piketty's study, addresses the question as to *why* inequality of wealth matters. This book argues persuasively that life is generally more secure for everyone in relatively equal societies. '[T]he differences between more and less equal societies are large – problems are anything from three times to ten times as common in the more unequal societies.'[24] The benefits of greater equality in health, education, low prison population, suicide rates, reported life-satisfaction, and more, are shared across larger proportions of the population in more rather than less equal societies. In other words, unless you are one of the über-rich, your life would probably be better if wealth, health, education and general wellbeing were spread more equally among everyone. If Britain were to concentrate on making citizen's incomes more equal, the rates of violence, obesity, imprisonment, addiction, broken families, vandalized neighbourhoods, and more, would probably decrease with positive consequences for everyone.[25]

The debate about economic equality is complex for many reasons, not least that equality means different things to different people (for example, some kind of proportionality in the way people are treated; formal equality under the law where all are treated the same; the absence of discrimination resulting from inherited skin colour, ethnic identity, sexuality, place of birth, or suchlike; equality of opportunity or outcome).[26] Economic equality in society is irrelevant for some if the poor are getting richer.[27] For others, the emphasis should be on harm caused not inequality per se, because not all forms of inequality are inherently unjust and some are more unfair than others.[28]

Christianity has tolerated extreme social inequality, including slavery, in the course of its history. Even so, the basic principle that we have been

---

24 Richard Wilkinson and Kate Pickett, *The Spirit Level: Why Equality is Better for Everyone*, Harmondsworth: Penguin, 2010, p. 173.

25 For a useful review, see Lynsey Hanley, 'The Way We Live Now' at www.theguardian.com/books/2009/mar/13/the-spirit-level.

26 For these designations of equality, see Julian Rivers, 'The Abuse of Equality', *Ethics in Brief* 11:1 (2006), http://klice.co.uk/uploads/Ethics%20in%20Brief/Rivers%20v11.1%20pub.pdf.

27 Deirdre McCloskey, 'Equality lacks relevance if the poor are growing richer', *Financial Times*, 11 August 2014.

28 Adam Posen, 'The economic inequality debate avoids asking who is harmed', *Financial Times*, 5 August 2014.

encountering in Jesus' teaching and that of the early Church is that the purpose of economic activity is to meet human needs, not to accumulate wealth for the few. This principle is rooted in the yet deeper truths that every human being was created equal before God, is included equally in Christ, and will be judged as such within the eschatological framework of eternity. Contextual gulfs between first-century Palestine, ancient Cappadocia, and the UK today, preclude any simple transference of meaning but demand, rather, the labour of interpretation amid and across difference. Neither Jesus nor the ancient Church could have had any conception of the characteristics of late capitalism, globalized markets, money flows, mass consumption, international markets, per se. But Jesus and the tradition frequently address questions about attitudes to wealth, the acquisition of wealth, its use and disposal, and more. Basil envisioned wells dug for the benefit of all in his allegory of wealth as water flowing pure and abundant for the whole community. At the heart of their teaching was that wealth is not only the stock of all assets held by private individuals, corporations and governments that can be traded in markets but a trust in the service of God and others.

In a useful summary of the ancient teaching of the Church, Stanley Harakas states: 'The Fathers observed that Christ did not seek the destruction of individual property or private ownership, but rather its sanctified use. In this view, wealth is a trust held by the individual in the service of God.'[29] While Christianity has not typically demanded that people be treated identically in socio-political terms, there have been clear limits to what social inequality might entail and especially when the love of money (not money itself) among the few produces grinding poverty for the many. Economic activity is not denounced as inherently wicked but seen to exist for the mutual wellbeing of all – one test of which today is whether it tends to increase or decrease economic inequality. Jesus' teaching and Christian tradition offer an important perspective on the relation between wealth and common good, especially where the cost of wealth accumulated in the hands of a few is a sick society in which few flourish to their full potential.

Is this anti-capitalist? Where capitalism means an economic system that subordinates people and human dignity to the means of production and accumulation of wealth, the reflections above suggest it to be indeed contrary to Christianity. Hence Pope John Paul II condemned capitalist practices where,

---

29 Stanley S. Harakas, 'An Eastern Orthodox Perspective on Economic Life, Property, Work, and Business Ethics', in *Spiritual Goods*, Bowling Green, Ohio: Philosophy Documentation Center, 2001, pp. 143–63, at p. 145.

man is in a way treated on the same level as the whole complex of the material means of production, as an instrument and not in accordance with the true dignity of his work – that is to say, where he is not treated as subject and maker, and for this very reason as the true purpose of the whole process of production.[30]

People matter more than profit. Profit should never be the end but only the means of economic endeavour. Where capitalism means the subordination of that which God has given to humanity in common for the corrupt exploitation of the many by the few, it conflicts with humanity's God-given project of living together for the good of all. If, however, our interest is with capitalism not as a thing but a process, continually in motion and evolving, the movement of capital and associated practices whereby money is invested and otherwise used to increase its value, the question becomes more complex. Consider David Harvey's comment when citing Karl Marx's *Capital*:

> Capital 'comes out of circulation, enters into it again, preserves and multiplies itself within circulation, emerges from it with an increased size, and starts the same cycle again and again'. The powerful sense of flow is palpable. Capital is process, and that is that.[31]

For our purposes, this means that it's difficult (and perhaps unwise) to reduce such a process to a fixed definition and hence difficult (and perhaps nonsensical) to denounce capitalism as if it were a single, transhistorical and transcultural phenomenon.

What matters more than fixing a definition and thereafter declaring Christianity to be anti-capitalist is what happens when wealth and its accumulation violates the practical truths entailed in God's gift of the world to humanity in common, denies that humanity is created in the image of God and every person for good, and that the end (*telos*) of the wealth forthcoming from the earth and human labour is to serve the common good, and results in poverty that impacts detrimentally on a person's body. Jesus did not require Zacchaeus to leave his job but required that he not defraud the taxpayers (Luke 19.1–10). The Good Samaritan had money available to advance the innkeeper what might be needed (Luke 10.25–37). In the parable about a nobleman returning from a journey to find that some of his servants have used his money well to realize a profit but others

---

30 John Paul II, *Laborem exercens*, 1981, 7.
31 David Harvey, *A Companion to Marx's Capital*, Vol. 1, London: Verso, 2010, p. 92.

have not, the nobleman is presented as expecting his servants to calculate for themselves the risk/benefit ratio, and make sensible investments (Luke 19.11–27).[32] Wealth is not merely a 'thing' but a complex set of responsibilities. The cost of wealth can be damnation – or the burden of using it well for common good.

It is not necessary to extract from the Gospels a blanket condemnation of all wealth creation. But three propositions and related implications flow from basic Christian convictions.

1 *God is good and God's will for good is the very truth of creation or fundamental reality of the universe.* Hence we must deny the fatalism that breeds indifference to the human costs of poverty, and refuse to accept defeat in the face of the persistent hardship of so many.

2 God's goodness and justice is *the end or goal of human history.* Hence we must resist the commonly accepted cultural worth that attaches to the trappings of wealth and power that flows from wealth and focus instead on the word of God which denounces all practices that crush the poor and anticipates the end times when many large and beautiful houses will be desolate (Isa. 5.9) and nomads shall eat among the ruin of the rich (Isa. 5.17).

3 God's goodness and justice place a *practical demand* upon every human being. God's word demands practical ways in which to resist both the occasional and systematic exploitation of the many to fill the storehouses of the few. The gospel excludes the privileging of some at the cost of the neighbour's good.

The practical task is to address the realities of UK society today in this light and, where necessary, question what we find. To this end, we might consider a recent government-sponsored report by the National Institute for Economic and Social Research and Landman Economics, published by the Social Mobility and Child Poverty Commission, which considered the prospects for reducing child poverty in the UK.[33] It predicts that, by 2020/1, if earnings rise in line with the latest forecast by the government's Office for Budget Responsibility, 21 per cent of families with children will be living in poverty on the relative measure – 11 percentage points

---

32 Bovon, *Luke 2*, p. 609.

33 Howard Reed and Jonathan Portes for the Social Mobility and Child Poverty Commission, *Understanding the Parental Employment Scenarios Necessary to Meet the 2020 Child Poverty Targets*, June 2014, www.gov.uk/government/uploads/system/uploads/attachment_data/file/318073/3b_Poverty_Research_-_Final.pdf. See also *Child Poverty Act 2010*, Ch. 9, www.legislation.gov.uk/ukpga/2010/9/pdfs/ukpga_20100009_en.pdf.

above the government target of fewer than 10 per cent of children living in households where net income is less than 60 per cent of median or typical household income, and 3.5 percentage points higher than the proportion living in poverty in 2010/11. Absolute child poverty in 2020 (defined as experiencing material deprivation) is forecast at 24 per cent.

Combine this with data on in-work poverty and the picture is dismal. The most recent Joseph Rowntree Foundation annual *Monitoring Poverty and Social Exclusion* report, written by the New Policy Institute, says that just over half of the 13 million UK citizens in poverty (surviving on less than 60 per cent of the national median income), are from working families. The study reports around 13 million people in poverty in the UK of whom around 6.7 million are in a family where someone works. The remaining 6.3 million are in workless working-age families or families where the adults are retired. *'This is the first time in the history of this data series where in-work poverty has made up the majority of poverty.'*[34]

Our GDP (Gross Domestic Product) as calculated by the International Monetary Fund compares favourably with other nations. Figures for 2012 ranked us sixth in a list of 185 nation states.[35] The UK has the sixth largest national economy in the world. Something is wrong when, in a country this wealthy, the number of people in low-paid jobs is rising and average incomes falling such that Oxfam reports:

> millions of families across the UK are living below the breadline ... 20,247,042 meals were given to people in food poverty in 2013/14 by the three main food aid providers. This is a 54 percent increase on 2012/13 ... Despite their best efforts, many people cannot earn enough to live on.[36]

Charitable giving might be necessary to address immediate hardship but problems of this scale suggest that policy decisions to ensure a flexible labour market are hurting the poor unacceptably. The data suggest that something is deeply wrong with the distribution of wealth in the UK today. The teaching of Jesus and of the Christian tradition about the acquisition, use and relative value of earthly wealth is clear: we won't get to grips with what is wrong until we renew our awareness of the common good.

---

34 Joseph Rowntree Foundation, *Monitoring Poverty and Social Exclusion* 2013. www.jrf.org.uk/publications/monitoring-poverty-and-social-exclusion-2013, p. 26. (Emphasis added.)

35 International Monetary Fund, *World Economic Outlook*, October 2012, www.imf.org/external/pubs/ft/weo/2012/02/.

36 The Trussell Trust, *Below the Breadline: The Relentless Rise of Food Poverty in Britain*, June 2014, www.trusselltrust.org/resources/documents/foodbank/6323_Below_the_Breadline_web.pdf.

5

'A Disposition to Preserve, and an Ability to Improve': Edmund Burke and the Common Good in a Revolutionary Age[1]

SAMUEL BURGESS

Edmund Burke was an Irishman, a Whig MP and a distinguished orator. He entered Parliament in 1765 and, though he was not a systematic philosopher, his writings and speeches have made a lasting impression upon subsequent political thought.[2] He was a champion of civil society, an advocate of the American colonists in their dispute with Britain and an outspoken critic of the French Revolution. Burke has been a seminal influence upon the conservative tradition, yet he has long engaged thinkers from across the political spectrum, exciting the interest of individuals as diverse as Samuel Taylor Coleridge, John Maynard Keynes and Winston Churchill. He repeatedly addressed a nation that was fractious and frustrated: many were disillusioned with the political establishment, antipathy towards the wealthy simmered and some rallied to the prophets of radical change. Burke himself was well aware of the creative tensions which constitute a nation's common life, but this did not lead him to the conclusion that the great structure of society should be wished away in a fit of frustration. Instead, he bade the people remember what they held in common, encouraging them to dwell on the common heritage that united them and not on the differences that divided them. Indeed, one of the reasons Burke has so much to say to us concerning the question of the common good is because his writings are so deeply concerned with

---

1 Edmund Burke, 'Reflections on the Revolution in France, and on the Proceedings of certain Societies in London relative to that Event', *The Works of The Right Honourable Edmund Burke*, 16 vols, London: C. and J. Rivington, 1826–7, Vol. V, p. 285.

2 Burke has received a substantial amount of public attention in recent years, including a biography by Jesse Norman MP. See Jesse Norman, *Edmund Burke: Philosopher, Politician, Prophet*, London: William Collins, 2013.

the shared life of the nation. In particular, his work offers us an expression of faith in the people themselves; both high and low, rich and poor. For Burke, the greatest share of sagacity was not apportioned to the individual but vested in the whole. As he put it, 'the individual is foolish ... but the species is wise'.[3] It is for this reason that Burke's vision of society did not conceive of a people pitted against a ruling elite but of a finely balanced body composed of interdependent parts.[4] He denounced those who hoped to engineer a new order by demagoguery, delivering orations on a perfect future from public platforms. It is precisely because of Burke's scepticism of great ideological schemes to recast society that he does not offer us a single prescriptive vision of the common good. Rather, in his writings and speeches we find an acute awareness of particular political and social principles which ought to be observed if the common good is to be cultivated. In this chapter I shall touch upon five of these principles, elaborating upon Burke's understanding of their importance, before offering a conclusion as to how Burke might help us preserve the common good today.

A respect for the customs, laws and institutions which have historically constituted a society

In Burke's 'Reflections on the Revolution in France', he expresses the belief that those characteristics which define a nation, from distinctive customs to long-standing laws and ancient institutions, should not simply be discarded without great thought and caution. It is because these civil institutions have served the 'common purposes of society' that they have achieved such longevity.[5] To destroy them would amount to pulling out the struts which uphold the great edifice of society. In Burke's view each generation receives a great inheritance of wisdom from the past and it is their obligation to preserve that wisdom for posterity. This led Burke to the belief that as 'temporary possessors' of the commonwealth no one generation should 'act as if they were the entire masters' of society. Burke's fear was that those who do so may well 'leave to those who come after them a ruin instead of an habitation'.[6] Such passages intimate that, for

---

3 Edmund Burke, 'On the Reform of the Representation in the House of Commons', *Works*, Vol. X, p. 97.

4 This is not to say that Burke did not believe in a social hierarchy; he clearly did. However, he argued that the aristocracy had a duty to be 'reconciler[s] between God and man' and 'amongst the first benefactors to mankind' in their administration of law and justice. See Burke, 'Appeal from the New to the Old Whigs', *Works*, Vol. XI, pp. 217–19.

5 Burke, 'Reflections on the Revolution', p. 125.

6 Burke, 'Reflections on the Revolution', p. 181.

Burke, the common good hinges upon a history. It involves a corporate identity that is transmitted from the past to the present, through customs, institutions and the self-understanding of a people. Burke denounced the machinations of the French revolutionaries with dismay because he believed that by

> changing the state as often, and as much, and in as many ways as there are floating fancies or fashions, the whole chain and continuity of the commonwealth would be broken. No one generation could link with the other. Men would become little better than the flies of a summer.[7]

Yet Burke was no mere traditionalist, paddling against the inexorable tides of change. He did not revere a given form of government simply because it represented the sediment of years. Burke spoke frequently of the natural law, which constitutes an important aspect of his thought.[8] He believed that 'We are all born in subjection – all born equally, high and low, governors and governed, in subjection to one great, immutable, pre-existent law' which is 'antecedent to our very existence'. For Burke, it is by this law that 'we are knit and connected in the eternal frame of the universe, out of which we cannot stir'. The natural law is one of the great axes around which the constituent components of his political thought orbit. Burke believed that the British state had emerged in accordance with this law and he saw the hand of providence actively ordering the state. The state was in some sense sanctified by virtue of its congruence with the natural law.

> This great law does not arise from our conventions or compacts; on the contrary, it gives to our conventions and compacts all the force and sanction they can have. It does not arise from our vain institutions. Every good gift is of God; all power is of God; and He who has given the power, and from Whom alone it originates, will never suffer the exercise of it to be practised upon any less solid foundation than the power itself. If, then, all dominion of man over man is the effect of the Divine

---

7 Burke, 'Reflections on the Revolution', p. 181.
8 The most comprehensive works on this topic are Francis P. Canavan, *The Political Reason of Edmund Burke*, Durham: Duke University Press, 1960; Peter Stanlis, *Edmund Burke and the Natural Law*, Lafayette: Huntington House, 1986. It should be noted that there has been much debate surrounding Burke's conception of natural law. For a succinct summary of the literature see Christopher Insole, 'Two Conceptions of Liberalism: Theology, Creation and Politics in the Thought of Immanuel Kant and Edmund Burke', *Journal of Religious Ethics*, 36 (2008), pp. 451–2.

disposition, it is bound by the eternal laws of Him that give it [*sic*], with which no human authority can dispense.[9]

In speaking of the ancient institutions and elevated offices of the British state in the same breath as divine providence, Burke was not advocating a British exceptionalism nor was he insinuating that the state was beyond reproach. Rather, he was arguing that the British nation had developed under the auspices of the divine law and, for that reason, it was not the prerogative of its citizens to raze it to the ground. Crucially, for Burke, a belief in providence did not preclude the importance of human agency. On the contrary, humans have a choice as to whether they will adhere to God's law or not. The French revolutionaries 'appear[ed] rather to resist the decrees of Providence itself, than the mere designs of men'.[10] Burke possessed a remarkable knowledge of British history and fervently believed that the distinguishing virtue, which had carved the contours of Britain's body of law and given form to its constitution, was prudence. He was clear that if a society is to live justly and create a forum for the common good then prudence is an indispensable political guide.

The belief that prudence ought to be the chief guide to political questions

For Burke, prudence was not only 'the first in rank of the virtues political and moral, but she is the director, the regulator, the standard of them all'.[11] When Burke spoke of prudence he was making a distinction between two different forms of reasoning: prudential and speculative. Aristotle had made the same distinction, arguing that while speculative reasoning was well suited to the deductive enquiries of mathematics and geometry it was simply not capable of adjudicating upon political and ethical questions. Burke's emphasis on prudence was in marked contrast to a strain of Enlightenment thought which was current among the French *philosophes*. This strain of thought believed there to be an ideal form of society which could be deduced abstractly from certain supposed natural rights, much like a mathematical equation; the *philosophes* heralded a bright new age which was to be ushered in by the use of such reason. Burke, by contrast, was convinced that societies should not be torn down and recast

---

9 Burke, 'Speech in the Impeachment of Warren Hastings', *Works*, Vol. XIII, pp. 166–7. Burke, as is typical of his age, speaks of 'man' and 'men' inclusively.

10 Burke, 'Thoughts on French Affairs', *Works*, Vol. VII, p. 85.

11 Burke, 'Appeal from the New', p. 98.

according to a prescriptive vision that had been rationally constructed by an intellectual elite. 'Is every landmark of the country to be done away', he asked, 'in favour of a geometrical and arithmetical constitution?'[12] Burke consistently made the point that the British system of government had never been drawn up according to an abstract theory. In his view such a project would most likely subvert the rule of law, upturn stable institutions and ultimately lead to anarchy, before ending in despotism.

Burke adamantly rejected the view that an ideal form of government could be rationally constructed, but he clearly professed the belief that there were morally better and worse societies. Prudence was the bridge between the natural moral law and the contingent set of circumstances in which any human society exists. By definition, prudential reasoning possesses a moral dimension and Burke was clear that prudence seeks the good within any particular set of circumstances: 'God forbid that prudence, the first of all virtues, as well as the supreme director of them all, should ever be employed in the service of any of the vices.'[13] For Burke, the role of the prudential statesman is to deliberate upon the moral course of action in particular circumstances without speculating upon utopian schemes to recast society at large. The common law offers a striking picture of this dynamic, as prudential judgements formalize the demands of justice in respect to a particular people with their own distinct context and concerns.

A belief in the supreme importance of the rule of the law

The rule of law was of central importance for Burke. The sovereignty of law was for him not simply a political issue, but a moral and religious one. He went so far as to call it 'blasphemy in religion' and 'wickedness in politics, to say that any man can have arbitrary power'. He ardently believed that 'man is born to be governed by *law;* and he that will substitute *will* in the place of it is an enemy to God'.[14] Adherance to the law and rejection of arbitrary power is a unifying thread which runs through the diverse commitments and stances of Burke's political career. Following Cicero, the common lawyers and the Anglican divines, Burke was quite clear that all human law is only legitimate if it remains within the bounds of the divine law. As we have seen, he believed that through the operation of prudence the unchanging demands of justice are appropriated to the

---

12 Burke, 'Reflections on the Revolution', p. 113.
13 Burke, 'Speech in the Impeachment', p. 275.
14 'Speech in the Impeachment', p. 169.

particular concerns of a particular people: 'the science of jurisprudence, the pride of the human intellect, which, with all its defects, redundancies, and errors, is the collected reason of ages, combining the principles of original justice with the infinite variety of human concerns'.[15]

Burke saw an intimate connection between the divine law and the common law, which shaped the life of the nation both in its political order and in its civil character.

Burke's belief in the divine law led him firmly to reject any doctrine propounding the unbounded autonomy of the individual. While Burke was undoubtedly an advocate of liberty, he was never an advocate of the libertarian freedom which conceives of each person as an island, unhindered by any impediment except the inconstancy of their own volition. He spoke of 'an extreme in liberty, which may be infinitely noxious to those who are to receive it, and which in the end will leave them no liberty at all'.[16] By contrast, he consistently extolled the virtue of a particular brand of liberty, namely that which is to be found under just laws. The British constitution was, for Burke, the legal framework within which the common good could be cultivated. He wrote of the constitution:

> Here it says to an encroaching prerogative, Your sceptre has its length, you cannot add an hair to your head, or a gem to your Crown, but what an eternal Law has given to it. Here it says to an overweening peerage, Your pride finds banks, that it cannot overflow: here to a tumultuous and giddy people, There is a bound to the raging of the Sea. Our Constitution is like our Island, which uses and restrains its subject Sea; in vain the waves roar. In that Constitution I know, and exultingly I feel, both that I am free, and that I am not free dangerously [sic] to myself or to others. I know that no power on earth, acting as I ought to do, can touch my life, my liberty, or my property ... I bless God for my safe mediocrity ... I cannot by Royal favour, or by popular delusion, or by oligarchical cabal, elevate myself above a certain very limited point, so as to endanger my own fall, or the ruin of my Country. I know there is an order, that keeps things fast in their place; it is made to us, and we are made to it.[17]

---

15 Burke, 'Reflections on the Revolution', pp. 181–2.
16 Burke, 'On the Reform of the Representation', p. 103.
17 'On the Reform of the Representation', pp. 103–5.

The constitution thus crystallizes and clarifies a universal order and appropriates it to a particular people with a particular story. As such, the constitution is an expression of the people's identity, in communion with each other and in communion with God.

Nowhere is Burke's vision of the people's common life within the constitutional order painted more vividly than in his redefinition of the *philosophes*' social contract. Burke argues that society is a contract of sorts but it is not something merely 'to be taken up for a little temporary interest'. Here he clearly had in mind the social contract of thinkers such as Locke and Rousseau, which, because it was voluntary, was also revocable. By contrast, Burke believed that all people are born into a network of obligations and duties, beginning with the duty to their family, which they cannot simply neglect. For Burke society as a whole is constituted by a far broader series of relations. He describes 'a partnership in all science; a partnership in all art; a partnership in every virtue, and in all perfection'. Crucially, Burke also believed it to be a partnership which extends between generations. He wrote, 'As the ends of such a partnership cannot be obtained in many generations, it becomes a partnership not only between those who are living, but between those who are living, those who are dead, and those who are to be born.' We might note that such an understanding of society radically redefines the locus of the common good. Yet Burke goes further still. We are told that:

> Each contract of each particular state is but a clause in the great primaeval contract of eternal society, linking the lower with the higher natures, connecting the visible and invisible world, according to a fixed compact sanctioned by the inviolable oath which holds all physical and all moral natures, each in their appointed place.[18]

Though Burke's notion of the social contract is often cited as evidence for his traditionalism, the religious element of this passage is often underplayed. For Burke, society entails a reciprocal obligation both between man and man as well as between man and God.[19] If we fail to understand this, we fail to understand Burke's view as to why we must obey the natural law, why tradition cannot simply be discarded and why the natural affections and duties into which we are born are to be taken so seriously.

---

18 Burke, 'Reflections on the Revolution', pp. 183–4.
19 Burke, 'An Appeal from the New', pp. 205–6.

An emphasis upon the importance of the natural and immediate affections of mankind

For Burke, man's created nature, endowed as it is with natural affections, was a part of the bedrock of civil society. Burke was certainly alive to the capabilities of human beings at their worst, but equally he remained optimistic as to the potential probity of human beings if they are governed by just laws and edified by right reason. He famously wrote:

> To be attached to the subdivision, to love the little platoon we belong to in society, is the first principle (the germ as it were) of public affections. It is the first link in the series by which we proceed towards a love to our country, and to mankind.[20]

Burke was arguing that we learn to love within the immediacy of our family units and civil associations. Subsequently, the ripples of this first education extend outwards in concentric circles of affection, ultimately leading us to a love of all humanity.

At a time in which the very foundations of society were being placed under the scrutiny of *philosophes*, Burke was clear that the created order contains a moral gravity which must not be abrogated if society is to flourish. Burke argued that although the physical causes which bring us into the world are 'unknown to us, perhaps unknowable', we can be sure that we are born with 'moral duties, which, as we are able perfectly to comprehend, we are bound indispensably to perform'. These duties exercise an authority over us 'because the presumed consent of every rational creature is in unison with the predisposed order of things'.[21]

The underlying thrust of such arguments was directed against the 'infamous gang'[22] of *philosophes*, and above all Rousseau, who asserted that man is born free, unencumbered by duties and obligations. Burke spoke scathingly of such philosophers, who profess a benevolence to all people in their political writings while simultaneously denying the first affections of mankind to their immediate kin, 'Benevolence to the whole species, and want of feeling for every individual with whom the professors come in contact.'[23] Burke was stressing the point that in order to love humankind we do not need to deny our parochial and familial affections. On the contrary, it is by these affections that we learn to love rightly.

---

20 Burke, 'Reflections on the Revolution', p. 100.
21 Burke, 'An Appeal from the New', pp. 206-7.
22 Burke, 'Letter to a Member of the National Assembly', *Works*, Vol. VI, p. 41.
23 'Letter to a Member', p. 35.

Rousseau taught that human beings are corrupted by social institutions but Burke was clear that the exact reverse is true; we are edified by them. Like Aristotle and Cicero before him, Burke believed that human beings are naturally social and civil creatures who are created to live in community. In the same manner that we are charged with duties to our parents, we are bound by 'the social ties and ligaments, spun out of those physical relations which are the elements of the commonwealth'. He clearly affirmed that a proper love for one's nation is a good and natural instinct; he believed that 'without any stipulation, on our part, are we bound by that relation called our country, which comprehends (as it has been well said) "all the charities of all"'.[24] Burke conceived of the nation as the arena in which the most elemental relations are allowed to flourish, develop and expand, the single cells of our social existence coalescing to form the sinews of civil society. The great community of civil society is then a product of the primary affections, duties and obligations into which we are born and in which we are nurtured. For Burke, it is within the natural units of family, friendship and shared interest that the common good is cultivated. His emphasis on the creative freedom of the individual to thrive within the small platoons of civil society is the basis of the conservative view that the state ought not to be too overbearing. Burke went so far as to say that, 'Without ... civil society man could not by any possibility arrive at the perfection of which his nature is capable, nor even make a remote and faint approach to it.'[25] This was because for Burke the very basis of civil society was religion, the great end of civil society being to unite human beings with each other and with God. Burke believed that in our human frailty we need religion to be present at every level of society, or else the whole edifice will crumble.

A reverence for the Church and the Christian Religion

The Church and the Christian religion were central to Burke's thought.[26] Burke defended the widely held English view that the Church was the 'foundation of [the] whole constitution, with which, and with every part of which, it holds an indissoluble union', 'church and state' being 'ideas

---

24 Burke, 'An Appeal from the New', p. 207.

25 Burke, 'Reflections on the Revolution', p. 186.

26 Ian Harris provides an excellent account of Burke's thought on this subject. See Ian Harris, 'Burke and Religion', in Christopher Insole and David Dwan (eds), *The Cambridge Companion to Edmund Burke*, Cambridge: Cambridge University Press, 2012, Ch. 7, pp. 92–103.

inseparable in [Englishmen's] minds'.[27] He said of the Christian religion, 'we will have her exalt her mitred front in courts and parliaments. We will have her mixed throughout the whole mass of life and blended with all the classes of society.'[28] In the *Reflections* Burke spends more time defending the Christian religion from the revolutionaries' desire to bring about its complete destruction than he does on defending any other aspect of society. Burke is unequivocal, 'religion is the basis of civil society and the source of all good and of all comfort'.[29] He further asserts that, 'We are Protestants, not from indifference, but from zeal.' He was horrified by the prospect of atheistic fanaticism because of his belief that 'man is by his constitution a religious animal'.[30] And, while he did see virtue in other religious traditions, he did not shy away from the view that some religions contained more truth than others. He argues that, while we no longer 'violently condemn … the Greek nor the Armenian, nor, since heats are subsided, the Roman system of religion, we prefer the Protestant; not because we think it has less of the Christian religion in it, but because, in our judgment, it has more'.[31]

Any Burkean account of the common good in Britain, ought to note that the Christian religion was integral to Burke's account of British society. This was not just because it was the religion which he believed to have soothed the savagery of the Anglo-Saxons and refined their manners and customs, but chiefly and simply because in Burke's eyes it was true. Burke was no secular liberal. He feared that the toleration which the revolutionaries professed would be used to stifle and persecute the Christian religion. In this fear he was to be vindicated.[32] He wrote contemptuously of 'these new teachers continually boasting of their spirit of toleration. That those persons should tolerate all opinions, who think none to be of estimation, is a matter of small merit.'[33] Burke's belief in the toleration of other religious traditions came from his own conviction that the true spirit of the Christian religion is one of generosity and love. He wrote, 'There are in England abundance of men who tolerate in the true spirit of toleration.' Such men 'think the dogmas of religion, though in different degrees, are all of moment, and that amongst them there is, as amongst all things

---

27 Burke, 'Reflections on the Revolution', p. 188.
28 'Reflections on the Revolution', p. 197.
29 'Reflections on the Revolution', p. 173.
30 'Reflections on the Revolution', p. 174.
31 'Reflections on the Revolution', p. 174.
32 See Charles A. Gliozzo, 'The *Philosophes* and Religion: Intellectual Origins of the Dechristianization Movement in the French Revolution', *Church History* 40:3 (1971), pp. 273–83.
33 Burke, 'Reflections on the Revolution', pp. 273–4.

of value, a just ground of preference. They favour, therefore, and they tolerate. They tolerate, not because they despise opinions, but because they respect justice.'[34]

Burke also defended a strong institutional role for Christianity in Britain. He speaks of 'our church establishment', calling it the 'first of our prejudices, not a prejudice destitute of reason, but involving in it profound and extensive wisdom'. Furthermore, it 'hath solemnly and forever consecrated the commonwealth and all that officiate in it'. In his view, 'This consecration is made that all who administer the government of men, in which they stand in the person of God himself, should have high and worthy notions of their function and destination, that their hope should be full of immortality.' He believed that religious conviction would help those in high office to look beyond the immediate gratification of economic profit and dismiss 'temporary and transient praise'. He thought that they ought to pursue 'a solid, permanent existence in the permanent part of their nature', offering their own example as 'a rich inheritance to the world'.[35] Burke proceeds to paint a succinct picture of how a religious influence upon society connects humanity with God. He argues that civil, religious and political institutions aid 'the rational and natural ties that connect the human understanding to the divine'. He believed that in so doing society 'build[s] up that wonderful structure Man' who 'when made as he ought to be made, is destined to hold no trivial place in the creation'.[36] For Burke then, human beings are capable of greatness and civil concord but only when their nature and reason are ordered rightly by true religion.

What does Burke offer us today?

Having unpacked five Burkean principles which might enable us to cultivate the common good, the question arises as to how these principles might affect our communities and our public policy today. Rather than engage in discussion of specific questions of public policy, we can perhaps point to some areas of public debate where Burke's distinctive voice still merits a hearing.

As we have seen, for Burke the common good is the particular expression of a people's common existence; the aggregated articulation of all the myriad civil, political and religious activities of a people. He welcomed a society that was rich, heterogeneous and creative. For Burke, the

---

34 'Reflections on the Revolution', p. 274.
35 'Reflections on the Revolution', p. 176.
36 'Reflections on the Revolution', pp. 176–7.

rich plurality of civil society did not preclude the possibility of a shared culture; diversity laid the foundation of a healthy community. Burke did not espouse multiculturalism but a variety of parts contributing to one shared culture. He was clear that this culture must be in continuity with a nation's history if there were not to be a radical rupture in identity which would eradicate moral norms, extirpate the wisdom of ancient customs and ultimately lead to ruin. Again and again, Burke's cautionary voice reminds us not to break faith with former generations. Burke teaches us today that if the common good is to be cultivated our society cannot simply be a fusion of alien cultures; it must respect our history and anticipate our future.

If Burke had one eye fixed upon the past, he also had an eye optimistically observing the horizon. By redefining the commonwealth to include our ancestors and the future beneficiaries of our labour, Burke consistently emphasizes the importance of stewardship. He reminds us that a great price has been paid for the liberties and laws we enjoy and he reiterates the point that they are not ours to squander or curtail as we choose. The bounds of our stewardship are delineated by the reach of the obligations we owe to our ancestors and our progeny. This realization has implications across a range of issues. One of the reasons Burke has the ability to galvanize the left and the right on particular issues is because his writings are rich with rebuke to an unfettered capitalism. In a society which has knowingly encumbered an emerging generation with an inordinate level of debt, Burke's admonition against those who choose to maximize their personal advantage at the expense of another generation rings clear. As an admirer of Adam Smith, Burke believed there was no contradiction between one's own self-interest and the ability to render a service to society. Yet Burke was also clear that there were moral limits to this doctrine: 'Let us not turn out everything, the love of our country, our honour, our virtue, our religion, and our security to traffic – and estimate them by the scale of pecuniary or commercial reckoning. The nation that goes to that calculation destroys itself.'[37] The pursuit of self-interest must be subject to law and, if the common good is to be realized, laws must be sanctioned by individuals who have some conception of what is virtuous and good. This principle of looking to the future, and not constructing a culture which prioritizes transient and immediate gratification, also has significant implications for environmental policy, public planning and indeed architecture.

---

37 Burke, *The Senator; or, Parliamentary Chronicle*, Vol. VII, London: C. Cooke, 1793, p. 593.

Burke's writings also help us to consider the role of Christianity in working towards the common good. As we have seen, Burke believed Christianity to be the bedrock of the British nation, her moral compass and her guiding light. Burke was clear that the great social institutions, both civil and political, which comprise the beating heart of the British nation, were bequeathed to his countrymen by the Christian faith. A cursory glance at the world today informs us of a variety of ideologies, religious and secular, which do not hold the liberties, laws and moral norms which our society has inherited from the Judaeo-Christian trad-ition. We might then remember that, for Burke, social concord was undergirded by a tolerance which emerged from Christian convictions, not from a secular state dogmatically asserting the equality of all religions. Burke remonstrated against those who believed 'we should uncover our nakedness by throwing off that Christian religion which has hitherto been our boast and comfort, and one great source of civilization amongst us'. He was keenly aware 'that the mind will not endure a void' and feared what might replace the Christian religion in Britain, should the nation cast away its faith.[38] In such passages Burke reminds us that a society will not be improved by legislation alone, but by a rejuvenation of its culture.[39]

Burke's work might be seen to sanction a renewed patriotism. For Burke the nation is not an ethnic or sectarian construct, but it is a 'social, civil relation'[40] that is rooted in the life of a land. We have seen that it is by participating in the life of the nation that human beings are led out of the dark valleys of selfish interest to the verdant uplands of communal life. It was, in part, because of their obsessive emphasis upon individual rights that Burke repudiated the views of the liberal innovators. The 'natural rights' proclaimed by the revolutionaries supposedly superseded sovereign jurisdictions. As a result, the revolutionaries arrogated to themselves a licence for unlimited change. Burke suspected that such supposed natural rights simply provided an excuse for the revolutionaries to refashion the nation in their own image. In response to such views, he consistently made the point that the only real rights of any efficacy are those concrete civil rights which have emerged from a nation's shared story and are ultimately derived from that divine order of justice which imparts true dignity and liberty to the lives of human beings. Furthermore, for Burke our civil rights are inextricably conjoined with duties. Burke is quite clear that, if the common good is to be achieved, we cannot abrogate our duties to the nation for they are incumbent upon us from birth. So too did Burke reject

---

38 Burke, 'Reflections on the Revolution', p. 174.
39 Burke, 'Reflections on the Revolution', p. 154.
40 Burke, 'Appeal from the New', p. 207.

a conception of equality as consisting in a drive to reduce all difference, to make all homogenous, to level all hierarchies and tradition. Burke was clear that true equality is found before God, equality before the common law being a pale reflection of the equality of all before the divine law. In this picture, a critical function of government is to create just laws and preserve the common good by means of effective representation. The state ought not then to be an idealistic and overbearing institution imposing a form of life upon a people, but the sovereign reflection of the common life, the undergirding assumptions, the literature, language and moral norms that a people have fostered in their shared civil existence. It is for this reason that a Burkean might question whether the sovereignty of the nation should ever be ceded to a foreign body, in which the inhabitants of the nation cannot see their own face, cannot implement their own laws and cannot freely choose the next chapter in their common story.

In Britain today we see a society which is struggling to find a common identity and a sense of national unity. Burke has much to say to us in our search for that fruitful equilibrium of interests which constitute the common good. Above all, he cautions us against human vanity, which hints at a golden future if only we cut loose our ancient anchors and chase an ever receding horizon. Burke tells us instead to preserve the good that has been given to us and to be prudent as we embrace change. Were he here today, he would perhaps echo Milton's famous exhortation to his fellow countrymen to 'consider what nation it is whereof ye are',[41] that we might recognize the lingering shadows of those who came before us, everywhere an active inheritance in our own lives: their inquisitiveness a stimulus to our commerce, their genius exhibited in our architecture, their religion refining our customs, their quarrels giving form to our constitution, their deaths memorialized in our liberties.[42] In our own age we may come to realize that the common good is not an innovation but an inheritance. If we hope to enrich the inheritance that has been handed on to us, then we should heed Burke's warning that a 'people will not look forward to posterity who never look backward to their ancestors'.[43]

---

41 John Milton, *Areopagitica*, London: A. Millar, 1738 [1644], p. 44.

42 It should of course be remembered that Britain has always been enriched by other cultures and civilizations which have been woven into the fabric of a distinctive British identity. Continuity with the past does not necessitate a narrow and parochial view of British history, but rather that the common heritage of the nation is not forgotten as we move forwards.

43 Burke, 'Reflections on the Revolution', p. 78.

6

The Common Good after the
Death of God

JON E. WILSON

God is dead! Long live the common good!

The hero of Friedrich Nietzsche's *Thus Spake Zarathustra* (1883–5) took
a journey from theology to godlessness. It was also, to begin with, a
journey from the solitude of the mountains to the sociability of the city.
Zarathustra's story began when he abandoned secular life 'to have enjoyment of his spirit and his solitude' in the forests and hills. But after ten
years, at the age of 40, he got weary of lonely philosophizing, and decided
to descend to talk with the people in the marketplace. On his climb down,
Zarathustra joked with an old hermit who had fled the company of men
and women as he had once done. The sage said he had abandoned human
society because he 'loved men too well', and became disappointed by their
imperfection. Instead of living among other people in the metropolis, he
disappeared into the woods to praise God alone. 'Could it be possible!'
Zarathustra wondered, 'This old saint has not yet heard in his forest that
God is dead!' Zarathustra went down to teach those who would listen
how to live a more worthwhile and worldly existence.[1]

Nietzsche's critique of Christianity was that it forced people to obey an
abstract and oppressive system of ethics which stopped them truly living.
For this late nineteenth-century German, the problem with Christianity was
that it asked people to replace the practical life of human beings, in their
greatness and particularity, with inhuman norms and rules. Christianity's
claim that everyone had an immortal soul made people reject the joy of
life on this earth for the uncertain prospect of happiness in the next. As
a result, it created a world of flat, stultifying uniformity, in which people
locked themselves up in an abstract and supremely individualistic world
of faith. Nietzsche, himself the son of a Protestant Pastor, argued that

---

1 Friedrich Nietzsche, *Thus Spoke Zarathustra*, Harmondsworth: Penguin, 1961, p. 41.

Christianity, like the liberal ethics to which it gave rise, forced people to put a dead, abstract conception of the individual before everything else.

In England, at least, religion continued to have a central place in public life long after Nietzsche's pronouncements. Most twentieth-century sociologists imagined that industrialization and modernization would inevitably lead to the decline of faith. But, as the historian Callum Brown argues, the endurance of Christianity in England confounded social science. World War Two was a conflict which most of its British protagonists saw as a struggle over Christian values. Religion was resurgent in the 1950s, as both church attendance, and a pious, Christian-centred public discourse expanded. Christianity remained, as Brown puts it, central to 'the nation's core religious and moral identity', but it was also crucial in defining the character of private lives. In 1900, there were 609 baptisms for every 1,000 live births; in 1956 that had only dropped to 602.

In England, God 'died' sometime around 1963: the time, for Philip Larkin, 'between the end of the "Chatterley" ban and the Beatles' first LP'.[2] The mid-1960s were years when taboos were being rapidly broken, and Christianity publicly challenged. Record complaints were received when the TV series *That Was the Week That Was* broadcast 'Which? A Consumer's Guide to Religions', recommending the Church of England as the Best Buy: 'a jolly good little faith for a very moderate outlay', it noted. The *Daily Mail* vehemently protested at a light-hearted satire of the Second Vatican Council. But the BBC's Director General stood firm against these criticisms, arguing that public attitudes were shifting, and it was his job to drag the corporation 'kicking and screaming into the sixties'. He was right. This was the start of a period which saw the 'immense and pro-liferating criticizability of things' noted by Michel Foucault 15 years later, when there was 'a sort of general feeling that the ground was somehow cracked, even and especially that which seemed most familiar and solid to us and closest to us'.[3] In England, Christianity was closest and first to be challenged. After 1963, every indicator of religious activity, from church attendance to marriage, went into free fall. Baptisms had fallen to 466 per 1,000 by 1970, then to below 200 by the 2000s. Many churches responded by trying to modernize, with the embrace of guitar music and dance nights. But the retreat of religion from the private and public life of people in England was undeniable.[4]

---

2 Philip Larkin, 'Annus Mirabilis', *Collected Poems*, London: The Marvel Press and Faber and Faber, 1988, p. 167.

3 Michel Foucault, *Society Must be Defended: Lectures at the Collège de France, 1975–6*, London: Penguin, 2003, p. 6.

4 For the 1950s 'religious boom' and 1960s bust see Callum G. Brown, *The Death of Christian Britain: Understanding Secularisation, 1800–2000*, 2nd edn, London/New York:

Since the 1960s, England has gone through a period of hyper-secularization. The decline of religious practice is evident in the life of individuals. Take my parents, for example. Growing up in deeply pious dissenting households in the Midlands in the 1940s and 1950s, they struggled to balance church and secular commitments in the 1960s and 1970s. They moved from church to church (and brought up non-believing children) to end up with a vague form of non-institutional religiosity in their early 70s. Unlike the USA, our everyday popular and political culture is not noticeably Christian, nor that of any other religion for that matter. Christianity remains the default religious identity for most people, 59.3 per cent in England and Wales in 2011, but fewer than one in ten Christians go to church even on Christmas Day. It is present on special occasions, in the life of national moments like Remembrance, in chaplaincies in institutions we visit in moments of crisis. But few are comfortable about religion having a strong place in everyday life. A recent poll showed 58 per cent of people didn't support public funding for faith schools. Often, it has been new migrant communities who have revived and sustained religious life. The arrival of more devout populations from Asia, Africa and Eastern Europe has allowed churches which would otherwise have closed to survive and proliferated new forms of congregation which otherwise were rare or absent: mosques and African Pentecostalist churches, for example. But these institutions and the idioms they've produced have not significantly altered mainstream religious decline. Often, they explicitly acknowledge their 'minority' status. Aside from the occasional secular use of the word 'mission', religious themes and idioms are absent from the ordinary political speech of our leaders. Prime Minister David Cameron's statement that Britain is a Christian country was so radically out of kilter with the rest of his politics that he was quickly attacked for trying to court the support of the religious minority.[5]

Institutional Christianity in Britain has been slow to respond to the crisis. The chapters in this book and the alliance of faith institutions exemplified by *Together for the Common Good* show how it has reacted. Church attendance has not bounced back. But at least since *Faith in the City* (1985) and the work of David Sheppard and Derek Worlock in Liverpool, religious leaders have come down from the mountain, rolled up their sleeves, and made the practical case that work in the town and the

Routledge, 2009 and Hugh McLeod, *The Religious Crisis of the 1960s*, Oxford/New York: Oxford University Press, 2007. Church of England ordinations started to drop from 1967. Catholic church attendance declined more slowly, steepening only in the early 1980s.

5 Toby Helm and Mark Townsend, 'Taxpayers cash should not be used to fund faith schools, say voters', *Observer*, 15 June 2014.

marketplace is essential to their calling. Religious institutions have often been far better at listening to the real voices of citizens than secular charities or political parties. The work of organizations like London Citizens and campaigns such as that for the living wage show how faith groups (with Christians, Jews, Muslims and others working together) have been active in a renewal of grassroots organizing, at a time when others have been stymied by abstract ethical norms and idioms.[6] Nietzsche would challenge the equality of every individual and the 'bias to the poor' which characterizes the resurgence of faith-based social practice. But he would have recognized the emphasis on life, and the concern with the irreducible particularity of each person's destiny as the right starting point.

So, despite the catastrophic collapse in the outwards signs of religious belief, we can't simply describe England as a secular society. Religious affiliation has declined. But faith groups have become significant public institutions in a new way. Religion is 'an intervening force in the affairs of this world', as Bhrigupathi Singh so nicely puts it,[7] in a way that wasn't the case 30 or 40 years ago. In England, the intervention of the faithful has grown in response to a crisis in economics and politics which exposed the failure of every kind of institution that treats individuals as abstract, self-interested and disconnected beings. In their thinking, if not always their actions, churches and other religious organizations have led the way in challenging the failure of modern institutions to recognize the conditions for sustainable human wellbeing. Against secular forms of market and bureaucratic governance which treat people as atoms and objects, a series of movements inspired by faith and the practice of congregation (including the network which inspired this book) have once more asserted the idea of the common good.

Drawn particularly from Catholic Social Teaching, the idea of the common good affirms the centrality of both love and freedom to human existence. We grow up and develop, in childhood as throughout the rest of our lives, in (hopefully) nurturing relationships. People are frail and fallible, and need to be cared for by others when young, old or ill. Yet we are rational, intentional beings, and gain satisfaction from living lives we can shape as our own. Our freedom is our own, but it is given to us from others. It does not originate at birth, but comes with the powers

---

6 For different perspectives on this move, see Luke Bretherton, *Resurrecting Democracy: Faith, Citizenship and the Politics of a Common Life*, Cambridge/New York: Cambridge University Press, 2014; Rowan Williams, *Faith in the Public Sphere*, London: Bloomsbury, 2012.

7 Bhrigupathi Singh, 'Rehabilitating Civil Disobedience', in Hent de Vries and Lawrence E. Sullivan (eds), *Political Theologies: Public Religions in a Post-Secular World*, New York, NY: Fordham University Press, 2006, p. 365.

and capabilities which our dependence gives us, at home, in school, in a supportive workplace, among friends. Our wellbeing depends neither only on the absence of restraint nor the possession of resources, as free-market liberals and technocratic social democrats would suggest. Instead, it relies on our participation within networks and institutions that share goods in common, in which we choose our own path in negotiation with others, but where our flourishing is woven into the fate of the whole group. It is a recognition of the practical truth behind the glib slogan 'we're all in it together'.[8]

In an age of pithy but meaningless political slogans, the absence of an abstract, normative ideal or definition for 'the common good' is singularly attractive. Its potential lies in its concern particularly with the practical forms in which power is exercised in human institutions. The common good is not a utopia, nor even a future state to be aspired to. Instead, it is a way of working which can be experienced in practice. It is a condition that has existed in the historical past and does exist in the present. It exists, for example, in the feeling people have when a whole group is involved in constructing a shared project and working well to a common purpose, in a church, school, business or political movement, for example. The argument is that it is present too rarely; our politics needs to be about extending it to more and further spheres of activity.

This idea of the common good offers a possible centre of gravity for a politics which can challenge the division and disconnection, the unaccountability of elites and limited prospects for the rest of us, which mark the condition of England now. But to thrive in a society in which 'God is dead' for most people and all but a few institutions are post-Christian, it needs to be nurtured in places beyond the church (or mosque (Hindu), mandir and synagogue, for that matter). After the disappearance of religion from so much of our private and public lives, the roots of faith institutions have become too weak to allow them to lead a transformation in our politics on their own. But those roots can become intertwined with other, secular, growths.

My argument here is that we do not need to invent a secular notion of the common good from nowhere. In England, it particularly connects to long-standing idioms and traditions which value civic self-government. These have become weakened over the last few decades, but they still endure in the practical life of local institutions and in public imagination.

---

8 The argument here is drawn from Alasdair MacIntyre, *Dependent Rational Animals*, London: Duckworth, 1999. My own development of it is in Jon E. Wilson, *Letting Go. How Labour Can Learn to Stop Worrying and Trust the People*, Fabian Ideas 632, London: Fabian Society, 2012.

Those institutions and idioms privilege the emergence of shared purposes out of face-to-face conflict and conviviality. They value an accommodation between different interests far more than moral certitude, conceiving the city as a space of continual conflict but also continually remade agreement. In that sense they are profoundly worldly traditions and idioms, interested in power as well as virtue. My argument here is that to flourish, the common good needs Machiavelli the politician as much as Aquinas the philosopher.[9]

Conversational commonwealths

England's municipal corporations were created in England's first great moment of secularization. There was nothing overtly ungodly, of course, about Henry VIII's dissolution of religious institutions and properties. Henry and his successors did not only enrich individuals but scattered the wealth and welfare functions of the Church across hundreds of secular institutions, in the process radically transforming the geography of English civic life. More than 100 city and town corporations were founded in the 1500s, to manage land and run grammar schools, hospitals, poor houses and almshouses and look after the wealth and welfare of urban England. Councils for 51 boroughs previously run by monasteries were incorporated during 1540–70. Forty-one schools were created, as chantry schools became King Edward Grammar Schools, and more than 75 hospitals given new secular foundations. The monarchy and its allies were sometimes hostile to the dispersal of authority which the proliferation of self-governing corporations seemed to entail. The Duke of Newcastle complained to Charles II that each was 'a petty state against monarchy'. Yet in reality, as Paul Slack argues, the central state had no choice but to work with these local institutions if it wanted to get its work done. Social action remained almost entirely the preserve of local bodies until the 1900s.

The local institutions of early modern England valued civil conversation above all else, and conversation created the common good. They were organizations where talk mattered, where decisions were only made after discussion which conformed to the norms of civil exchange. They created what Phil Withington describes as 'a vernacular civic humanism', which sometimes made explicit reference to Cicero, and emphasized the place of polite, virtuous interaction. As Paul Slack argues, the idea of the 'common

---

9 I'm indebted to Maurice Glasman for this expression, as so much else.

weal' (more rarely the 'common good') was central to the operation of a network of local institutions.[10]

The world of politics and public action was constituted by this plethora of conversational commonwealths, by municipal corporations, guilds, parish vestries and manorial courts in which a large proportion of the male population participated. This was a world in which citizenship meant active involvement in the debates within particular institutions. Mark Goldie estimates that one-half of the adult male population held some kind of public office every ten years.[11] What we would call 'the state' was made up of a jumble of local institutions. Between the 1500s and 1700s, 'the state' was, as Phil Withington puts it, 'an amalgam of jurisdictions, offices, privileges, communities, and corporations encompassing, often on semi-autonomous and competitive bases, a range of public participants, languages, and interests'. The public realm was made by active citizens participating in institutions which forged their own local sense of the common good. It was made, of course, by religious speech too. But its closest connection was perhaps to the urban world of free and argumentative Protestant communities which John Milton championed in his defence of a free press *Areopagitica*.[12]

England's culture of civic participation endured into the twentieth century. In many cases, the municipal corporations of the seventeenth and eighteenth centuries became the great cities of the Victorian and Edwardian age. In others, new councils were created, taking advantage of the opportunity in the 1835 Municipal Corporation Act for new cities to be created. It was England's towns and cities, not Whitehall or Westminster, which provided the most effective and dynamic response to the challenges of industrialization well into the twentieth century. Britain's urban centres thought themselves to be self-governing polities, autonomous but linked together to constitute the uneven fabric of national life. Cities imagined their town halls as parliaments, their residents as the citizens of minirepublics. In the late nineteenth and early twentieth century, it was these which began to develop public services – sewage systems, schools, heat,

---

10 Phil Withington, 'Agency, Custom and the English Corporate System', in Henry French and Jonathan Barry, *Identity and Agency in England, 1500–1800*, Basingstoke: Houndmills, 2004, p. 210; Phil Withington, *The Politics of Commonwealth: Citizens and Freemen in Early Modern England*, Cambridge/New York: Cambridge University Press, 2005; Paul Slack, *From Reformation to Improvement*, Oxford: Clarendon Press, 1998, pp. 5–29 and *passim*.

11 Mark Goldie, 'The Unacknowledged Republic: Office-holding in Early Modern England', in Tim Harris (ed.), *The Politics of the Excluded, c.1500–1850*, Basingstoke: Palgrave, 2001, pp. 153–94.

12 David Marquand, *Mammon's Kingdom: An Essay on Britain, Now*, London: Allen Lane, 2014, pp. 157–9.

power, lighting. For many, local civic patriotism was a more powerful form of attachment than the imperial identity which the central state tried to propagate.[13]

One of their greatest moments was the movement in the 1900s to create the civic universities, at Liverpool, Manchester, Birmingham, Leeds, Sheffield and Bristol. These were secular institutions, admitting men (and later women) without reference to religion. They offered an alternative model to the elite education of Oxford and Cambridge, stressing the connection of higher learning with, and not its separation from, practical, urban life. They were true universities, teaching the full spectrum of university subjects, with centres of world-leading scholarship. But they focused on the practical disciplines – engineering for example – seen as necessary for the common good of their region to flourish. For R. B. Haldane, the philosopher–politician who led the civic university movement in parliament, civic universities existed to ensure that the highest, most noble forms of life could flourish in the provincial towns of England.[14]

I do not want to draw normative principles from historical practice. England's cities were good and bad, sometimes ruled by profoundly corrupt oligarchies as well as virtuous leaders. While their authority lasted, they were sites of dispute and conflict, often fractious, occasionally (particularly in their early years) violent. But, I think, that is the point. Cities were places where the self-interest of one set of individuals or factions came into contact with other individuals or interests. The endurance of urban institutional life allowed conflict to be transformed into shared ways of working, sometimes leading to the dominance of one group by another, at other times to a genuinely inclusive form of the common good. Initially, these institutions were male, and restricted to a small elite. But the late nineteenth century saw their opening to involvement by working class men and women: female ratepayers could vote in local institutions from the 1870s, long before they had the vote in parliament. England's urban institutions offered the space for excluded groups to organize, challenge and contest the effort of elites to dominate, in the process creating a local culture of conviviality and mutual respect. Common

---

13 Philip Harling, 'The Centrality of Locality. The Local State, Local Democracy, and Local Consciousness in Late-Victorian and Edwardian Britain', *Journal of Victorian Culture* 9:2 (2004), pp. 206–34; Simon Szreter, 'Britain's social welfare provision in the long run', in Armine Ishkanian and Simon Szreter (eds), *The Big Society Debate: A New Agenda for Social Policy*, Northampton, MA: Edward Elgar, 2012; Jonathan Rose, *The Intellectual Life of the British Working Classes*, New Haven and London: Yale University Press, 2001.

14 R. B. Haldane, 'The Civic University', in *The Conduct of Life and Other Addresses*, London: John Murray, 1914, pp. 63–96.

action emerged from conflict. The common good was the creation not of a unifying set of ideologies or values, but shared forms of sociability, common rituals and local forms of practical patriotism.

E. P. Thompson showed in *The Making of the English Working Class*[15] that working class political leaders created institutions which emulated but democratized existing forms of organization. Associations of labouring men were modelled on guilds, clubs and corporations, but opened membership to previously excluded groups. Later in the nineteenth century, Trade Unions created forms of solidarity and community based on the organization of labourers within (not in opposition to) the particular structures of capitalist life. As Patrick Joyce demonstrates, working class institutions, including eventually the Labour Party, reflected a 'particularistic sense of industry and place' in which a person's town, industry and workplace offered overlapping sources of solidarity. Working class identity was not the product of a stark and oppositional sense of economic interest, as Marx argued, but emerged from dispersed centres which were connected to one another by political organization. In the late nineteenth century unions saw themselves as nurturing a culture of solidarity and friendship which often overlapped with the social duty of elites. The argument they made was a constructive one, that industry was made by the action of labourers and trade unions as much as factory owners. Unions certainly often fostered a sense of the different interests of labour and capital. But that sense of plurality was the starting point for a politics concerned with 'class harmony rather than class war'. This was a form of organization interested in the conditions for social inclusion, able to exist alongside forms of identity (including patriotism) 'of a non-class sort' as Joyce notes. Before the Great Depression at least, the concerns of the working class movement were never narrowly material or economic, but they ranged across the broader political conditions of a decent life. The freedom which came from participating in institutions governed by debate and argument was still central. In 1906 the *Cotton Factory Times* quoted Milton's *Areopagitica*, '[gi]ve me above all the liberties, the liberty to know, to utter, and to argue freely, according to Conscience'.[16]

---

15 E. P. Thompson, *The Making of the English Working Class*, London: Gollancz, 1980.

16 Patrick Joyce, *Visions of the People. Industrial England and the Question of Class, 1848–1914*, Cambridge: Cambridge University Press, 1991, pp. 139–40.

Politics, conflict and the common good

Perhaps one could argue the culture of English civic participation created a good set of conditions for what Hannah Arendt (perhaps the late twentieth century's most important Nietzschean philosopher) called political action. Arendt's starting point was the same as Nietzsche's: the plurality of human wills and desires in a world without divine direction. Unlike Nietzsche, Arendt saw collective action as necessary for human flourishing. Politics gives life without God meaning and stability. Without it, people retreat into the chaotic inner life of the mind, succumbing to a fleeting succession of thoughts and impressions with little connection to external reality. It was only through political action that people had the possibility of doing something which could outlive their existence, of acting in a way that would be remembered. The paradox, for Arendt, is that collective action is fluid and unpredictable and has no single author. Unlike the act of making things with one's hands, collective action is incapable of being controlled by any one individual. To be possible, it requires institutions which allow people to make binding commitments to one another, where they can develop sufficient trust to make promises which they keep despite the vicissitudes of fortune.[17]

For Arendt, the classic instance of those institutions were the city-states of ancient Greece and the assemblies of Revolutionary America, places where individuals debated and argued to create a common destiny by 'sharing word and deeds' in practice. What marked these institutions, like the cities of England before the 1920s, was their reliance on what Arendt calls the 'divisibility of power'. The genius, for Arendt, of the American (rather than French or Russian) Revolution was its recognition that power came from the dispersal of authority between different places and parties. That recognition came in part from the American Revolution's reliance on radical idioms which celebrated autonomous self-government of English localities. Within this tradition, the common good could not be produced by the command of a single sovereign, but needed 'power [to be opposed] to power, force to force, interest to interest, as well as reason to reason, eloquence to eloquence, and passion to passion', as the revolutionary John Adams put it. Tension between separate, rival political forces was not destructive but creative, becoming 'an instrument to generate more power, more strength, more reason', as Arendt notes.[18]

---

17 Hannah Arendt, *The Human Condition*, Chicago/London: University of Chicago Press, 1958.

18 Hannah Arendt, *On Revolution*, London: Faber and Faber, 1963, p. 151.

The civic tradition Arendt wrote about did not rely on an idea of the people or nation as 'one and indivisible'. That tradition's opponent was the idea that power could be located in a single, sovereign point, capable of representing the plurality of human intentions with a single will. Arendt's first full-length book, *Origins of Totalitarianism*, was a disquisition on the catastrophic consequences which follow the effort to deny the unpredictable plurality of human affairs as the necessary basis for all human action. To this effort, she attributed the emergence of anti-Semitism, imperialism and, eventually, Nazism, whose effects Arendt had so disastrously experienced herself. However different its different effects (and the British Empire and fascism are not the same thing) Arendt saw elements of totalitarianism in all attempts to found sovereign power on the existence of a homogenous people or, as the Nazis called it, *Volk*. Her point was not that we should celebrate plurality. Nor did she make the liberal argument that freedom relies on a political structure in which difference is tolerated. Instead, she thought that solidarity, community, agreement and common action were always possible. But they needed to be actively created from the stories we tell and the promises we make.

The civic tradition which Arendt championed imagined the nation as a confederation of separate forces, a multiplicity of parties and polities which sometimes act in tension, sometimes in unity. In that sense, it articulated a conception of politics appropriate for the fractured, incomplete, plural character of human existence identified by Nietzsche and both godly and ungodly philosophers, poets and novelists since. From its perspective, the common good is a necessity, because it is only through common activity that fallible human beings can create stable forms of meaning and action. But the common good is always also a struggle to produce, always difficult, always the result of creative effort. The result of the patient, constructive work of creating relationships and building institutions, it is always vulnerable to the fickle vicissitudes of political and economic fortune. Nonetheless, it has offered and can again offer the basis for a vibrant national common life.

Conclusion: Nurturing a sense of the common good

Present-day politics is too ready to skip over the chaotic singularity of particular experience, taking refuge in abstract vocabulary and vague statements of values. Political leaders speak in platitudes which seem to offer the promise of action, but leave us practically stranded with little sense of who we should be talking to to change things. The languages of liberal ethics and utilitarian instrumentality which pervade our political culture don't provide sufficient grip on the real world to offer effective tools for transformation. Moral indignation at the erosion of living standards or corrosion of cherished institutions don't offer sufficient purchase for action, either.

By contrast, the language and practice of the common good does, I think, offer the possibility of a practical politics. Unlike liberalism and utilitarianism, it can be easily translated into a story about doing things in really existing institutions. The danger, though, is that it is soaked up by the vague language of mainstream politics, and becomes just another set of normative prescriptions with no relationship to real action. As a politically engaged scholar writing from a 'godless' perspective, my anxiety (I will put it no more strongly than that) is that a theological orientation might assist in the evasion. It has the potential to offer an ethical critique of the present which is too remote from the world of politics and power we need to engage with to get things done.

This chapter has offered my answer to that anxiety. It does so by telling a practical, historical story about the existence of institutions which, I've suggested, were able to nurture a sense of the common good. That story offers suggestions about the kind of political actions needed to put the common good into practice now. But it also offers one possible point of connection between a growing, religiously inspired movement for change focused on the common good and possible secular allies.

7

Evangelicalism and the Language(s) of the Common Good

JONATHAN CHAPLIN

Introduction

A faith-based movement to renew a vision of the common good for the UK needs to engage the evangelical movement. As the fastest-growing wing of the Church, present in many of the toughest (as well as the leafiest) neighbourhoods of the nation, it has the potential to make distinctive and powerful contributions to the common good; indeed it is already doing so. In turn, it too needs to learn from other wings of the Church with longer common good traditions.[1]

I use the term 'common good' here broadly to refer to all aspects of the public welfare of British society. It is true that a key impetus to the recent revival of common good language in the churches (and beyond) has been the severe grassroots impact of the government's austerity programme since 2010, many of the victims of which are encountered first-hand by local congregations. But the term should not be used as a code word for an 'anti-austerity campaign', or for some narrowly partisan stance. What the common good requires of us today may be radical in its implications, but we must remain open to insights on the common good from those representing conservative or traditional political leanings. As it happens – and contrary to what much of the secular, and some sections of the Christian, media like to suggest – British evangelicals are not particularly politically conservative.[2] Evangelicals are well-represented in the Christian groups in most UK political parties, and their voting habits are not far out of line with those of the general population. A Theos report shows that even their

---

1 Evangelicals were not well represented at the Together for the Common Good (T4CG) Conference in Liverpool in 2013, but T4CG is seeking to embrace them. I was unable to attend so I am very grateful to Chris Lawrence, who did, for valuable suggestions on this chapter. Thanks also to Andrew Bradstock and David Landrum. The usual disclaimer applies.

2 For example, the 'Evangelicalism' pages of the *Guardian*'s 'Cif belief' site give no sense of the diversity of the British movement.

more conservative representatives do not make up anything like a US-style 'religious right'.[3] While many have 'social conservative' leanings on issues like marriage, family or bio-ethics, many also adopt centrist or centre-left stances on economic and environmental issues.[4]

I want to suggest that there are in fact several conceptions of the common good in contention today in the evangelical movement and in the churches generally, as well as in the wider public. The term calls for clearer definition than has often been on offer, but the first step in reaching that goal is to take the measure of the diversity of usages, and evangelicalism is one place to start.

A movement re-engaging with the common good

Evangelicalism has profoundly shaped the common good of modern British society, yet unlike Catholicism and Anglicanism it has never developed a profound account of the common good.[5] Since its emergence in the early eighteenth century, the movement has made deeply formative contributions to the public life of this country, yet at no point did it develop a distinctive or consistent language of 'the common good' by which to name or guide what it has been doing.

Evangelicalism has been marked much more by its periods of energetic social activism than by the depth or coherence of its social theology.[6] The story has been frequently told of how evangelicals in the eighteenth and nineteenth centuries initiated or lent vital support to a plethora of initiatives for social and political reform.[7] Often these interventions were launched from the platform of dynamic local churches or voluntary associations, some of which then coalesced into larger campaigns for state action against various social 'sins' – the slave trade, prostitution, poverty, lack of education, poor housing, sanitation and health, drunkenness, child

---

3 Andy Walton, *Is there a 'Religious Right' Emerging in Britain?*, London: Theos, 2013.

4 See, e.g., the work of the Jubilee Centre. Michael Schluter and John Ashcroft (eds), *Jubilee Manifesto: A Framework, Agenda and Strategy for Social Reform*, Leicester: InterVarsity Press, 2005.

5 On Anglicanism and Catholicism, see Malcolm Brown (ed.), *Anglican Social Theology: Renewing the Vision Today*, London: Church House Publishing, 2014. On Nonconformity, see Lesley Husselbee and Paul Ballard (eds), *Free Churches and Society: The Nonconformist Contribution to Social Welfare 1800–2010*, London: Continuum, 2012.

6 On why, see my 'Evangelical Contributions to the Future of Anglican Social Theology', in Brown (ed.), *Anglican Social Theology*, pp. 102–32.

7 David Smith, *Transforming the World? The Social Impact of British Evangelicalism*, Carlisle: Paternoster, 1998; John Wolffe (ed.), *Evangelical Faith and Public Zeal: Evangelicals and Society in Britain 1780–1980*, London: SPCK, 1995.

labour and other forms of factory exploitation.[8] Until the end of the nineteenth century evangelicals were conspicuous by their *presence* in, and often leadership of, an array of initiatives intended to address palpable social ills. They were prominent contributors to the 'Nonconformist Conscience', the widely influential public ethos which decisively shaped Victorian national life (often, if not always, for good).[9]

There was, however, a lengthy and regrettable retreat from the movement's strikingly activist history, running roughly from the 1910s to the 1960s.[10] During this period, and for a variety of doctrinal, sociological and institutional reasons, large sections of the British movement (the Salvation Army being one shining exception) abandoned their proud history of common good activism and retreated into a doctrinally narrow, ecclesially defensive and socially passive mentality. Many of its foremost proponents, overreacting to the 'earthly' preoccupations and 'liberal' theology of the Social Gospel movement, reduced the gospel to the offering of a purely interior salvation of the 'soul', obscuring that it is much more the incorporation of the converted believer into a redeemed community called to bring the healing and transforming power of the gospel to the whole of human life.[11] This amounted to an abject disavowal of the movement's remarkable legacy of public engagement and an eclipsing of its earlier, at times quite stirring, vision of biblical wholeness.

The movement has still not fully recovered from this amnesiac phase. However, abridging a long and patchy story, the tide began to turn in the 1970s when the British movement found itself confronted by a variety of internal and external challenges, prompting it to abandon its introversion and isolationism. It began to reclaim its earlier commitments to social and political engagement – to a vision of the gospel impinging on all aspects of the personal and common good.[12] The result is that, today, many parts of the movement have once again become significant contributors to

---

8 David Bebbington, 'Evangelicals, Theology and Social Transformation', in David Hilborn (ed.), *Movement for Change: Evangelical Perspectives on Social Transformation*, Milton Keynes: Paternoster 2004.

9 David Bebbington, *The Nonconformist Conscience*, London: George Allen & Unwin, 1982; Kenneth D. Brown, 'Nonconformist Evangelicals and National Politics in the Late Nineteenth Century', in Wolffe (ed.), *Evangelical Faith and Public Zeal*, pp. 138–54.

10 David O. Moberg, *The Great Reversal*, London: Scripture Union, 1973; David Bebbington, 'The Decline and Resurgence of Evangelical Social Concern 1918–1980', in Wolffe (ed.), *Evangelicals and Public Zeal*, pp. 175–97.

11 But there were significant exceptions. See Ian Randall, 'The Social Gospel: A Case Study', in Wolffe (ed.), *Evangelical Faith and Public Zeal*, pp. 155–74.

12 This shift is reflected in global evangelicalism. See Brian Stanley, *The Global Diffusion of Evangelicalism: The Age of Billy Graham and John Stott*, Nottingham: InterVarsity Press, 2013, Ch. 6.

faith-based (as well as secular) social and political action, operating in many social contexts and on a wide range of issues. Evangelicals are again making significant contributions to the common good in many local communities and in broader public settings.[13] Alongside this renewed activist impetus has emerged a new generation of evangelical social theologians seeking to offer intellectual resources to the movement and to engage more broadly in ecumenical and public debates.[14]

Concerns about the common good are thus now routinely expressed by evangelical activists and thinkers. It remains the case, however, that no distinctive evangelical account of the idea has yet crystallized out of the smorgasbord of current, often admirable, interventions in the field. Yet, this is not at all to imply that the movement has had nothing to contribute to reflection on the meaning and practice of the common good. On the contrary, I will suggest below that what has been occurring since the 1970s is that a variety of contrasting understandings and practices of social engagement – five distinct 'visions' of the common good, each with their own language – have emerged from various corners of the movement. While the specific term 'common good' is not yet as prevalent in evangelical language as it is in Catholic and Anglican discourse, a series of notions are being employed that clearly enter 'common good territory'. Some of these complement what other wings of evangelicalism (and other wings of the Church) are offering, while others diverge quite sharply from them. There is far from a united front in the movement over what the common good requires, or even means.[15] But that is true of most con-

---

13 Major changes in this direction have also been occurring in the USA and in ways sharply diverging from the 'religious right'. See Marcia Pally, *The New Evangelicals: Expanding the Vision of the Common Good*, Grand Rapids: Eerdmans, 2011.

14 See. e.g., the work of Oliver O'Donovan, Nigel Biggar, Robert Song, Brian Brock, David Clough; and biblical ethicists Christopher J. H. Wright, N. T. Wright, Richard Burridge.

15 American evangelical leader Andy Crouch writes that the term 'being fine-sounding and vague ... easily becomes political pabulum to promote whatever policies the speaker wants to advance', 'What's So Great About the "Common Good"?', *Christianity Today*, 12 October 2012 (www.christianitytoday.com/ct/2012/november/whats-so-great-about-common-good.html?start=1). Sojourner Community founder Jim Wallis, author of *On God's Side: What Religion Forgets and Politics hasn't Learned about Serving the Common Good*, Grand Rapids: Brazos/Oxford: Lion, 2014, invoked common good language in a lecture at Davos in January 2014 (www.youtube.com/watch?v=PscDRX5XUjQ). He was attacked by an American evangelical for failing to define the term (www.aei-ideas.org/'values'-talk-at-davos/). While some British evangelicals (e.g. Archbishop Justin Welby) deploy common good language positively, others remain sceptical. Michael Schluter, founder of the Jubilee Centre, holds that the concept 'lacks granularity' (private communication). Evangelical social activist and T4CG participant Greg Smith poses important questions about the term in 'The Common Good: Who and What Is It Good For?' (http://togetherforthecommongood.co.uk/viewpoints/blog/reader/the-common-good-who-and-what-is-it-good-for.html).

fessional traditions in the UK – as witnessed by the contrasting readings of Catholic Social Teaching found in this book. I propose that these differences arise not mainly from different formal definitions of the concept but from different broader visions of a flourishing human society, of what are the most important components of the common good of such a society – the crucial 'goods' we need to hold in common – and of where it is most under threat today.

I offer below a preliminary sketch of these five signature languages of the common good and the larger substantive visions underlying them. They are not wholly distinct and many prominent evangelical individuals and organizations cannot be lined up straightforwardly with any one of them; they are tendencies rather than sharply defined positions. But they may help to explain the complexities of British evangelical engagement with the common good. Moreover, given that the typology may well have parallels within other confessional traditions, it may also shed light on why the notion of the common good means so many different things to different sections of the Christian community as a whole. Yet I hope it also points to possibilities of conversation and convergence around common good concerns both within and beyond evangelicalism.

Five evangelical languages of the common good

Each of the five visions can be captured in terms of an epithet that conveys the heart of its understanding of 'gospel faithfulness' in the public realm:

1 Practising individual discipleship in the secular realm
2 Restoring the biblical roots of a Christian nation
3 Promoting social justice in an age of global capitalism
4 Allowing the Kingdom to transform every aspect of culture
5 Building a gospel community as an alternative to the world.

Many evangelicals (and others) might immediately retort, 'But I support all of the above!' That could be a credible claim for any individual, but important differences between the larger tendencies emerge on closer examination.

Practising individual discipleship in the secular realm[16]

From the late 1960s, a desire began to stir in some British evangelical circles to break with the movement's half-century of withdrawal from social engagement. Key leaders began to urge that fidelity to the gospel requires individual believers to practise faithfulness and integrity well beyond the narrow confines of their personal lives, friendships and local churches. Attention was concentrated initially on the need to equip individuals for discipleship in workplace and professional settings (including politics), for example by maintaining high standards of integrity, trustworthiness and selflessness. This was coupled with an encouragement to engage with broader social concerns by demonstrating personal compassion through support for charitable or welfare organizations. Given the largely middle and upper-class composition of the post-war evangelical leaders who supported this move, there were, however, initially few engagements with working class people or with the trade union movement.[17]

This approach assumed a largely individualist approach to social change. Outside churches, Christians might meet for fellowship in professional or caring settings, but there was no expectation of seeking a common mind on issues they were confronting, exploring a structural or critical analysis of their social and professional settings, or envisaging any larger transformation of society (and, regrettably, this is still the default approach of too many UK evangelical churches today). Yet even from this limited outlook the goal was to bring society as a whole gradually closer to the will of God through the cumulative, organic impact of the faithful witness of individual believers. Although this vision did not yet embrace a clearly articulated understanding of a 'common good', it was at least now recognized that Christians did bear a responsibility for re-engaging with 'secular' concerns. From these initial stirrings much else was to follow.

Restoring the biblical roots of a Christian nation

Not long after the appearance of the first vision, another sprang into life announcing larger ambitions. Prompted by a sharpened awareness of the pace of secularization in British public life, evangelical voices were raised – notably the National Festival of Light (NFOL) – calling the nation back

16 The term 'secular' here refers to 'the world outside the church' rather than to 'secularism' or 'secularization', more critical meanings which are central to other visions.

17 For example, evangelical involvement with the Industrial Mission (IM) movement was minimal. On IM see Peter Cope and Mike West, *Engaging Mission: The Lasting Value of Industrial Mission for Today*, Guildford: Grosvenor House, 2011.

to its Christian roots. Particular concern was expressed at manifestations of the 'permissive society' in moral relativism and sexual libertarianism – both amply advertised in the media – and at the rising materialism and individualism of post-war consumer society. The movement was inspired by a concern that if the nation were to continue to abandon its historic biblical moorings, not only the lives of individuals but also the common good of the nation itself would be imperilled.

This, then, was not an individualist vision of social change but a corporate one requiring concerted Christian action behind agreed political initiatives to stem the process of de-Christianization and shore up what was left of the legacy of a biblically formed culture. There was no retreat from long-standing evangelical commitments to religious liberty and equality, nor any calls for reversals of the recent liberalization of laws on divorce or homosexual practice. Yet there was a 'neo-Christendom' assumption at work that the unity, identity and stability of the UK depended on it remaining a substantially Christian nation in which biblically based morality effectively guided public life. The hope was that this legacy could be shored up not only through evangelism and individual Christian witness but also through social reform across a range of strategic fronts such as sexual behaviour, family life, religious education and worship in schools, Sunday trading and others.

Yet without a clear or compelling strategy for actually realizing these goals in the face of hostility from secularist opponents and indifference from many other Christians, the prospect of launching a wide-ranging national movement of Christian public renewal began to seem increasingly improbable by the 1980s. Accordingly, protagonists began to rethink their aims and strategies. The NFOL reinvented itself as the organization CARE (Christian Action, Research and Education), which dropped the former restorationist 'Christian nation' language and repositioned itself as an educational and campaigning group focusing on a specific set of public issues attracting evangelical concern. Initially it maintained a focus on family and sexual issues and religious education but subsequently took up issues such as religious liberty, gambling and poverty, bioethics, slavery and sex trafficking.

However, since 2000, the 'Christian nation' vision has undergone a marked revival, prompted especially by the growing clashes between the claims of religious liberty and the expanding reach of equality, human rights and anti-discrimination legislation.[18] A series of high-profile legal

---

18 A balanced assessment of these clashes is found in Christians in Parliament, *Clearing the Ground Inquiry*, Westminster: Christians in Parliament, 2012, and Nick Spencer, *How to Think about Religious Freedom*, London: Theos, 2014.

cases in which Christians have claimed (often justifiably) that their 'right to manifest' their faith in public has been unjustly curtailed by this expanding area of law has galvanized evangelical opinion behind a range of new organizations.[19] Such groups vary in aims and language but they are committed to campaigning (and litigating) in defence of a biblically based morality in the face of increasingly secularized law and public policy. They argue that without such foundations – defended, critics should note, through the democratic actions of concerned Christian citizens rather than being 'imposed' theocratically from above – the nation's long-standing commitments to key principles such as religious liberty, gender equality or hospitality to strangers, will be placed in jeopardy. In addition, such groups have given voice to the growing concern among many evangelicals about the expanding public claims of Islam. Some have launched attacks on 'multiculturalism' – characterized as an enfeebling cultural relativism which refuses to challenge threats to core British values – for undermining the unifying Christian cultural capital on which national identity depends.[20] Anglican former bishop Michael Nazir-Ali and former Archbishop of Canterbury George Carey are among the more prominent public spokespersons of this vision. Advocates claim to seek a wide-ranging transformation of the moral and political practices of the nation, and in that sense the scope of their concerns mirrors that of the fourth vision described below.[21] Yet their energies are currently overwhelmingly concentrated on issues of religious liberty, marriage and family, bioethics, education and Islam. As I heard one prominent representative put it: 'we need to take a stand in the areas where the Gospel is most directly under assault today'.[22]

19 For example: Christian Concern, the Christian Legal Centre, The Christian Institute and, in opposition to the same-sex marriage bill, Campaign for Marriage (C4M). Not all might accept the full 'Christian nation' position as described here; and some would endorse elements of the other visions.

20 See Michael Nazir-Ali, *Triple Jeopardy for the West: Aggressive Secularism, Radical Islam and Multiculturalism*, London: Bloomsbury, 2012. For a more positive account of multiculturalism, see Jonathan Chaplin, *Multiculturalism: A Christian Retrieval*, London: Theos, 2011.

21 See, e.g., the comprehensive range of issues covered in John Scriven, *Belief and the Nation*, London: Wilberforce Publications, 2013.

22 Elaine Graham, in *Between a Rock and Hard Place: Public Theology in a Post-Secular Age*, London: SCM Press, 2013, Ch. 5, reads such voices as engaged in a purely defensive form of 'evangelical identity politics'. Her criticisms are sobering but I find this a rather one-sided account.

Promoting social justice in an age of global capitalism

Also in the 1970s, another distinctive vision of the common good began to gather steam. Evangelicals engaged in urban ministry at home began to awake to the realities of social and economic deprivation in Britain's inner-cities, while evangelical missionaries abroad found their evangelistic strategies challenged by escalating third world poverty and oppression.[23] These contextual prompts were fuelled by, and fuelled, a rediscovery among leading evangelicals of the radical biblical call to practise justice, mercy and compassion for the poor, vulnerable and marginalized.[24] Two powerful impulses emerged. One was a commitment to 'holistic mission' (akin to 'integral human development' in Catholic Social Teaching), in which it was insisted that 'evangelism and social action' must go hand in hand if the fullness of the biblical gospel was to be upheld.[25] The creation of the development organization Tearfund (originally an acronym for 'The Evangelical Alliance Relief Fund') and its offshoot Traidcraft exemplified this new integral missiology. Another was a new engagement with political campaigns for structural economic change, nationally and globally. Over time many (not all) supporters of this new wave of 'prophetic social justice evangelicalism' increasingly drew on the diagnoses of those who saw globalizing capitalism as a (perhaps the) chief manifestation of a 'secularized' society, since the 'neoliberal' ideology underpinning it was directly antithetical to the demands of biblical justice. For such advocates, it is here that the gospel is 'most directly under assault'. They do not describe their goal as 'restoring a Christian nation' but as 'following Jesus by working for global justice'. In time, many proponents also found themselves drawn into support for related causes such as environmental protection, peace-making and opposition to the arms trade. Advocates of this vision are increasingly open to working ecumenically and with secular

---

23 A leading evangelical urban pioneer at home was (Bishop) David Sheppard. See *Built as a City: God and the Urban World Today*, London: Hodder & Stoughton, 1973, while pioneers abroad are represented in Vinay Samuel and Chris Sugden (eds), *Sharing Jesus in the Two Thirds World*, Grand Rapids: Eerdmans, 1983.

24 See, e.g., Ronald Sider, *Rich Christians in an Age of Hunger*, London: Hodder and Stoughton, 1978; Dewi Hughes, *Power and Poverty: Divine and Human Rule in a World of Need*, Nottingham: InterVarsity Press, 2008; Joel Edwards, *An Agenda for Change: A Global Call for Spiritual and Social Transformation*, Grand Rapids: Eerdmans, 2008; Marijke Hoek and Justin Thacker (eds), *Micah's Challenge: The Church's Responsibility to the Global Poor*, Milton Keynes, Paternoster, 2008.

25 See, e.g., Vinay Samuel and Chris Sugden (eds), *Mission as Transformation: A Theology of the Whole Gospel*, Oxford: Regnum, 1999; James A. Grant and Dewi A. Hughes (eds), *Transforming the World: the Gospel and Social Responsibility*, Nottingham: InterVarsity Press, 2009.

agencies, while most seek nevertheless to maintain clear biblical foundations for their radical stances.[26]

Allowing the Kingdom to transform every aspect of culture

The third vision just sketched has strong affinities with the fourth, and could perhaps be seen as one specific outworking of it. Yet the fourth has more comprehensive concerns, and on some points stands in tension with the third and in partial agreement with the second.

The first stirrings of this comprehensive vision occurred early on in evangelicalism's recovery of interest in the common good. As the first vision began to make headway in evangelical circles in the 1970s, some pioneering voices were already calling for more.[27] For example, from the worlds of business and politics prominent voices argued that mere individual workplace integrity or social charity were not enough and that broader structural assessments of the goals and organization of industry, the professions and public policy were needed.[28] From the early 1980s, John Stott, Rector of All Souls, Langham Place, London, began to lead a wider movement for more critical and comprehensive engagement in all areas of society and culture.[29] Prominent leaders like Stott called for serious exploration of what Christian discipleship might mean for many fields of society, culture, politics, the academy and the arts. They found themselves inspired by a recovered awareness of what the 'Lordship of Christ', the 'Kingdom of God' and the 'new heavens and earth' might mean not only for personal salvation but also cultural transformation. It was in this period that many new evangelical organizations (such as CARE) were formed, each seeking to contribute a 'biblical perspective' on some aspect of society.[30] This flowering of a new 'evangelical associationism' was clear

---

26 Founded in the 1970s by 'vision four evangelicals', Greenbelt Festival now represents a 'post-evangelical' rendition of vision three.

27 An influential early voice was American writer Francis Schaeffer, founder of L'Abri Fellowship. See also Alan Storkey, *A Christian Social Perspective*, Leicester: InterVarsity Press, 1979.

28 See, e.g., H. F. R. Catherwood, *The Christian in Industrial Society*, London: Tyndale Press, 1964; Sir Fred Catherwood, *Pro-Europe?*, Leicester: Inter-Varsity Press, 1991; Norman Anderson, *Lawyer Among the Theologians*, London: Hodder & Stoughton, 1973.

29 See, e.g., Stott's influential book *Issues Facing Christians Today*, Basingstoke: Marshall Pickering, 1984 (4th edn, 2006).

30 See e.g., Jonathan Burnside, *God, Justice and Society: Aspects of Law and Legality in the Bible*, New York: Oxford University Press, 2011, and Alan Storkey, *Jesus and Politics: Confronting the Powers*, Grand Rapids: Baker, 2005.

evidence of the movement's re-engagement in many dimensions of the common good.[31]

The concerns of this vision are not only with issues of social justice but with every way in which the contemporary secularized culture of modernity is seen as having fallen away from God's comprehensive good purposes in creation and redemption. The power of the gospel must be allowed to transform the whole of human life and culture, including the arts, business, education, technology, the media, the professions and government.[32] Arguably much in line with Catholic Social encyclicals, all these arenas are seen as equally important components of a complex and integrated common good of an entire society. There is no dichotomy between supposedly 'moral' issues like marriage and bioethics and 'structural' issues like economic justice, and there should be no antagonism between champions of the former and advocates of the latter. The Church must somehow address all of them, and in coherent ways. In doing so, it will often adopt a countercultural posture, but as American evangelical 'transformationist' Tim Keller puts it, it will serve as a 'counterculture for the common good'.[33]

Building a gospel community as an alternative to the world

Representatives of the fifth vision often strongly echo the social justice concerns of, especially, the third. Yet the fifth vision has been nurtured by a distinctive strand of (mainly American) neo-Anabaptist social theology pioneered by John Howard Yoder and Stanley Hauerwas. This influence lends to this vision a more consistently 'anti-system' cast than is seen in any of the others. Unfairly dubbed by critics as 'separatists' proposing a withdrawal from social engagement, in fact its representatives advocate a *different method* of engagement, one in which the church plays the central role as an alternative community witnessing to the radically alternative values of the gospel.[34] The Church is to be a dynamic, corporate, countercultural embodiment of the message of Jesus.

---

31 On evangelical associationism, see my 'Evangelical Contributions', and John Milbank, 'Foreword' to Pally, *The New Evangelicals*, pp. x–xviii.

32 The UK Evangelical Alliance's range of concerns now spans over a dozen different areas of culture and public policy (www.eauk.org) suggesting that at least the leadership of mainstream British evangelicalism now seeks to exemplify vision 4.

33 Tim Keller, 'A New Kind of Urban Christian', *Christianity Today*, 1 May 2006, www.christianitytoday.com/ct/2006/may/1.36.html.

34 In Hauerwas' famous line: 'The church does not *have* a social ethic, it *is* a social ethic.'

Known initially for its commitment to pacifism, this vision now calls for radical fidelity to the gospel in many areas of social life.[35] While this brings it closer to vision four, its key distinctive is that such discipleship is to be performed first from the platform of the believing community rather than from positions of influence within the existing structures of society (business, politics, the academy and so on). Many advocates of this vision hold that such structures are so pervasively corrupted by a secularized, violent, capitalist, liberal culture, that seeking to work through such structures – and thus to conform to their autonomous norms – will not bring genuine transformation and might even amount to conniving with 'idolatry'. Concentrating on conventional political action to promote social justice – through the 'worldly' tools of mobilization, lobbying, partisan campaigning, wielding government power and so forth – would be spiritually compromising and futile.[36]

Since adherents to this vision disavow transformative aspirations for society as a whole, they are suspicious of the universalist language of 'the common good' or 'social justice'.[37] They warn that employing these generic notions risks obscuring the distinctiveness of the Christian message – as if the awkward particularity of Jesus is better left aside. On this vision, it is *the Church* – when it is being faithful – which is the site of the true common good, since only the gospel establishes genuine community, while secular liberalism pulverizes it. Only the Church is the 'true *polis*'. If the fruits of the Church's embodiment of the common good spill over into wider society, well and good. So it is worth noting that advocates of this vision do indeed entertain the possibility that a truly faithful Church might indeed contribute to the long-term healing and transformation of a culture. But that will only happen if the Church maintains a clear spiritual (not necessarily social) distance from the 'powers of the age'. The Church, they might say, must 'work *apart* from the world, *for the sake of* the world'. But the capacity of the Church to contribute to what a secular society itself deems its 'common good' is no test of its biblical faithfulness. Advocates of this vision are therefore likely to be awkward conversation partners in any broad conversation about 'the' common good.

---

35 See the wide range of public engagements called for in *The Blackwell Companion to Christian Ethics*, ed. Stanley Hauerwas and Samuel Wells, Oxford: Blackwell, 2004.

36 The 'After Christendom' books series published by Paternoster represents a variant of this vision. Its contributors urge serious engagement with the political system, yet one practised in 'subversive' mode. See, e.g., Jonathan Bartley, *Faith and Politics after Christendom: The Church as a Movement for Anarchy*, Milton Keynes: Paternoster, 2006.

37 See Stanley Hauerwas, *After Christendom: How the Church is to Behave if Freedom, Justice and a Christian Nation are Bad Ideas*, Nashville: Abingdon Press, 1991.

Conclusion: evangelical contributions to an ecumenical common good?

I hope that this fivefold typology will shed light on why contemporary evangelicalism harbours competing understandings of the common good of British society and of the principal threats to it that require a concerted Christian response. I have made no attempt to evaluate these understandings but only to put them on display in order to help explain why British evangelicals reveal such divergent 'common good' enthusiasms.[38] But I noted above that, to the extent that this diversity is reflected in other confessional traditions, the typology may also help illumine why there are significant disagreements about the common good among British Christians generally. I now want to consider a further distinctive feature of many evangelical common good interventions, and then offer three concluding reflections on what an evangelical contribution to a movement for the common good might entail.

The additional feature I want to consider is a pronounced tendency within evangelicalism (at least in visions 2 to 5) towards the adoption of 'countercultural' stances towards wider society, or at least some crucial aspects of it. An instinctively antithetical posture towards 'the world' seems to be lodged within the movement's DNA, rooted in a sharp sense of the 'spiritual warfare' between the gospel and the fallen world. This posture manifests itself in a variety of ways and is directed towards a diversity of targets. What targets are selected, and thus which way evangelicals tend to lean on the existing political spectrum, depend largely on what they take to be the chief manifestations of 'fallenness' in the societies they inhabit and thus what beliefs and practices stand most in need of 'prophetic' critique: whether atheism, moral relativism, sexual libertarianism and rising Islam (vision 2); globalized capitalism (vision 3); the secularized culture of modernity (vision 4); or a corrupt democratic liberalism (vision 5).

Of course, a readiness to take antithetical stances – sometimes towards similar targets, sometimes towards different ones – is also evident in Catholicism and Anglicanism. Yet the deep influence of 'incarnational' and 'sacramental' models of social engagement in these two traditions generates a powerful impetus to seek commonality with those outside the Church and feeds a greater optimism that a shared common good can

---

38 My account of escalating evangelical diversity is far from complete. See, e.g., Robert Warner, *Reinventing English Evangelicalism, 1966–2001*, Milton Keynes: Paternoster, 2007. Since this book appeared, further diversity, and increasing debates over the boundaries of the movement, have emerged, not least over the issue of same-sex relationships.

be discerned with society at large.[39] Such traditions are more naturally consensus-oriented than much of evangelicalism has classically been. For many Catholics, grace 'elevates', rather than 'judges', nature; for many Anglicans, the Church stands alongside (or even, for many in the Church of England, *within*) the nation, rather than over against it. Behind this contrast lies, for example, evangelicalism's classical Protestant caution about the capacity of shared human reason to discern a universal natural morality ('natural law'). Rather, since reason is as radically corrupted as every other human capacity, it can be expected to produce intellectual and spiritual splintering rather than a tendency towards convergence. And in an increasingly plural society this will give rise to the presence of radically competing conceptions of the common good, imposing significant limits to agreement and cooperation, limits which it is dishonest to deny. While this may be a somewhat oversimplified depiction of the contrast, we do need to reckon with a recurring tension between the predominantly 'priestly' posture of much Catholicism and Anglicanism and the instinctively (or at least episodically) 'prophetic', countercultural stance of much evangelicalism.

I conclude with three reflections. First, in the light of the above, can we, perhaps, hope for a constructive process of mutual enrichment and challenge to take place between the incarnational and the prophetic impulses, as evangelicals share more fully with their ecumenical partners in a movement for the common good? On the one hand, evangelicals may need to become better listeners for, and practitioners of, the possibility of ecumenical convergence, and convergence between Church and wider society, where these truly exist.[40] This is already happening on the ground in many local contexts and in the work of several national organizations with evangelical roots (Tearfund and Oasis Trust, for example).[41] On the other hand, their partners may need to be more receptive to evangelical interrogations of accounts of the common good that seem to sidle up too comfortably to conventional secular wisdom (whether of left, right or centre).

Second, notwithstanding the deep-rooted contrast just described, it is increasingly clear today that the diversity of understandings of the common good within evangelicalism is also replicated (in their own vernaculars) in

---

39 As Anna Rowlands put it in her T4CG keynote address, 'the language of the Common Good … seeks to be a way of speaking that unites rather than divides' (http://togetherforthe commongood.co.uk/conference/t4cg-conference-sessions.html).

40 For a helpful evangelical appropriation of Catholic 'common good' language, see Nicholas Townsend, 'Government and social infrastructure', in *God and Government*, ed. Nick Spencer and Jonathan Chaplin, London: SPCK, 2009, pp. 108–33.

41 It is also well advanced in the USA. See Pally, *The New Evangelicals*, p. 220.

other confessional traditions. If so, then the debate about what the common good requires of the Church today may be less and less one between evangelicals and 'the rest'. Rather it may increasingly be between advocates of *each of the five visions* sketched above, whichever confessional tradition they happen to hail from. And if that is the case, then the question facing the churches can perhaps be phrased thus: 'Which insights of each competing vision of the common good need to be affirmed and harnessed in pursuit of a broader, more comprehensive, if always internally contested, ecumenical vision capable of speaking effectively – sometimes consensually, sometimes oppositionally – to a secular, plural society with which we share a common life and destiny?'

Third, a word about common good as 'substance' and common good as 'process'. Many within the common good movement have argued that the common good is not first about the *content of substantive social visions* (which, they stress, is very difficult to agree on in a plural society) but rather about the *quality of the conversations* about such visions. It is not a prescriptive model but rather a 'way of doing politics' – a practice of inclusive dialogue about what goods we hold in common and how to protect and nurture them.[42] The five visions described above are, however, quite clearly substantive in nature. Each is an attempt to identify the central concerns of a social vision of what makes for a flourishing human social order according to God's design, and to work it out in contemporary Britain.

Yet, within the main confessional traditions of the Church, including evangelicalism, also lie powerful injunctions to seek that vision *collaboratively*, through processes of corporate deliberation. In each, albeit in different ways, the whole people of God – the *laos* – is accorded an indispensable role in the discernment of what the common good requires at any time. Indeed for any community which affirms something like the Pauline vision of the 'Body of Christ' with its many diverse yet equally valued members, this must be so: a biblical ecclesiology must issue in a

---

42 The T4CG website adopts such a position: http://togetherforthecommongood.co.uk/resources/resources/articles/whats-the-common-good.html. The site acknowledges that the common good does need to be discerned in the light of core 'principles', such as those articulated in Catholic Social Teaching, yet it stresses that it is 'revealed through the "best possible conversation"'. It is, to me, doubtful whether according such priority to conversation over content adequately reflects 'common good' discourse in official Catholic Social Teaching documents, but I leave that aside here. The site also states: 'Pursuing a definition [of the common good] is therefore unlikely to lead to clarity and may generate division rather than unity.' However, first, the substantive 'principles' referred to here already place robust parameters around what might be accepted as furthering the common good; and, second, the absence of any definition risks reducing the common good to whatever participants in a conversation can agree it shall be.

participatory politics. Indeed the very idea of a 'common' good implies that such a good can only be identified when all members of a community have been given space to testify to their own experiences, struggles and insights. That will inevitably require open, often difficult, sometimes 'antithetical', conversations enabling a continual negotiation of conflicting perceptions and interests, in which not every claim can be affirmed but yet where all voices are at least afforded the possibility of a hearing. Only out of such an inclusive dialogue can a truly 'common' good emerge; and if that is so within the Christian community, it will be no less so in wider society.[43] Those arguing that the common good can only be approached through a dialogical practice point to a vital truth, one which must not be suppressed by those who might seek to define the content of the public common good pre-emptively for everyone else. What follows regarding the prospects for common perception and action will depend on the specifics of the issues and participants and cannot be predicted in advance. Most likely a broad-based ecumenical movement for the common good will involve a shifting, patchwork quilt of multiple coalitions in which each partner will fall in behind those instances of common action that their convictions and constituencies can currently endorse (which, however, might evolve through further cooperation). Generous attentiveness, mutual forbearance and the absence of recrimination will thus be at a premium within such a movement.

---

43 As Maurice Glasman put it in his T4CG conference speech: 'there cannot be a peace that we can have that doesn't involve reconciling estranged interests ... [T]he language of the common good is going to have to be around this reconciliation of interests between capital and labour, between faithful and secular'. (http://togetherforthecommongood.co.uk/conference/t4cg-conference-sessions.html).

8

Social Action that Crosses Boundaries and Overcomes Barriers: A Muslim Perspective on the Common Good

TEHMINA KAZI

On Remembrance Day in 2011 a wide range of Muslim and non-Muslim groups decided to come together to show their opposition to Al-Muhajiroun, who were intent on publicly burning poppies in disrespect for the memories of British soldiers. The Islamic Society of Britain joined forces with British Muslims for Secular Democracy, and many others, to organize a counter-protest. This did not in the end go ahead, but only because Al-Muhajiroun were banned the night before by the Home Secretary.[1] However, this newly formed coalition was instrumental in bringing about a sea change among British Muslim organizations and others in countering radicalism. It also crystallized the form and nature of our collaboration with non-Muslim organizations, towards the pursuit of shared goals.

April 2013 saw another significant event: the inaugural meeting of the 'People Like Us' Interfaith Project at the Woolf Institute in Cambridge.[2] Here was a meeting that enabled good practice to be shared on issues which unite all communities in Britain: bereavement, education, work and family. In front of a hugely diverse audience, a humanist funeral celebrant was able to reach out and connect with a recently bereaved Muslim. Not once did any particular group use the project to advance their own ideology; the emphasis was always on individuals enriching the collective with their own practical expertise, without denying or dampening their individuality in any way.

---

1 www.channel4.com/news/theresa-may-bans-muslims-against-crusades-group.
2 www.woolf.cam.ac.uk/news/detail.asp?ItemID=606.

Both projects epitomize what the common good should look like in twenty-first-century Britain. Traditional interfaith dialogue has been overtaken by cross-community initiatives that prioritize social action. These projects, like many of the most successful collaborations, are propelled by a sense of urgency and a keen awareness of some injustice. However, they part company with forms of civic engagement – such as protests against the Iraq war or boycotts of Israeli goods – that have become familiar in British Muslim circles, in three important ways.

First, they show a willingness *as Britons* to tackle concerns in our midst – including threats to universal values, social cohesion and public order in Britain – rather than issues that are primarily linked to foreign policy. The impetus behind this is not necessarily a desire to combat anti-Muslim sentiment (although that is a beneficial by-product), but a shared conviction that this is the right thing to do. Mehdi Hasan summed this up well in a *Guardian* article in 2012:

> We have allowed ourselves to be defined only by foreign policy and, in particular, by events in the Middle East for far too long. British Muslims can make a positive contribution to British society, but first we have to stop our navel-gazing and victim mentality. We must let the people, press and politicians of this country know that we are as British as we are Muslim, and we care about our shared future.[3]

Second, they signify a radical departure from tribalism in British politics, transcending Left–Right squabbles. Instead of defining the group's political and religious identity against some nebulous other, a more holistic world view is adopted.

Third, they provide a blueprint for the building of working relationships with other groups and individuals who hold a wide range of religious, non-religious and political beliefs. These individuals don't just work with each other for the sake of a 'drop of diversity', or for other opportunistic reasons, but because our efforts as individuals cannot be divorced from the wellbeing of society as a whole. Sherman Jackson rightly asks in the 2014 Ibrahim El-Hibri lecture, 'Even if Jews and Christians can do it on their own, how do we fit into each other's schemes?'[4]

---

3 www.theguardian.com/commentisfree/2012/apr/02/muslims-step-outside-antiwar-comfort-zone.

4 'Beyond Tolerance and Dialogue: Can the Abrahamic Faiths Vindicate a Role for Religion in Public Life?', 2014 Ibrahim El-Hibri Interfaith Lecture by Dr Sherman A. Jackson, King Faisal Chair of Islamic Thought and Culture, Professor of Religion and American Studies and Ethnicity and Director of the Center for Islamic Thought, Culture and Practice at the University of Southern California, www.youtube.com/watch?v=mDEac8zkVik.

The common good, the individual and the collective

A widely quoted Catholic definition of the common good is: 'The sum of those conditions of social life which allow social groups and their individual members relatively thorough and ready access to their own fulfilment.'[5] The secular philosopher John Rawls defined the common good as: '[c]ertain general conditions that are in an approximate sense equally to everyone's advantage'.[6] In practice, even countries with the highest levels of social capital don't always reach consensus about *which* conditions would benefit all of their residents equally – or even to what degree. From a Muslim perspective, the aforementioned Catholic definition would serve better to bring both individual and societal interests to fruition, synthesizing the two without inordinate pressure or contrivance.

Commentators often claim that our most fundamental social problems grow out of a widespread pursuit of individual interests. However, in many British Muslim communities, endemic social problems occur when the interests of particular individuals conflict with the predominant communitarian ethos (same-sex marriage is a prime example). Some communities expect total compliance with the traditional status quo, enforcing this in a variety of ways: setting rigid criteria for the 'in-group' which purport to be religiously inspired; maintaining hierarchical power structures that actively exclude and stigmatize those not deemed to be part of the in-group; treating all dissenting views as an attack on the established order. Dilwar Hussain's analysis of British Muslim civic engagement in *British Muslims: Between Assimilation and Segregation* uses Maslow's hierarchy of needs to show why this may be the case. Maslow ranks 'deficiency needs', such as physiological needs, the need for safety, a sense of belonging, and esteem, ahead of 'growth needs', like self-fulfilment and enabling the fulfilment of others. 'To transpose this on the Muslim community', writes Hussain, 'it may be somewhat unrealistic to expect the community to engage with contributing to the wider society, for example, when it is still at the level of securing its own existence and at the stage of meeting physiological or security needs.'[7] However, truly strong communities actively embrace pluralism, dynamism and creativity, rather than seeing these qualities as

---

5 Vatican II, *Gaudium et spes* (*Pastoral Constitution on the Church in the Modern World*), 1965, 26.

6 John Rawls, *A Theory of Justice*, revd edn, Oxford/New York: Oxford University Press, 1999, p. 217 (see also pp. 205, 213).

7 Dilwar Hussain, 'Councillors and Caliphs: Muslim Political Participation in Britain', in Mohammad Siddique Seddon, Dilwar Hussain and Nadeem Malik (eds), *British Muslims Between Assimilation and Segregation, Historical, Legal and Social Realities*, Markfield, Leicester: The Islamic Foundation, 2004, pp. 173–200, at p. 192.

threats. They are able to reconcile individual expression and contentment with the ongoing fulfilment of obligations to the collective.

Islamic concepts that relate to the common good

'Most Muslims', it has been said, 'share inherited conceptions of ideas of the common good.'[8] There are two key concepts in Islamic jurisprudence which either tally with the common good, or seek to devise a strategy for its implementation. The term *maslaha* was used by the Andalusian scholar Al-Shatibi (d. 1388), as the closest approximation of the common good.[9] While this concept didn't apply to questions of worship, it was deemed relevant to relationships between humans; everyone should strive for the best public solution in terms of cooperation with others, on a macro and a micro scale. Muhammad Masud quotes the story of the time when a Granadan Sultan imposed a tax for the building of a security wall around the city. Ibn Lubb, the chief *mufti*, ruled that this tax was not in accord with the *Sharia*. Al-Shatibi responded by issuing a *fatwa* justifying the tax on the grounds of *maslaha* (public interest), which for him was a basic principle for legal reasoning.[10] He analysed *maslaha* in terms of three sub-categories: *daruriyat* (the necessities of human life in this world and the hereafter), *hajiyat* (that which is complementary to the necessities), and *tahsiniyat* (that which is commendable). Keeping in line with the social action theme, this chapter will focus on the third category, which relates to 'noble habits' that go beyond the regular duties of a Muslim. These include the sort of charitable donations which exceed what is considered to be obligatory in Islam, eloquent and polite speech, and strong *adab* (manners or etiquette). This ties in with one of my favourite concepts in Islam: *ihsan*, or striving for excellence in work and social interactions.

---

8 Armando Salvatore and Dale F. Eickelman (eds), *Public Islam and the Common Good*, Leiden/Boston: Brill, 2004, p. xix.

9 See 'Muhammad Khalid Masud, 'Abū Ishāq al-Shātibī', in Oussama Arabi, David S. Powers and Susan A. Spectorsky (eds), *Islamic Legal Thought*, Leiden/Boston: Brill, 2013, pp. 354–74, esp. p. 361, where Al-Shatibi's definition of *maslaha* is quoted: 'That which relates to what sustains human life, the accomplishment of livelihood, and the acquisition of emotional and intellectual requirements.' See also pp. 356–9, where *maslaha* is translated as 'public interest' and 'human welfare'. Muhammad Qasim Zaman writes, '*Maslaha* (or, more precisely, *maslaha 'amma*, "public interest") can, broadly speaking, be understood as the "common good", though it is more accurate to see it as a means, or a legal criterion, through which the common good is realized.' (The '*Ulama* of Contemporary Islam and their conceptions of the Common Good' in Salvatore and Eickelman, *Public Islam*, pp. 129–56, at pp. 131–2.) [Cf. Esther Reed's account of Thomas Aquinas on the common good (p. 59): 'The common good is not pre-determined, but is about the conditions necessary for the flourishing of all.' Eds.]

10 Muhammad Khalid Masud, 'Abū Ishāq al-Shātibī', p. 359.

A second key concept is *istislah*. This fulfils the practical side of the *maslaha* equation; it literally means 'to seek the best public interest'. It is a device employed by Muslim jurists to solve pressing social problems where answers do not easily spring from the pages of religious texts. Theoretically, it has the potential to bring both communitarian benefit and benefit to particular individuals.

However, the classical formation of *istislah* is nullified if a certain measure infringes upon one or more of the *maqasid al-sharia* (goals of the Sharia). These are traditionally said to be religion, life, reason, family and property, with some scholars adding honour to the list. Any legal and political system which fulfils these goals can be considered 'Islamically correct'. Tariq Ramadan, for instance, writes, 'For me, as a Muslim living in a minority in another society, everything in that society that is just should be seen as itself part of the Sharia.'[11] Many scholars deem states like the United Kingdom to be better at upholding these public goals than majority-Muslim countries. Cambridge University scholar Michael Mumisa states: 'It is my opinion that the British legal and political systems as they stand at the moment meet the goals of the Sharia',[12] while his colleague Tim Winter (Abdal-Hakim Murad) writes:

> Muslims may be unhappy with the asylum laws here, but would one wish to claim asylum in any Muslim country that currently springs to mind? We may not approve of all the local rules of evidence, but if we are honest, we will surely hesitate to claim that a murder investigation is better pursued in, say, Iran or Saudi Arabia, than in English jurisdiction.[13]

Continuing with the governance theme, *taaddudiya* (pluralism) was a key feature of the Constitution of Medina. The Prophet Muhammad (pbuh) legislated for a society where Christians and Jews enjoyed equality before the law – including the freedom to practise their own religion and culture – in exchange for political loyalty. *Shura*, or consultation, was a very important procedure in political decision-making, and does not get enough credit as a tool of governance. Genuine pluralism both precedes it, and is perpetuated by it: *shura* is a wellspring for *ikhtilaf*, or differences in opinion that permit Muslims to tailor certain edicts to

---

11 Tariq Ramadan, 'Islamic Views of the Collective', in M. Ipgrave (ed.), *Building a Better Bridge: Muslims, Christians and the Common Good*, Washington, DC: Georgetown University Press, 2008, p. 79.

12 Michael Mumisa, 'Does Islam allow British Muslims to vote?' (2013). See, www. conservativemuslimforum.com/downloads/pdf-version.pdf, p. 9.

13 http://masud.co.uk/ISLAM/ahm/loyalty.htm (2003).

their own circumstances, while causing the least amount of harm. This does not apply to the major tenets of Islam, but still represents a radical departure from neo-orthodox Islamic positioning. Contrary to popular belief, freedom of thought is actively promoted in Islam, rather than seen as a necessary evil. The Qur'an states in Surah Hud, verse 118: 'And had your Lord so willed, He could surely have made all human beings into one single community: but (He willed it otherwise, and so) they continue to hold divergent views.'

Such ideas are clearly controversial among those who only support forms of governance that have explicitly 'Islamic' labels. The term *khalifa* is taken by such people to mean a civil and religious leader of an Islamic state. Contrary to the rhetoric of several extremist groups, the Islamic state is a purely historical concept. Not only is there no mention of a state in the Qur'an, but only 350 out of the Qur'an's 6,200 verses relate to law and jurisprudence. The meaning of the term *khalifa*, as I understand it, is far more humanistic: men and women have been created as vicegerents (*khalifas*) on earth, tasked with upholding peace, a just social order, and respect for the environment. Nadeem Malik writes, 'The concept of *khalifah* (vice gerent) applies to both individuals in their duties to God, to one another and to the earth, as well as to those in positions of power and to those who appointed them.'[14] It is thus a term which includes, within its purview of responsible stewardship, a concern for the common good. Another concept which makes this reading of *khalifa* possible is one of my other favourite concepts in Islam: *amanah*, or holding things in trust. This radically reorients popular concepts of ownership: it states that everything in the world only belongs to humans for a limited time, before such things return to God, and that individuals must do their best to discharge all relevant responsibilities during that period. Accountability, honesty and diligence are just some of the values enshrined in this concept. The Qur'an says in Surah Anfal, verse 27: 'O you, who believe, do not betray God and His Messenger, and do not knowingly violate your trusts.'

The concept of *amanah* establishes a framework for active citizenship, with clear delineations of individual rights and responsibilities, in relation to all other sentient beings and the planet. The fact that so many individuals have failed in their caretaking duties – as is evident in the political, social and environmental crises we see around us – is all the more reason to reinvoke and popularize an interpretation of the common good that is compatible with a large swathe of religious traditions, yet is robust enough to exist independently of them.

---

14 Nadeem Malik, 'Friends, Romans, Countrymen?', in *British Muslims*, p. 169.

Finally, the concept of *asabiya* (social solidarity) may either be used in furtherance of the common good, or against it. The positive interpretation takes it to refer to a flourishing community spirit, where individuals interpret and implement universal values in the ways that suit them best. Consequently, other individuals and communities are neither chastised nor ostracized for realizing these values differently. The negative interpretation of *asabiya*, however, endorses tribalism and parochial self-interest. This is a feature of contemporary British Muslim political activity that Muslim civil society practitioners and organizations should work harder to discourage. They should make it clear that Muslims are invited to reflect on and learn from the universe in its entirety, rather than restricting their focus to religious texts, or initiatives which only promote narrow and sectarian interpretations of Islam. The next section describes the political environment which will help us realize this vision.

British Muslims, procedural secularism and the common good

'Contextualizing Islam in Britain' was a research project conducted by The Centre of Islamic Studies at Cambridge University in which a diverse group of Muslim participants was asked the question 'What does it mean to live faithfully as a Muslim in Britain today?' The report of their discussion noted the importance for UK Muslims of 'procedural secularism' (as distinct from 'assertive' or 'ideological secularism'), which 'protects the equal rights of all citizens, while freely allowing religious citizens to participate fully and robustly in open debate in the public sphere'.[15]

The relation between procedural secularism and pluralism has been explored by experts such as Jacques Berlinerblau. Berlinerblau claims that his understanding of secularism does not in any way denigrate religion, but rather stresses the core secular goal of enabling citizens to live peaceably with other citizens whose creed is different to their own.[16] While many political scientists have articulated pluralistic visions of a secular society, Berlinerblau goes several notches further by embracing the symbiotic relationship between religious communities and secularists. He describes how their respective success as civic actors is often dependent on each other, and outlines a programme to revive secularism which actively includes and empowers people of faith.[17]

15 Cambridge Centre of Islamic Studies, *Contextualising Islam in Britain II* (2012), p. 92. See www.cis.cam.ac.uk/assets/media/cib2-complete-report.pdf.

16 See J. Berlinerblau, *How to be Secular: A Call to Arms for Religious Freedom*, Boston: Houghton Mifflin Harcourt, 2012.

17 Berlinerblau, *How to be Secular*, pp. 193–208.

Secularism in the UK can only thrive on the basis of specific pacts that different communities make with each other. Non-religious groups and individuals should move towards greater cooperation with liberal and progressive religious stakeholders. The onus is also on religious groups and individuals to forge common ground on contentious issues such as women's rights, LGBT rights, freedom of expression and the establishment of good interfaith – and, crucially, intrafaith – relations. Certain commentators have argued that these issues have become a stick with which to beat religious minorities, but I think this analysis encourages a victim mentality and exculpates religious communities of all responsibility for the injustices in their midst.

Proponents of ideological secularism often cite the negative role that religion can play when it comes to issues like the rights of women, minorities and LGBT people. This is used as grounds to object to the inclusion of religion – or even of values that purport to be religious – in the public sphere at all. When hardline religious activists and preachers speak out against women's rights and use supposedly religious arguments, this furthers such misconceptions. Some extreme acts have more to do with culture than religion. For example, forced marriage is a negative cultural practice. Although associated with Islam, it is actually at odds with Islamic history, which includes examples of the Prophet Muhammad ending marriages in which consent had not been sought.[18] However, it would be a whitewash to attribute all of these negative practices to culture alone. Several theological arguments are usually advanced on the alleged impermissibility of marriage between Muslim women and non-Muslim men, for example, even if the wife in a non-Muslim married couple later decides to convert to Islam. Fortunately, there are experienced and confident Islamic scholars like Dr Usama Hasan, who have rebutted these arguments in public.[19]

It is my firm belief that interpretations of Islam which impose normative rules on others – and can only be properly understood in the context of religious morality – should not be granted legitimacy by public bodies. Subjective 'in-group' truth claims remain compatible with democratic ideals as long as they provide not only personal inspiration but also inspiration for civic activity. However, they erode the very foundation of democratic discourse when they are either applied to others (including members of

---

18 The following is from the *Hadith*: Abdullah ibn Abbas narrates, 'A virgin came to the Prophet (pbuh) and mentioned that her father had married her against her will, so the Prophet (pbuh) allowed her to exercise her choice.' (Translation of *Sunan Abu-Dawud*, 'Marriage' (*Kitab Al-Nikah*), Book 11, Number 2091).

19 http://unity1.wordpress.com/2012/01/13/what-happens-to-a-marriage-if-one-of-the-couple-converts-to-islam/.

the 'out-group') without their consent or are consensually applied yet still contravene modern equality and human rights standards. One example of this was the Universities UK guidance from December 2013, which authorized external speakers to dictate gender segregation at university events. This guidance was later withdrawn after protests from a coalition of secular activists and groups, including British Muslims for Secular Democracy. The Equality and Human Rights Commission put out its own guidance in 2014 to confirm that the practice of gender segregation in public universities did indeed violate equality law, even if segregation was entered into voluntarily.[20]

We should develop an understanding and appreciation of equalities that transcend the benefits it can provide for our own 'in-groups'. This means acknowledging the six protected equality grounds – gender, age, disability, race, religion and sexual orientation – and respecting their rights, but also insisting that each group upholds their responsibilities vis-à-vis the others. For example, this means that a religious group which believes gay marriage to be sinful is entitled to hold such a view, but is never entitled to prevent other religious organizations from holding same-sex wedding ceremonies if they so wish. They should also expect to be robustly challenged on those views. By the same token, an employer who finds Islam repugnant should never be able to bully their Muslim employees without facing serious penalties.

If the majority of British Muslims do indeed support procedural secularism as a system, then how are they to regard individual activists from non-Muslim backgrounds, and how are they to regard the possibility of forging wider links for the common good? I think this boils down to two things. First, we need to clarify the values we subscribe to. Second, there must be greater emphasis on interfaith social action, as opposed to interfaith dialogue.

One exponent of Islamic values, Shaykh Manwar Ali, has commended the 'British values' of creativity, openness, tolerance and adaptability. He would see values such as these as 'Islamic', adding to them the values of human dignity, understanding the narrative of the other and knowing how to frame grievances. The overarching value for an Islamic thinker like Manwar Ali would be the need to build strong communities.[21] Far from advocating withdrawal from society, mainstream Islamic scholarship regards civic engagement – and its attendant rights and responsibilities

---

20 www.equalityhumanrights.com/commission-tackles-gender-segregation-universities.

21 www.neweuropeangeneration.eu/uploads/9/4/5/4/9454102/islam_and_secular_democracy_manwar_ali.pdf.

– as highly desirable for Muslim citizens. Contrary to popular belief, this holds equally true for Muslims who consider themselves to be orthodox or conservative.

This leads to a second point. Within a procedural secular state such as Britain, Muslims have rights and responsibilities that are in keeping with Islamic teachings. As British Muslims, we are able, for the most part, to practise our faith in an atmosphere of respect and security, with recourse to established anti-discrimination provisions if this is not the case. Since 2012, I have been involved with the Measuring Anti-Muslim Attacks Project, which is a prime example of such provision.[22] Many other European countries have far worse problems in terms of the scale of anti-Muslim sentiment, yet they do not have designated reporting and mapping mechanisms for such crimes, let alone anything that has buy-in from national governments, or mainstream organizations like Victim Support or Neighbourhood Watch.

More needs to be done to highlight this area of thought, and how it can be used as inspiration in the lives of British Muslims today. Civic participation does *not* mean abusing democratic rights to further interests that are in themselves thoroughly undemocratic, tribalistic and parochial.[23]

Human rights principles and Sharia law

The Equality and Human Rights Commission promotes five human rights principles under the acronym 'FREDA'. These are: fairness, respect, equality, dignity and autonomy. While these broad principles find generous backing from all the major world religions, many religious texts – including Islamic ones – would not be compatible with contemporary understandings of equality and human rights. This is particularly pertinent when it comes to contentious issues like same-sex marriage, and the operation of Sharia councils in the UK.

According to the jurisprudential schools in Islam, the actual purpose of Sharia law is to serve the best interests of human beings, towards a wide range of general moral objectives contained in the Qur'an and Sunnah. Examples include racial equality, freedom of conscience, or the right of women to own property. As we have seen, many of the practices and deci-

---

22 See http://tellmamauk.org/.

23 The petition calling for Maajid Nawaz's removal as a prospective Liberal Democrat parliamentary candidate in March 2014 – for tweeting an innocuous cartoon – was a pertinent example of this. See www.theguardian.com/commentisfree/2014/jan/28/speaking-islam-loudmouths-hijacked.

sions that pass for Islamic jurisprudence in Britain today end up furthering the opposite of these goals. This happens for a number of reasons.

First, many of the contemporary British arbiters of Sharia law ignore the fact that specific rulings in the Qur'an are contingent on particular historical circumstances, several of which do not exist in the modern age.

Second, too many people do not bother to approach the Qur'an and Sunnah in a holistic manner, from a well-informed intellectual and moral perspective. Now, I am not making excuses for the anti-women traditions in some Islamic texts. It is indisputable that these exist, alongside the ones that could be considered empowering to women. However, since the power dynamics within British Muslim communities often swing heavily in favour of patriarchal norms, it is inevitable that the anti-women parts of religion will end up being reinforced. Further, even gender-neutral rulings on issues such as women's access to mosques may be read in a way that is demeaning to women, while explicitly pro-women aspects of Islam – such as a wife's right to stipulate no housework in an Islamic marriage contract[24] – end up being downplayed or ignored. Couple this with the fact that many British Muslim women are not aware of their rights – from either a non-religious secular perspective or an Islamic one – and it is not difficult to see how this would lead to widespread injustice.

Third, many of the judges in Sharia councils are not qualified for nor experienced in the appraisal of domestic matters from a secular perspective that is concordant with modern equality and human rights standards. There have been cases where women find it much harder to get divorces than men do, and are charged twice as much for such a service. Any sensible arbiter would realize that this goes against fundamental principles of equality, and would insist on changing such rules. However, since there is no legal framework governing Sharia councils (as opposed to Muslim arbitration tribunals, which operate under a clause in the Arbitration Act), individuals who have been adversely affected by their decisions often find it hard to gain redress. We need statutory and institutionalized protection for people who have been adversely affected by the decisions of Sharia councils. Any quasi-judicial mechanisms which encourage insularity – and undermine the rule of law – should be strictly monitored and regulated. At best, they do nothing to further the common good. At worst, they are completely inimical to it.

---

24 See Iqbal A. Ansari, 'Muslim Women's Rights, Goals and Strategies of Reform', in Zakia A. Siddiqi and Anwar Jahan Zuberi, *Muslim Women, Problems and Prospects*, New Delhi: MD Publications, 1993, pp. 45–52, at p. 50.

Examples of good practice

I would like, finally, to give some good examples of good practice, to show how Muslims are working at the local level for the common good. Rumi's Kitchen is an interfaith soup kitchen in Cricklewood. It is largely run by Muslims, but has volunteers with a diverse range of beliefs and serves everyone, regardless of their background or beliefs. Another example would be the 'People Like Us – Interfaith' initiative mentioned above, which has now led to further collaborations. For instance, one of the humanist panellists in Cambridge, Trevor Moore, invited me to join a panel with British Humanist Association trustee Alom Shaha, Jewish interfaith worker Abigail Kay and Revd Paul Collier at Alleyn's School in November 2013. We used it as an opportunity to explain our respective beliefs, how we came to hold them, and most importantly, what they had enabled us to achieve.[25] Another example would be the Three Faiths Forum's 'Women ARTogether' project, where women from different faith backgrounds used their passion for art to break down barriers. This later evolved into a spoken word bonanza, called 'Female Voices'.[26] As I write, the British Humanist Association is planning an event on finding common ground between humanists and Muslims.

The vast majority of theologians happily propagate and even spearhead these kinds of initiatives. For instance, Shaykh Hamza Yusuf has enthusiastically participated in interfaith youth conferences.[27] However, there remains a fringe of religious leaders who see diversity as a threat to their authority. The irony is that these same individuals could potentially be the greatest beneficiaries of interfaith activity, if they realized its true benefits. Exclusivist approaches to religious diversity – and the arrogance that usually accompanies them – are not only the biggest threat to interfaith relations, but do tremendous damage to intrafaith relations too. In December 2009, a mosque application was refused by Walsall Council after receiving more than 800 complaints. Rather than being the handiwork of 'Stop the Islamification of Europe' or some other far-right group, the protesters were mainly Sunni Muslims, and the mosque application in question was submitted by the Ahmadiyya Muslim Association UK.[28] The Ahmadis are a minority sect in Islam, whose members have faced severe human rights abuses in majority-Muslim countries (espe-

---

25 www.meetup.com/Central-London-Humanists/events/149852062/?value=EXTERNAL +EVENT+-+Encountering+Faiths+and+Beliefs.

26 www.flickr.com/photos/3ff/sets/72157636656384334/.

27 www.halaltube.com/interfaith-youth-work.

28 www.spittoon.org/archives/4076.

cially Pakistan, where the amended Hadood Ordinances treat them as heretics).[29] As ostensibly similar diaspora communities in a contemporary British context, this very public display of animosity must be unintelligible to most outsiders. More crucially, the aforementioned protesters have, knowingly or unknowingly, breached a fundamental tenet of our civic code: the importance of reciprocity when upholding the civil rights of particular minority groups. For no matter how people evaluate belief systems that are different from their own, equal treatment before the law is what places us on common ground.

This sort of approach is more likely to take us beyond the parameters of mere tolerance for other groupings, into a mindset where we can actively champion the rights of people who seem different from ourselves. These differences may manifest themselves in terms of personal views, practices and lifestyles. For example, British Muslims for Secular Democracy campaigned against two anti-Semitic preachers who were invited to speak at Green Lane Mosque in December 2009.[30] Non-religious groups and individuals, such as human rights activist Peter Tatchell, have also played a significant role in this process. Tatchell is well known for his interventions against the subjugation of Balochis in Pakistan, a minority group far removed from his experiences as one of the leading LGBT rights activists in London. Interfaith and intercultural activities can provide a major impetus for this kind of empathetic advocacy work, as long as they implement the central teaching of most belief systems, that is the just and ethical treatment of other people, including those who happen to be different. In building and maintaining such relationships, social media can be a vital enabler, but it is no substitute for real-life collaborations. We need social action that crosses boundaries and overcomes barriers. Just because two individuals or organizations cannot find complete consensus, particularly on issues of individual belief and doctrine, however, it doesn't mean that they should discount each other's potential as allies in furtherance of the common good.

---

29 www.newstatesman.com/asia/2011/04/pakistan-laws-women-religious.
30 www.bmsd.org.uk.

9

The Church of England and the Common Good

MALCOLM BROWN

When the Roman Catholic Bishops' Conference of England and Wales published *The Common Good* in 1996, it was seized upon with alacrity by many socially active Anglicans who saw immediately that it represented both a new phase in Roman Catholic/Anglican understandings and opened the door to a major set of resources for all socially concerned Christians. For Anglicans who had worked happily alongside Catholic colleagues throughout the divisive years of Thatcherism, *The Common Good* told us that the Catholic hierarchy, not just our local Catholic friends, stood in solidarity in the struggle for better communities and a better politics, and for many of us the paper was our first insight into the living tradition of Catholic Social Teaching which we had hitherto encountered only through the unmediated language of encyclicals. The Church of England had made its most effective post-war impact on social issues through *Faith in the City* of 1985, but now *The Common Good* helped us address some of the perceived deficiencies of *Faith in the City* such as its rather weak theological undergirding and jejune belief that policy revisions would inevitably follow the uncovering of facts.

The Common Good achieved something that, at that moment, the Church of England was probably not equipped to do. Anglicans were only just beginning to recover an authentic tradition of social theology following *Faith in the City*'s (and numerous activists') flirtation with liberation theology. This had, through the 1980s, tended to obscure the pre-existing Anglican social tradition and had not translated easily into the secularizing culture and largely middle-class Church of the time. In most of its official work on social issues, the Church of England had gone on using the Anglican social theology of William Temple, epitomized in his *Christianity and Social Order* (1942), but without giving much attention to the way in which Temple's popular little book had grown out of his solid and orthodox grounding in Christian doctrine. Through this neglect,

Anglican activists tended to lose a clear connection between Christian theology and social action.[1] By the 1990s, the popular perception that the Church of England was in the vanguard against the divisive free-market ideologies of Thatcherism had exposed the underlying beliefs of Anglican activists to unprecedented scrutiny and they had been, theologically speaking, found wanting.[2] *The Common Good* reminded Anglicans that an alternative social vision, and a rationale for action, could be grounded firmly in a theological tradition – the challenge they faced was to (re)discover an authentic social theological tradition of their own.[3]

Seek the common good

But, of course, the theme of the common good had not hitherto been absent from Anglican consciousness. Liturgical reform in the 1960s had reshaped the intercessory prayers in the communion service, introducing the well-known petition that we might 'honour one another and seek the common good'. This form of words has persisted through *Series 3*, the *Alternative Service Book* of 1980 and into *Common Worship*, now current. Importantly, this line follows the petitions for the Queen and all in authority. The pursuit of the common good is thus stressed as an aspect of personal discipleship but also part of God's calling to the social and political structures.

In comparing the intercessory prayers of today's liturgy with that of the Book of Common Prayer, the more recent texts suggest a Church with a greater awareness of its distinctiveness within a society whose conception of the good is no longer seen as identical with the Christian vision. Whether this was conscious on the part of liturgists in the 1960s is a moot point – the fact remains that that decade saw the accelerating collapse of established social structures and shared assumptions about class, society, sex, gender and many other former givens. It was the 1960s which made mainstream the idea that freedom from the past, social and physical

---

1 The connection between Temple's systematic theology and his social theology in *Christianity and Social Order* lay largely unexamined until Wendy Dackson's important study (Wendy Dackson, *The Ecclesiology of Archbishop William Temple (1881–1944)*, Lewiston, NY and Lampeter: Edwin Mellen Press, 2004). As Dackson points out, *Christianity and Social Order* had become a blueprint for Anglican political thought, and activism had eclipsed serious theological enquiry.

2 See, Henry Clark, *The Church Under Thatcher*, London: SPCK, 1993.

3 For a more detailed examination of this historical background and the present state of play see Malcolm Brown (ed.), *Anglican Social Theology*, London: Church House Publishing, 2014.

mobility, and the overturning of social norms constituted liberation for all, and old Anglican assumptions about the virtues and continuities of establishment came under direct fire. The so-called 'new morality' provoked many in the Church of England to a sincere (though much mocked) quest for relevance, but while this revealed an impressively energetic and intellectually inquisitive movement within the Church, it also bore witness to a certain shaken-ness in the face of confident and iconoclastic individualism. The specific liturgical petition for the common good may have reflected, consciously or otherwise, a sense that such a concept could no longer be taken for granted as structures of mutuality withered and the good of the individual began to take precedence.

The radical shift to economic liberalism in 1979, when Margaret Thatcher became prime minister, has usually been presented as a decisive moment when social consensus was forcibly ended and wealth reasserted itself as the arbiter of morality, with a selfish individualism coming to replace the egalitarianism of the 1960s social revolution. This is too simple a picture. The late 1950s and early 60s had seen the most decisive moves from the shared experiences and values of class and region, moulded by the industrial era's focus on production, to the sharper-elbowed individualism of a nation of consumers.[4] Part, at least, of Thatcherism's prospectus was about restoring a more settled and deferential social order. One reason why this aspect of her vision was not realized was that her economic policies were themselves ideologically grounded in an even more deeply atomized individualism – a new phase of liberalism rather than a reversion to any pre-liberal understanding.[5] However, it was not immediately apparent that both social liberalism and economic liberalism were, so to speak, drinking from the same glass. True, Alasdair MacIntyre had assembled the building blocks for this critique of liberalism in the very early 1980s, well before the neoliberal economic experiment had really taken root, but it would take 30 or more years for his ideas to gain even minimal traction in the field of practical politics and social action. And it remains that tensions between different kinds of liberalism – social liberals celebrating individual freedom in morals but deploring economic freedom in the market, and economic liberals taking more or less opposite positions – continue to bedevil serious analysis of the strengths and weaknesses of liberal ideas.

---

4 See, David Kynaston, *Modernity Britain: A Shake of the Dice, 1959–62*, London: Bloomsbury, 2014.

5 See Charles Moore, *Margaret Thatcher: The Authorised Biography*, Vol. I, London: Penguin Books, 2013.

The contextual point, however, is that differing modes of liberalism in political and cultural life have conspired together, over many decades, to create a public consciousness which elevates the notion of the autonomous individual over conceptions of the common good. And this, inevitably, introduces profound missiological challenges for all churches as the vocation to make the gospel intelligible in every generation, and the inevitability that Christian people will, to a greater or lesser extent, receive their formation within the narratives of the dominant culture, push towards the 'liberalization' of the Church's mission, while the obligation to witness to the categories and patterns of thought formed by Scripture and centuries of pre-Enlightenment tradition act as a powerful countercultural corrective. This dilemma is acutely felt today in the churches' struggle with rapidly changing understandings of sexuality.[6] Whether 'liberal' or 'conservative' in theology, almost all can recognize that rapid social change, set against the assumptions behind the churches' teaching, prompts a major rethinking of the demands of mission.

The missiological challenge facing the churches today is largely about negotiating the positive and negative aspects of liberal individualism against the template of a gospel ethic forged in a pre-modern social context, recognizing that the Enlightenment itself derived from the solidly Christian formation and motivation of figures such as Locke.[7] It is perfectly possible to construct from the gospels either an individualist ethic or a communitarian ethic – the emphasis on personal conversion working in tension with the notion of the people of God, although the tension has many other dimensions. Anglicanism, in whose complex and confused origins and history the desire to hold together incompatible doctrines, practices and attitudes is very much apparent, may be surprisingly well equipped to negotiate an ethic of the common good among the current travails of competing liberalisms and their numerous critics.

The parish and the common good

One particularly Anglican factor sharpens the missiological question acutely. That is the organization – and indeed the deep ecclesiology – of the Church of England as a Church organized on a geographical, rather

---

6 *Report of the House of Bishops Working Group on Human Sexuality* (the Pilling Report), London: Church House Publishing, 2013, pp. 10–14.

7 Jeremy Waldron, *God, Locke and Equality: Christian Foundations in Locke's Political Thought*, Cambridge: Cambridge University Press, 2002.

than primarily a doctrinal principle: in short, the notion of the parish.[8] The idea that the Church of England is there for all the people of the land, serving them through a close identification with every local community and drawn together across differences through the unifying structure of the diocese, runs very deep in Anglican self-consciousness – certainly in England. The strapline on the Church of England's website has, for some years, read 'A Christian Presence in Every Community'. One might quibble about different interpretations of 'Christian', what constitutes 'presence' and how one defines 'community', but aspiration goes a long way to shape identity. Were the parochial system to break down, or the geographical coverage be broken, the Church of England would have an acute identity crisis.

Close to the heart of the parochial model is the sense that, in serving the whole community, the church is there to perceive, articulate and build up the common good of the people of that place. The parish becomes a dimension of belonging and identity which mediates between the individual and the nebulous concept of society as a whole. The parochial model is more an instinct than a formulated principle, but no less potent for that. In an age of accelerating change, flux and mobility the parish ideal preserves the significance of face-to-face encounters, across classes and generations, which are increasingly uncommon in other contexts. The parish has been a powerful framework for conceiving the common good in manageable dimensions, but has become increasingly countercultural as the globalizing imperatives of late capitalism tend to detach identity, value and meaning from any conception of place at all. It is another example, at a structural rather than ethical level, of the Church of England having to decide whether to go with the flows of culture or to resist in the name of unchanging verities. Alternatives to the parish system, based on the concept of the network rather than the place, claim to represent how people today 'really live'. But the proponents of the networked church rarely explain how the warp and weft of the net are to be defined other than through implicit notions of 'people like us' – the common good is not a concept that has yet been mapped properly onto the network model.

---

8 It may be overstating the case to describe the Church of England as essentially defined geographically and some would argue that its foundations are in fact doctrinal and expressed in the 39 Articles. This is a fair, but incomplete, point. Given that there is a broad doctrinal framework captured in the 39 Articles, the Church of England's self-consciousness is far more explicitly formed by the idea of being the Church for the people of England, expressed in the parochial model. Most Church members are concerned with the role of their church in its community: few recall much about the 39 Articles.

The common good and the wellbeing of the Church

A saying attributed to William Temple – that the Church is one of the few institutions which exists for the sake of those who are not its members – is still much repeated in Anglican circles.[9] This is a succinct expression of the principle that the common good is integral to the Church's mission. In print, Temple's understanding of the pursuit of the common good as mission was more subtle. In *Christianity and Social Order*, he noted that:

> If we have to choose between making men Christian and making the social order more Christian, we must choose the former. But there is no such antithesis. Certainly there can be no Christian society unless there is a large body of convinced and devoted Christian people to establish it and keep it true to its own principles.[10]

Nevertheless, the pursuit of the common good and the evangelistic mission of the Church have often been perceived as antithetical. Some of this is little more than an institutional inability to multitask, but at a deeper level the historic antagonism between different Anglican traditions often made this a point of partisan distinction. Back in the 1980s, evangelicals frequently raised the spectres of the 'social gospel' and 'salvation by works'.[11] Yet in the recession which followed the banking crisis of 2008, evangelicals, including Anglican evangelicals, were among the vanguard in the growth of projects and programmes serving the common good. And whereas, in the 1980s, evangelicals decried as mere wishful thinking the claim by liberal Anglicans that social action was implicitly evangelistic since it constituted a non-verbal expression of Christian distinctiveness, precisely the same missiological claim is being made today by socially active evangelicals. For complex reasons yet to be analysed thoroughly, there has been a marked shift in British evangelicalism which has had a profound and positive effect on the Church of England's ability to commit to the common good. Jonathan Chaplin has suggested that this renewal of evangelical social action is partly about reconnecting with

---

9 This saying is not found in any of Temple's published works, but is believed to have been used by him in a number of unpublished sermons. Those who knew him suggest that it is certainly the sort of thing he would have said. (Author's conversations with Ronald Preston and Jack Keiser, mid-1990s.)

10 William Temple, *Christianity and Social Order*, Harmondsworth: Penguin, 1942 (London: Shepheard-Walwyn/SPCK, 1976, pp. 114–15).

11 As the term 'social gospel' is of American provenance with little UK salience, it is possible that English evangelicals in the 1980s were buying much of their theological ammunition from across the Atlantic.

evangelicalism's own history, but that it is more visceral than consciously theological.[12] It remains that Anglican evangelical action in pursuit of the common good is now a force to be reckoned with and, paradoxically, part of its strength may lie in the fact that evangelicalism in Western democracies is generally comfortable with the structures and principles of capitalism and business. This is not to suggest that evangelicals do not critique capitalism and commerce, but to make the more general point that contemporary evangelicalism is more content to work with the currently dominant enterprise model of action than are some more liberal strands of churchmanship which tend to be, sometimes inflexibly, nostalgic for the post-war consensus around the state's overriding responsibility for the welfare of the people.

The Church of England pursuing the common good today

In 2010, the Archbishops' Council set out three 'Quinquennium Goals' for the five-year life of the new Synod. These were intended to focus the work of the Church at national level and to express the key priorities for the period. The goals were: numerical and spiritual growth, reimagining ministry and serving the common good. The Synod papers which outlined these goals went to some trouble to stress that growth and pursuing the common good were not in opposition to one another.[13] While the old antithesis between evangelism and service is much weakened, it has not disappeared and a downward trend in the statistics of Church membership always exerts a strong pull towards the proverbial 'bums on pews' as the only worthwhile objective. But the Synod papers echoed Temple's dictum that while a flourishing Church is a necessity if the common good is to be served, a Church which does not serve the common good can hardly be said to be flourishing in an authentic way.

As the Quinquennium draws to a close, the goal of serving the common good has been pursued in multifaceted ways. At one end of the spectrum, it is important not to underestimate the small-scale, local, often unsung, work that churches and their members undertake. This is where Christian character, formed and nurtured in the life of a congregation, impacts upon a wider community most indelibly. Small acts of neighbourliness become increasingly countercultural the more individualistic a culture becomes

---

12 Jonathan Chaplin, in Brown (ed.), *Anglican Social Theology*, pp. 102–32.

13 GS 1815 *Challenges for the New Quinquennium*, 2010 (www.churchofengland.org/media/1163101/gs%201815.pdf), and GSMisc 995, *Challenges for the New Quinquennium: Next Steps*, June 2011 (www.churchofengland.org/media/1287487/gs%20misc%20995.pdf).

and, because many Christians act as good neighbours more by instinct than theology, there is some risk that they and the Church will fail to give proper weight to the way this aspect of discipleship serves the common good. As Temple said, 'Nine-Tenths of the work of the Church in the world is done by Christian people fulfilling responsibilities and performing tasks which in themselves are not part of the official system of the Church at all.'[14]

But the Church's pursuit of the common good takes on more organized and structural forms as well, and the parishes of the Church of England have long been responsible for social action and social care projects of great variety – some of purely local salience while others multiply and grow. The most prominent recent story concerns the creation of foodbanks. The Synodical Quinquennium beginning in 2010 coincided closely with the five-year term of the Coalition government elected in the same year, and thus the goal of pursuing the common good coincided with austerity policies and acute tightening of the welfare system. The outcomes of government policies, exacerbated by chaotic implementation of welfare reforms which sometimes, despite seeking laudable objectives were applied crudely and punitively, was that increasing numbers of claimants had to choose between heating their homes or feeding their families, while others found themselves penniless for significant periods after falling foul of the regime of sanctions for minor oversights or systemic failure to sort out their case.[15] In response, and almost always led by churches, numerous local communities set up foodbanks as a 'last resort' source of food for those with no alternative. Many church foodbanks were sponsored by the Trussell Trust, a church-related charity, but others were independent local ventures backed by congregations and other volunteers. Foodbanks quickly became symbolic of the failures of the government's welfare reform programme.[16] But the church-run foodbanks epitomized an interesting and complex tension in the Church's work for the common good.

---

14 Temple, *Christianity and Social Order*, p. 39.

15 Unpublished research on foodbanks by the Church of England's Mission and Public Affairs Division in Partnership with Oxfam, Child Poverty Action Group and the Trussell Trust.

16 The Lords Spiritual (Church of England diocesan bishops who are members of the House of Lords) took a strong lead in raising critical questions about the government's welfare reform programme. Contrary to the claims of ministers and much of the media, their stance was not one of resistance to change – indeed they clearly recognized the need for reform and backed the principles behind universal credit and the priority of work. Their concern was rather that a punitive rhetoric directed at all claimants was misleading, created the conditions for excessively harsh treatment of vulnerable people and obscured serious delivery failures. The bishops led the debate in the Lords during which the cap on individual welfare benefits was rejected, only for it to be reinstated in the Commons.

While churches were right to celebrate a very considerable achievement, and to be glad that, thanks to their efforts, people in danger of starvation were being fed, the distinction between foodbanks as temporary crisis-alleviation and foodbanks as a permanent feature of the welfare landscape was easily blurred. It requires a degree of subtlety to be simultaneously proud of a very considerable achievement and deeply ashamed to live in a country where such work is a necessity if the basic standards of a civilized society are to be maintained at all.

Justin Welby's appointment as Archbishop of Canterbury in 2013 brought to Lambeth Palace the first incumbent to be respected for his grasp of modern economic issues.[17] His experience on the Parliamentary Commission on Banking Standards convinced him that a major element in the crash of 2008 was not just that financial institutions were under-regulated but that the principles of the market itself had been flouted by the banks becoming big and few enough to act as an effective cartel. The solution lay less in regulating the market than in generating true competition – and this was not just a task to be urged upon government but one which could be addressed at local level, not least with the input of the churches. Out of this analysis came Welby's 'Task Group on Responsible Credit and Saving' which sought to put the Church of England's weight – both practical and exhortatory – behind the development of more robust and effective Credit Unions which would compete in certain sectors of the financial market with both the banks and the payday lenders.

Leaving aside the details and impact of the task group's work, this initiative is an important development in the Church's pursuit of the common good for two main reasons. First, Welby recognizes that the market is not, in principle, an enemy of the common good, but that without external and moral constraints, it ceases to operate competitively and damages both the social fabric and the conditions for the market itself to flourish. Welby grasps the distinction between the market's theoretical benefits and its tendency in practice to undermine its own virtues. Second, the Credit Union model, although often adopted as part of an anti-poverty strategy, functions most effectively for the less well-off when a broad cross section of society is embraced and participates. Rather than, on the one hand, distinguishing 'them' (the poor, vulnerable or needy) from 'us' who seek to help them or, on the other, privileging bottom up initiatives which are conceived as being 'of the poor' rather than 'for the poor', Credit Unions give concrete substance to notions of mutuality and interdepend-

---

17 Although William Temple's close association with Keynes gave him a good second-hand grasp of economics, Welby's pre-ordination experience as treasurer of an oil company gave unprecedented weight to his reflections on the financial crash and the banking system.

ence. Credit Unions are a good market choice for the better off as well as the poor, at least for certain financial functions. They serve the least well-off best when the better-off join in. There is something very explicitly 'common' in this vision of the good.

The tension between state and voluntary action

These examples contain within them a tension, deep in the life of the Church of England. On the one hand, many in the Church remain stalwart supporters of the Beveridge model of the welfare state. Indeed, Temple's *Christianity and Social Order* might be described as laying out the principles which Beveridge then fleshed out in policy terms and Nye Bevan enacted. More than that, Temple popularized the term 'welfare state' and understood it, not primarily as a system of social security but as the very rationale for the state itself – a better political vision than the totalitarians' power state, or the minimal state which had contributed to, and failed to ameliorate, the Great Depression. In contrast to those options, a state which seeks to secure the welfare of all citizens is a state to which the Christian (who always has a higher allegiance) can give at least provisional support. So, the principles of the welfare state itself, and not just the Beveridge post-war settlement, have Christian roots which, arguably, reflect the centrality of the common good in Anglican consciousness.

The practical outworking of the Beveridge report cannot but be inadequate for addressing a very different set of social stresses today. Consequently, the disputes that attended the inauguration of Bevan's welfare state continue to re-echo. Many still argue that the welfare system eclipses the proper role of charity and voluntarism, diminishing the salience of those intermediate institutions which once stood between the individual and the state and which theologians such as J. N. Figgis understood as crucial to a flourishing society.[18] This is not just the stance of the radical right which would happily substitute an all-powerful corporate sector for an overpowerful state. Beveridge himself followed his first report with another entitled *Voluntary Action*.[19] His point was that, while modern society had outgrown the charitable structures which had hitherto sought to protect the vulnerable, necessitating coordinated state action on

---

18 See: J. N. Figgis, *Churches in the Modern State*, London: Longmans, Green and Co., 1914.

19 William Beveridge, *Voluntary Action: A Report on Methods of Social Advance*, London: Allen and Unwin, 1949.

welfare, the state's system could not be a substitute for a rich culture of neighbourliness and voluntarism.

The twentieth-century history of Anglican social thought embraces this tension between the central state as guarantor of the common good and the common good subsisting essentially in a local voluntarism informed by religious commitment. This tension has been obscured to some extent by the close relationships between the key players. Temple and Beveridge knew each other at Balliol where Temple's fellow Rugbeian, R. H. Tawney was also a contemporary. When Temple was writing *Christianity and Social Order*, he shared the drafts with both Beveridge and Tawney (also with J. M. Keynes) and modified the text in the light of their comments. The fact that the 'Temple tradition' of Anglican social theology was dominant in the Church of England through the post-war period into the 1980s was largely due to the influence of Ronald Preston who, as a young man, had worked with Temple through the Student Christian Movement and studied for his first degree in economics at the LSE under Tawney. John Atherton, who wrote his doctoral thesis on Tawney under Preston's supervision and succeeded Preston at Manchester Cathedral, kept the tradition close to the centre of the Church's life to the very end of the twentieth century through his work at the William Temple Foundation and on the Church's Board for Social Responsibility.[20] It looks at first sight like a very tight-knit cohort.[21] But that impression conceals important degrees of difference. Temple broadly associated himself with the notion of Christendom (although not with the fervour or nostalgia of Demant).[22] In looking to the state as the only viable way to deliver the people's welfare, he nonetheless envisaged the state giving due recognition to the Church as providing its moral foundation and he took more or less for granted that Britain was, and ought to be, a Christian nation. Tawney was more sceptical of the Christendom approach. As he put it, 'The tradition of universal allegiance which the church – to speak without distinction of denomination – has inherited from an age in which the word "Christendom" had some meaning, is a source not of strength but of weakness.'[23] For Tawney, the Church of the twentieth century had (or ought to have had) a closer resemblance to the pre-Constantinian Church

---

20 See, for example: John R. Atherton, *Social Christianity: A Reader*, London: SPCK, 1994.

21 I have to declare an interest here, my doctorate, which brought Temple and Preston into dialogue with MacIntyre, having been supervised by Atherton.

22 See: V. A. Demant, *Religion and the Decline of Capitalism*, London: Faber and Faber, 1949.

23 R. H. Tawney, *The Acquisitive Society*, quoted in Atherton, *Social Christianity: A Reader*, p. 125.

– 'a sect, and a small sect, in a Pagan society'[24] witnessing to social virtues very different from those of the surrounding society. The common good, therefore, was not to be entrusted simply to governmental policies but was found in the quality of relationships to which the Church should bear witness in its own life.

Taking his two reports together, Beveridge might be seen to embody this tension. But unlike his report on welfare, *Voluntary Action* never translated into a programme and fell from view. Even in the work of Preston, although the strand of voluntarism is not absent and his critique of Christendom theologians like Demant is sharp, commitment to a Beveridge/Temple trust in the state as guarantor of welfare, and to welfare as the justification for the citizen's allegiance to the state, remains a dominant motif.[25]

In the late twentieth century, some of these theological tensions returned to prominence as the perceived failings of liberal theology were challenged by the pugnatious work of the American Stanley Hauerwas (whose eclectic formation embraced the Mennonite, Methodist, Roman Catholic and Anglican traditions) and the English Anglican, John Milbank. Both have been interpreted as standing somewhere in the Christendom tradition of Demant, but their Christendom is not to be associated with the state-oriented programme of Temple, being much closer to Tawney's 'sectarianism' and conscious rejection of Constantinianism. Quite how a Hauerwasian or Milbankian theological ethic translates into practical action for the common good is, as yet, less clear. Yet it is their style of theological ethics, reconnecting the internal life of the Church with its witness to God's social order, rejecting liberalism and its works and attempting to break down the secular/sacred division, which is most congruent with some important emergent strands of political thought today, and which also seeks the rebuilding of community and localism in ways which respect the deep historical role of Christianity in forging local and national identity. We shall consider this later.

The common good, the Church and politics today

The political question today, however, is not about delicate balances between public, private and voluntary sectors, but about the very legitimacy of the concept of a welfare state – less about state provision *and* voluntary

---

24 Tawney, *Acquisitive Society*, p. 125.
25 See, for example, the Church of England Board for Social Responsibility report, *Not Just for the Poor*, London: Church House Publishing, 1986, which was largely authored by Preston.

action than about voluntarism as an alternative to a comprehensive state welfare structure. Those who put voluntarism before state action can also claim theological foundations, appealing to the biblical model of the early Church which supported its own poor (Acts 2.45) and to the long history of the Church of England as a prime agent of social care whose proper vocation to this work had (as some argue) been usurped by a state that had overreached itself.

Something of this approach is exemplified in a report from the Res-Publica think-tank published in July 2013, which sought to map the (considerable) extent of the Church of England's contribution to social welfare and argued that the Church should act as a prime contractor to the government to deliver social services of all kinds.[26] Leaving aside questions of the Church's capacity to handle major commercial contracts, the limitations of any essential service provided mainly by volunteers and the experience of other voluntary agencies that the corporate sector could always win contracts awarded solely on cost terms by lowering standards unacceptably, the report certainly appealed to a significant Anglican constituency. But there is no consensus within the Church, at present, about where the proper boundary lies between public, private and voluntary provision in the shared task of building up the common good. This is a debate, not about the common good as a theological and practical priority, but about the means and mechanisms to achieve the good. One cause for concern in the Church is that significant partnerships between Church and government (or the corporate sector) usually value the Church instrumentally but misunderstand its deeper vocation. In other words, such partnerships put the Church on the back foot in ensuring that the notion of the common good as an imperative of discipleship, rather than just an objective of social policy, is heard and understood.

The challenge within the Church's own ranks can be discerned in the enthusiasm with which some accept, sometimes with alacrity, an instrumentalized evaluation of the Church's objectives and social significance. This is hardly surprising when the surrounding culture is so deeply utilitarian, but it militates against an approach to the common good which goes deeper than enumerating progress towards measurable targets. What may possibly preserve the Church from subservience to an instrumentalist, target culture is precisely the burgeoning of social action in the evangelical idiom in which Christian distinctiveness is seen as a highly prized virtue. But theological resistance to culture, rather than general acquiescence, needs to be explicitly nurtured against many odds.

---

26 James Noyes and Phillip Blond, *Holistic Mission: Social Action and the Church of England*, London: ResPublica, 2013.

Are we fighting a losing battle?

It is an interesting question whether the trend towards greater individualism – indeed, the onward march of the liberal Enlightenment project
as a whole – is inexorable and triumphant or in deep trouble. MacIntyre's
analysis of liberalism's ills, and his positing of alternatives grounded in the
recovery of community, practice, tradition and narrative, has infiltrated
numerous disciplines in the academy and is widely recognized (though
less often practised) in political and civil life.[27] The question is whether
this represents an early indication of a widespread realignment of social
attitudes, or merely an irrelevant cul-de-sac. MacIntyre gave tremendous hope to theologians and to religious traditions with his prescription
of 'another, no doubt very different, St Benedict'[28] as the way through
liberalism's impasse, and it could be argued that the persistence, indeed
the revitalization, of religion – contradicting most secularization theories
– is some kind of testimony to MacIntyre's perspicacity. But at grassroots,
so to speak, the portents are more confusing. The initial hopes that the
financial crisis might have sparked a new economics and a new politics
(rather as the Depression of the 1930s led to Temple and Beveridge's work
and ultimately the welfare state) remain unfulfilled. The hegemony of neoliberal economic thinking has only been scratched, and the emergence of
new schools of thought robust enough and sufficiently tested to be put
into practice, seems distant. Many have drawn the connection between
the increasing marketization, commodification and consumerization of
the economy and the loss of community resilience, mutuality and a sense
of the common good and, despite the depth of the economic crisis, little
seems to be arresting this trend. Janan Ganesh, writing in the *Financial
Times* in August 2014, celebrated London's ethnic and other diversities,
but went on to note that:

> From opinion polls to the compendious British Social Attitudes Surveys,
> the evidence suggests that voters born since Thatcher took office are
> the most individualist on record. Their attitudes to religion, family, the
> National Health Service, welfare, homosexuality, and even neighbour-
> liness are a libertarian's dream. If the future this points to is a rootless
> and postmodern society in which nothing is sacred, London got here
> long ago.[29]

27 Alasdair MacIntyre, *After Virtue: A Study in Moral Theory*, 2nd edn, London: Duckworth, 1985.

28 MacIntyre, *After Virtue*, p. 263.

29 Janan Ganesh, 'A censorious creed that gnaws away at the Conservative vote', *Financial
Times*, 11 August 2014.

Is that the future we all face? London exceptionalism may mean that other regions and localities hold out against this trend, but it would be a rash person who felt confident that the trend could be reversed. And, as David Hollenbach has argued, a particular understanding of pluralism, the growth of individualism and the allied emphasis in politics on diversity and freedom (understood in individualistic terms) constitute a major challenge to the concept of the common good. He notes that, 'the good that can be achieved in the shared domain of public life is hidden from view as protection of individual, private wellbeing becomes the centre of normative concern'.[30] All this suggests that, so to speak, Hayek is still ahead of MacIntyre in accurately describing the trajectory of our culture. It was Hayek who celebrated the transition from a 'tribal society' in which individual identity was formed in the relationships of the community, to a 'Great Society' where impersonal and amoral structures such as the market took the place of shared moralities (and, it has to be said, tribal suspicion of the other).[31] Hayek, along with Milton Friedman, was the philosophical driver behind Thatcher's economic experiment (although Robert Nozick surely had something to do with it, even though he is not celebrated in her pantheon),[32] and it was this economic ideology, for which there was no admitted alternative, which has shaped social attitudes to consumption, community, competition and identity. Against gross, and growing, economic inequality, the New Labour governments of Blair and Brown fought back with an emphasis on equality in terms of identity politics, itself profoundly informed by liberal individualism and abandonment of social normativity. Political discourse on left and right alike, despite differences, drew equally strongly on themes of liberal individualism and bequeathed us an atomized society and culture that seems heedless of what has been lost in the process – notably, a conception of the common good.

Arguments about the common good struggle to gain a hearing against strident assertions of the virtues of individualism and the primacy of choice. As a recent example, during the Parliamentary passage of the Falconer Bill on assisted suicide, the *British Medical Journal* published an editorial which claimed that, 'In recent years, respect for autonomy has emerged as the cardinal principle in medical ethics' – an assertion which calls into question the extent to which the editors of the BMJ were aware of contemporary developments in the subject.[33] Similarly, what-

---

30 David Hollenbach, *The Common Good and Christian Ethics*, Cambridge: Cambridge University Press, 2002, p. 10.

31 See: F. A. Hayek, *The Road to Serfdom*, London: Routledge and Kegan Paul, 1944.

32 Robert Nozick, *Anarchy, State and Utopia*, Oxford: Basil Blackwell, 1974.

33 *British Medical Journal*, 2014, 349: g4349, 2 July 2014.

ever the theological rights and wrongs of the Church of England's stance in opposition to same-sex marriage, the public debate was conducted solely in terms of freedom of choice and equality (understood as being expressed through identical treatment) versus prejudice. The Church of England and Roman Catholic attempts to explore the public virtues of heterosexual marriage – in other words, to examine the consequences for the common good of redefining marriage to include same-sex couples – were assumed to be no more than a smokescreen for bigotry. This is not to argue that the Church's stance was right: only that the context did not seem promising for a renewed public discourse which might elicit the nature of the common good.

Allies – and reasons for optimism

But the picture is not devoid of hope. The Church of England is not alone in seeking to reassert the political priority of the common good. It has allies, and not just among other churches with a congruent social tradition. On both sides of the House, politically, there are emerging groupings for whom a commitment to the common good is the key to renewing politics and economics with sufficient robustness to address the post-crash problems. While these groups remain somewhat fluid, key figures include Phillip Blond, whose Red Tory project informed Cameron's Big Society theme in the 2010 election and which, despite the Conservatives' reversion to a Thatcherite rather than a Burkean strand of Toryism, is not yet dead on their backbenches and, for Labour, Lord Maurice Glasman and Jon Cruddas. Blond, Glasman and Cruddas all draw, to a greater or lesser degree on the social traditions of the churches – in the case of Cruddas, specifically on Catholic Social Teaching. How their ideas will fare as we approach another general election is a tricky question. Most observers reckon that it will be two more Parliaments at least before such ideas become mainstream, if they ever do. But the Church of England is starting to align itself with these Labour and Tory thinkers who are aiming to restore the common good to a central position in political discourse. The House of Bishops has been exposed to some of the thinkers themselves and, in July 2014, the General Synod debated a paper on the common good which drew the explicit link between the Church's commitment to the common good and the need to support and contribute to the emerging political ferment around this and related themes. This has given the Church a position from which it can speak and act in the run up to the election. It looks beyond politics as a Dutch-auction of policy initiatives, aimed at distinct demographics, towards a more fundamental rethinking of political philosophy organized around a conception of the common good.

The optimistic outcome would be the emergence of a public politics and a new economics in which the common good featured strongly as a governing theme congruent with Christian social theology and which maintained a place for the churches, and religion more generally, within its conception of what a good society might look like. And, while the concept of religious establishment is deeply unfashionable, the Church of England's commitment to the concept of the nation, and its physical presence in terms of plant and people in every community, still give it a degree of salience in any politics of the common good, provided that that politics is not deaf to the history of how the people and communities of England, despite diversity and disunity, came to be who they are.

PART 3

The Market and the Common Good

Markets and the Common Good

BRIAN GRIFFITHS

The purpose of this chapter is to examine the question of whether or not markets contribute to the common good. It is a question to which there are widely different responses.

> The market generates order, promotes the common good, and teaches every virtue necessary for civilization apart from those left to the spiritual realm ... the market itself actually serves to do all those things that previous generations of intellectuals imagined could only be accomplished through the political sphere ... the market is the greatest force for achieving the common good: it is a moral teacher, it is humane, it is socially directed and future orientated in a way that no political institution, socialist or democratic, can ever be.[1]

> Today's markets are constituted by states, sustained by states, protected by states and sometimes imposed by states ... without the state's laws, police officers, courts, prisons, patents, Fraud Offices, food and drug regulations, air safety controls and rules forbidding insider trading, there would be no markets ... The doctrines that legitimize untamed capitalism tell us virtually nothing about the way in which it works.[2]

The first of these quotes is from an essay, 'Markets as Extended Communities', by Jeffrey Tucker, a research fellow at the Acton Institute, which is written from the perspective of Catholic Social Thought and which is part of a *festschrift* to Michael Novak. The second is from a book by a former Labour MP, David Marquand, entitled *Mammon's Kingdom* and subtitled, *An Essay on Britain, Now*. While he writes from the perspective of 'an unbeliever', he is at the same time sympathetic to Christian ethics.

---

1 Jeffrey Tucker, 'Markets as Extended Communities', in Samuel Gregg (ed.), *Theologian and Philosopher of Liberty: Essays of Evaluation and Criticism in Honor of Michael Novak*, Grand Rapids, MI: Acton Institute, 2014, p. 21.

2 David Marquand, *Mammon's Kingdom: An Essay on Britain, Now*, London: Allen Lane, 2014, p. 81.

From a Christian perspective the idea of the common good is an intuitively appealing concept. It resonates with the teaching of Jesus ('love your neighbour as yourself'), Paul ('let us do good to all people') and the prophets of the Old Testament ('seek the welfare of the city'). The welfare of the community in the Old Testament depended on the covenant between God and his people. Each and every person was valued for who they were: the structures of the society enabled them to flourish materially; the people worshipped the one true God. The ideal of the Church in the New Testament is that of a community consisting of people from differing ethnic backgrounds, social classes and income levels. It is God's new society and a paradigm for all human societies. The concept of the common good is explicit in Catholic Social Thought and implicit in the teaching of other churches. Because it originates in Greek thought and has been taken forward in a secular context, by for example John Rawls, it is a way of bridging the secular/sacred divide in public debate.

However, for an economist trained in the tradition of Adam Smith and the value of a market economy, as most economists in the UK and the USA have been, the pursuit of the common good raises a series of difficult questions. In the light of the financial crisis of 2007–8 can it ever be the case that markets contribute to the common good? Can the actions of free individuals pursuing their own interests but without any common objective lead to public benefit? What is the relationship between income distribution and the common good? Is greater equality irrelevant if the poor are growing richer? Is greater intervention by the state in economic life an inevitable consequence of pursuing the common good? In what way, therefore, do markets contribute to the common good?

Before tackling these questions, we need to be clear what we mean by the common good. In modern economics the concept of the common good is utilitarian. Each individual has a unique set of tastes, preferences and choices. For an economist the common good is seen as the sum of all these sets of preferences. Welfare economics has developed as a specific field within economics which explores the implications of this approach.

Many writers, especially Roman Catholic philosophers and theologians such as Jacques Maritain, have pointed out that the common good which starts from the basis of classical or Christian thought is a much greater and richer concept than that implicit in liberalism. Maritain defines the common good of political society as,

> the sum or sociological integration of civic conscience, political virtues and sense of right and liberty, of all the activity, material prosperity and spiritual riches, of unconsciously operative hereditary wisdom, of moral

rectitude, justice, friendship, happiness, virtue and heroism in the individual lives of its members.[3]

My working assumption has been that to pursue the common good is to strive to ensure that certain arrangements are in place in our common life together in society which will enable the integral development of all people. By integral development, I mean the development of the whole person, involving the opportunity to work, to participate in the communities (or 'little platoons' as Edmund Burke called them) which constitute society and to the spiritual development of each person with its implications for our spiritual life together.

I wish to argue in this chapter that markets do contribute to the common good in a number of ways.

The anthropology of Smith and Hayek

One reason markets contribute to the common good is that they enable human qualities such as creativity, enterprise and adventure to flourish. Put differently, markets go with the grain not against the grain of human nature.

Adam Smith is widely considered the father of the modern market economy and Friedrich von Hayek its most influential advocate in the twentieth century. Even though their contribution to economic thinking was separated by more than a century and a half, Smith and Hayek have much in common. The economic order they championed was far greater than a market economy. In the case of Smith it was 'the natural system of liberty'; for Hayek 'the spontaneous extended human order created by a competitive market'. What is interesting for our purpose is that the case they made for markets was not simply based on economics. They saw markets within the context of a political and social order which valued liberty, respected the dignity of the human person and enabled human flourishing.

In making the case for a market economy both started with a certain view of the human person. In his early work, Smith stressed the fact that each person was endowed with 'certain moral sentiments' such as prudence, sympathy, benevolence, self-control, charity, friendship, generosity and gratitude. When it came to explaining the growth in the wealth of nations Smith stressed those aspects of human nature which were of

---

3 Jacques Maritain, *The Person and the Common Good*, London: Geoffrey Bles, 1948, pp. 37–8.

particular relevance to wealth creation. One was the observation that 'the propensity to truck, barter and exchange one thing for another', was a characteristic of human nature, so that 'every man ... lives by exchanging, or becomes in some measure a merchant'. Another was the 'desire of bettering our condition', which 'comes with us from the womb and never leaves us till we go into the grave', which he encapsulated in the expression 'self-interest':

> It is not from the benevolence of the butcher, the brewer or the baker that we expect our dinner, but from their regard to their own self-interest. We address ourselves not to their humanity but to their self-love and never talk to them of our own necessities but of their advantages.[4]

Hayek was a great admirer of Smith and in the last chapter of his final book, *The Fatal Conceit*, postulated that our civilization, of which a market economy is an integral part, is the result of a process of cultural evolution. It resulted from 'conforming to certain traditional and largely *moral* practices [italics in original] which enabled those groups that followed them to be "fruitful, and multiply and replenish the earth, and subdue it" (Gen. 1.28)'. This was a remarkable statement as Hayek made it abundantly clear that he was an agnostic in matters of faith.

> So far as I personally am concerned I had better state that I feel as little entitled to assert as to deny the existence of what others call God, for I must admit that I just do not know what this word is supposed to mean. I certainly reject every anthropomorphic, personal or animistic interpretation of the term, interpretations through which many people succeed in giving it meaning. The conception of a man-like or mind-like acting being appears to me rather the product of an arrogant overestimation of the capacities of a man-like mind.[5]

In the light of this, his emphasis on the importance of moral practices in leading to the development of the market economy and his reference to the book of Genesis, which records God's mandate to humankind to work and take responsibility for developing the resources of the physical world, is surprising. However, in recognition of the role that he believed religion had played historically in the cultural development of the extended market order, he suggested that such practices should be called 'symbolic truths'.

---

4 See Adam Smith, *The Wealth of Nations*, ed. Andrew Skinner, 2 vols, London: Penguin, 1970, Vol. 1, pp. 117, 126, 119.

5 F. A. Hayek, *The Fatal Conceit*, London: Routledge, 1988, pp. 6, 139.

In making the case for a market economy, therefore, Smith and Hayek both started with a certain view of the human person. They did not start with some abstract, rational, maximizing individual, 'economic man', solely concerned with the costs and benefits of any decision they faced, regardless of whether it concerned the choice of a brand of coffee, a marriage partner or the sale of a human organ. This approach is most associated with the Nobel Prize-winning economist, Professor Gary Becker of the University of Chicago, and is a form of reductionism, in which human behaviour is analysed solely in economic terms. The consequence is that it excludes all other influences. In recognizing this, Becker made it clear that 'although a comprehensive *framework* is provided by the economic approach', there were certain things which he excluded from his analysis of choice, including values and their frequent unexplained shifts, custom and tradition, and the compliance which can be induced by social norms.[6]

By basing their analysis on a certain view of the human person, Smith and Hayek rejected both the view of the person as static, immobile and passive, a mere serf working on a feudal manorial estate, and of the person as simply a component of some vast impersonal, state machine which was the experience of Communist societies, in which the good of the individual was subordinated to the interests of the state.

Their starting point was that of resourceful human beings, men and women 'made for action' as Smith argued,[7] real people committed to enterprise and work, seeking improvement for themselves and their families and in the process contributing to the common good. The person was by their nature the subject of economic life and not as in feudalism, slavery and Communism its object. As an economic system, markets had grown up to serve the needs of persons and not the other way around.

It is because of this that freedom in economic life is an essential condition for the common good. Within the Judaeo-Christian tradition the human person is created in 'the image of God' (*imago dei*), possessed of unique dignity, with the capacity to be creative, enterprising and innovative but at the same time responsible and accountable. People cannot realize their full development in a political and economic order that deprives them of freedom, especially their economic freedom. When people are denied freedom, human flourishing will wither. So will economic prosperity. The failure of economic systems such as feudalism, slavery and Communism to

---

6 Gary Becker, *The Economic Approach to Human Behaviour*, Chicago/London: University of Chicago, 1976, p. 14.

7 Adam Smith, *The Theory of Moral Sentiments*, ed. Knud Haakonssen, Cambridge: Cambridge University Press, 2002, p. 124.

match the performance of market economies and enable people to emerge from poverty is a consequence of a defective view of the human person.

Farmers markets and the 'invisible hand'

Markets are social institutions, places where exchanges take place on a voluntary basis. A market is not a place where if I win you lose. A market transaction is beneficial to both sides. A second reason markets promote the common good is that they coordinate the different interests of people engaging in voluntary transactions.

One of the simplest forms of markets is a farmers market, typically held on a weekday morning in any small town or some part of any large city in this country. Consumers are attracted to the market because they can buy, producers because they can sell. No person consciously plans the entire outcome – something Smith spoke of as the 'invisible hand'.[8] The market is an institution which brings together the diverse interests of buyers and sellers to the mutual benefit of all. Markets are successful because they coordinate the diverse interests of buyers and sellers.

Each participant in the market will have their own personal interests. Some may be shopping for the best price. Others will be prepared to pay a premium for a quality product. Some may value the local convenience of a small village market more than greater choice at a distant shopping centre. Certain stalls may promote new products, others sell old favourites. Some products may be home grown, others imported from different continents. Some may be of the finest quality, others the essential basics. The important point is that markets are successful not because those who buy and sell have common objectives but because markets coordinate the different preferences of all concerned, without central direction. A farmers market may be a simple structure but the basic principle of coordination applies to all markets and is the basis of their value to society.

The image of farmers markets is an idyllic one. These are small, local markets selling simple products in which exchange is personal. What you see is what you get. However, even for small markets to be successful there must be trust between buyers and sellers. Trust is an essential element in any successful market and is based on keeping promises, 'my word is my bond'. If someone promises to deliver something, you trust that they will keep to their word. Trust is based on honesty, reliability and integrity.[9]

---

8 Smith, *Wealth of Nations*, Vol. 2, p. 32.

9 See, Onora O'Neill, *A Question of Trust*, The Reith Lectures, 2002, Cambridge: Cambridge University Press, 2002, esp. Ch. 3, 'Called to Account', pp. 43–59.

Without trust a market cannot function. It is because trust is so important that farmers markets are largely self-regulating. Any attempt by stalls to cheat or deceive their customers will quickly be found out. Consumers can check prices and quality at other stalls and the information is then spread by word of mouth throughout the market. The result is that honest stallholders who depend on repeat purchases will have a strong incentive to police the market and drive out stallholders who cheat in various ways, causing harm to the future success and reputation of the market. Making markets work, therefore, requires cooperation on certain rules and regulations in order for markets to be trusted. Because of this, suppliers who make up the market have a mutuality of interest.

A third reason markets promote the common good is that they encourage, even force, suppliers to anticipate, respond and adapt to the changing needs of consumers. Clothes shops respond to changing seasons. Food shops respond to new dietary standards. Financial markets developed derivative products to hedge uncertainty. Payday loans grew rapidly to meet the huge demand for short-term credit. Technology firms anticipated the demand for tablets, iPhones and digital music. All of these are examples of the way in which retailers, banks, manufacturers, service providers and exchanges acting from self-interest serve the interests of others. A system of market exchange will ensure that firms which treat customers with disdain fail to respond in this way, invariably decline and either fail, are taken over by other firms, or else are propped up by government financial support.

Sub-prime markets, market failure and regulation

Farmers markets form a sharp contrast to the sub-prime credit markets whose failure sparked the financial crisis of 2007–8. By definition, borrowers in sub-prime markets carry a much higher risk of default than in prime markets and because of this, interest rates are higher than for low-risk borrowers. In the years leading up to the crisis, loans in these markets were known in the US as 'liars' loans' (borrowers lied about their employment and income), 'ninja loans' (no income, no job, no assets), 'no doc loans' (borrowers produced no evidence to document their income and assets) and 'piggyback loans' (more than one loan to buy the same property).

By the time the loans were packaged into bundles, mixed up with other kinds of loans, sold on a number of times and then chopped up into smaller units through securitization, the products became extremely complex. The fact that the products turned out to be quite different from what was stated on the label of the packages is what made many of these securitized loans toxic. Unlike small, personal, local markets, selling simple products, the sub-prime markets grew to be large, global, impersonal, selling complex products which lacked transparency. Trust collapsed. Financial institutions failed. Governments launched expensive bailout schemes. Property values dived. Homeowners unable to repay their loans were subject to repossession orders.

The strength of the case that markets contribute to the common good should never be used to deny or disguise the reality of market failure. In the case of sub-prime mortgages, market failure was the result of a number of factors. One was the dishonesty of borrowers who made false statements regarding their income, assets and job prospects, which meant that the risks associated with these assets were priced incorrectly. Another was the irresponsible lending and mis-selling of products by banks and mortgage providers. Banks expanded their leverage (the amount they lent relative to their capital) on the presumption that they were 'too-big-to-fail', the problem of moral hazard. A further cause of failure was the huge pressure the US government brought to bear on financial institutions to increase their lending to sub-prime borrowers.

Markets can fail for other reasons. There may be an asymmetry of information between customers and suppliers. In some markets there may only be one supplier, a monopoly. In other markets a small number of firms may attempt to rig prices. In both cases prices will be higher and output lower to the detriment of the consumer. Firms may also impose costs on third parties, such as through pollution which those parties did not choose to incur and for which they were not compensated by the polluting firm.

To many people, and especially politicians, the obvious response to market failure is greater regulation. In some instances the case for regulation may be obvious. If the market failure is large and persistent, such as happened with the financial crisis of 2007–8, there is certainly a case for government intervention. In the UK, Gordon Brown and more generally the leaders of G-20 countries deserve great credit for the bold steps they took to deal with the crisis and for the process of initiating reform of financial regulation. However, economic research on the issue of regulation suggests that in general we should be cautious about imposing additional regulation too quickly to remedy market failures.

In the first place, there is 'government failure' as well as 'market failure'. In some cases a government response may make the problem worse. The recent classic case in the US is that of Fannie Mae and Freddie Mac, two quasi-governmental institutions which were set up to oversee the supply of mortgages in the residential housing market, because it was argued that the private sector left to itself would not provide sufficient mortgages to lower income families. There is clear evidence that both of these companies took on excessive risk in issuing large numbers of mortgages to sub-prime borrowers.[10]

Next there are the unintended consequences of regulation itself. When seat belts were first made compulsory in the US, it became apparent that one impact of the new law was that cars tended to be driven faster. This is not to suggest that the seat belt regulation was wrong but that the consequences of its introduction were not necessarily those intended. In other words, drivers decided that travelling at a certain speed without seat belts gave rise to an appropriate degree of risk. If they were forced to accept less risk, they would simply drive faster. Research also found that the same principle held in the regulation of banks. If banks judged that the capital they were required to hold was excessive, they would hold more risky assets. If they were prevented from doing so, their return on equity would fall and their growth would slow and capital would move to other less regulated institutions.

Economists who have studied regulation and collective action have tended to reach three conclusions.

The first is that regulation tends to be introduced for the benefit of large firms, not small firms. The most important asset the state has is its power to coerce. Hence a private company which can get the state on its side can use that power to increase its profits. Many firms would like to do this but it is costly. If a group of large firms organize themselves and agree on a strategy, the benefits to them are substantial. Small firms and consumers find it much more difficult to organize themselves because the costs are high relative to the benefits. The second conclusion is that the most powerful interests lobbying for regulation are generally firms which already have government support. The third is that because it is costly to organize large numbers of small firms or individuals the groups which are likely to lose out include taxpayers, women and the elderly.

10 Gretchen Morgenson, Joshua Rosner, *Reckless Endangerment*, New York: St Martin's Griffin, 2012; Anna J Schwartz, 'Origins of the Financial Market Crisis of 2008', *The Cato Journal* 29:1 (2009), reprinted in P. Booth et al. (eds), *Verdict on the Crash: Causes and Policy Implications*, London: IEA, 2009.

Competition and rivalry

When economists speak of the success of markets they mean *competitive* markets. Competition is at the heart of the case for the market economy. Many people think the case for markets is based on private ownership. It is not. Private ownership is a necessary but far from sufficient condition. The performance of monopolies and cartels falls short of that of competitive firms, because they fail to produce at the lowest possible cost and sell for the lowest possible price.

At first sight, competition sits uneasily with the notion of working together for the common good. Competition and the common good might seem to be diametrically opposed concepts. In the public's mind, competition is perceived as rivalry between large firms fighting for market share, keeping out competitors and lobbying for government regulations. The common perception is that competition produces aggression, rivalry, conflict, cheating and discrimination – all of which are anathema to a Christian conscience. The irony is that the economist's conception of competition views rivalry, price wars, predatory tactics and market abuse between and by firms as incompatible with competitive markets. These are the stuff of oligopolistic structures and price rigging. There are two different concepts of competition in economics, that of the neo-classical tradition and that of the Austrian school. In traditional, neo-classical theory perfectly competitive markets are ones in which all firms are viewed as price takers, who have no effect on the market price. The conditions required for perfectly competitive markets are severe: there has to be a large number of buyers and sellers, perfect knowledge of the present and the future with no obstacles to market participants adjusting to changed circumstances and with no barriers to entry or exit. The result is that an individual firm in a perfectly competitive market cannot arbitrarily raise the price at which it can sell, otherwise it would go out of business. At a simple text-book level this theory is static.

In the rival Austrian theory of competition, the focus is on entrepreneurs engaged in a discovery process much like scientists might be. In this sense it is a dynamic not a static approach. Prices act as signals. Price rises suggest that more of what they produce is being demanded. As market participants respond to higher prices they also learn more about the plans of other firms. This leads them to revise their own plans accordingly. They then discover they face new prices to which they have to respond, and so on.

Unlike the neoclassical theory, the competitive process is dynamic and in some versions no equilibrium position exists. In the Austrian approach, the key to understanding competition is the constantly changing information which a firm receives from implementing its own sales and production plans. Markets are continually generating new information for both producers and consumers.

In both approaches, competitive markets are favourable to the common good because they result in the lowest sustainable prices, given existing information and the fact that they stimulate innovation.

From a practical perspective, the less barriers to entry firms face and the more existing participants recognize that if they raise prices they will encourage new entrants into the industry, the more existing firms are effectively price takers. From a public policy perspective both approaches predict that the lower the barriers to entry are, the greater the benefits of competitive markets to the population at large. One key objective of policy therefore should be to encourage new entrants by removing barriers to entry and in many sectors allowing the entry of foreign firms into the market.

The moral limits of markets

One final issue relevant to markets and the common good is whether the range of activities which take place through markets should have boundaries placed around them. In 1970, Richard Titmuss argued in his book *The Gift Relationship* that blood is best collected from voluntary donors rather than commercial blood banks for two reasons: the poor would be exploited and commercialization would undermine the spirit of altruism which donors displayed. This would erode a sense of cohesion in society because replacing altruism with payment would lead to changes in attitudes, motives and relationships in other areas.[11] Later Michael Walzer put forward the thesis that certain goods and services have a social meaning and identity, independent of their utility and monetary value, which is why they are not traded on markets. Among the examples of things which cannot be traded in the USA he included heroin, prizes, criminal justice, votes in political elections and human beings, who should never be bought and sold as slaves.[12]

More recently, Michael Sandel has argued that we live in an era of market triumphalism where everything is for sale: a prison cell upgrade for $82 per night in Santa Ana California, surrogate motherhood during

11 Richard Titmuss, *The Gift Relationship*, London: George, Allen and Unwin, 1970.

12 Michael Walzer, *Spheres of Justice: A Defense of Pluralism and Equality*, New York: Basic Books, 1983, pp. 100–3.

pregnancy at $6,250, which is outsourced to India, and in South Africa $15,000 to shoot an endangered black rhino. His argument is that we have drifted from a market economy to a market society and in this society everything is up for sale. Because market mechanisms and norms have been extended to areas previously run on non-market lines he concludes that markets have crowded out morals.[13] David Marquand views the introduction of 'marketization' into such areas as nothing less than a radical social transformation. In education companies sponsor schools, local democracy is displaced and the ethos of public service is undermined. His book is an analysis of contemporary British society and its title is the essence of his conclusions, *Mammon's Kingdom*.[14]

The moral limits of markets is a complex subject and there are no easy answers to some of the issues. However, I believe a number of things can be said.

First, there are certain commodities (food, clothes, consumer durables, phones, tablets, cars and so on) and certain services (taxis, hairdressing, restaurants, hotels, entertainment) that are best left to markets and the private sector, even though certain markets will require consumer protection regulation to provide necessary information for informed choices.

Next, and at the other extreme, are certain things which should not be traded in markets. Michael Walzer's examples are a start. Other additions to the list are more contentious: abortions, assisted dying, sale of human organs, surrogate pregnancies, cannabis. For some, trading in these also should be prohibited. For others, it is permissible, subject to a regulatory framework which places them outside the market and subject to certain standards and public scrutiny. Discussion of what should be included in this list will take us far beyond any consideration of markets themselves.

Third, over the past 50 years there has been an unambiguous change in the culture of our society. It is probably an exaggeration to describe it as 'market fundamentalism' or 'Mammon's Kingdom', let alone a change from a 'decent society' to one which worships the three great idols of a 'new Holy Trinity; choice, freedom and the individual'.[15] However, there can be no question that there has been a major change in the values of the moral economy, and this was, in my judgement, one of the underlying causes of the recent financial crisis. The change in cultural values in the past half-century cannot I believe be explained simply by privatiza-

---

13 Michael Sandel, *What Money Can't Buy*, London: Allen Lane, 2012.
14 See note 2.
15 See Marquand, *Mammon's Kingdom*, pp. 183–99.

tion or deregulation but has its roots in the retreating 'sea of faith' which Matthew Arnold described so well.[16]

Fourth, the introduction of certain business principles and, where, appropriate market opportunities into the way public services, such as education, health, public administration, policing and community care are provided, has great potential benefits and should be welcomed.

Some have suggested that the professions which provide these services have their own ethical standards which only professionals in those fields are fully able to judge. For example, in the BBC Reith Lectures for 2002 Baroness O'Neill argued that:

> Teachers aim to teach their pupils; nurses to care for their patients; university lecturers to do research and to teach; police officers to deter and apprehend those whose activities harm the community; social workers to help those whose lives are for various reasons unmanageable or very difficult. Each profession has its proper aim, and this aim is not reduced to meeting set targets following prescribed procedures and requirements.[17]

While Baroness O'Neill is correct to stress the importance of a professional ethic, the fact is that professional services have to be delivered through organizations which can be well run or badly run and that, however virtuous members of professions may be, they have certainly not been negligent in pursuing their own self-interests. I have no doubt that in certain instances the introduction of targets and procedures has been overdone, but this should not prevent professionals from embracing the tools and techniques of business in order to provide a more efficient service.

Conclusion

Markets contribute to the common good in three ways. First, they coordinate the diverse interests of millions and in an increasingly complex global economy of billions of people. This is something which no planning, government, or international authority could replicate, simply because it would never have access to the necessary information. Second, markets incentivize producers to anticipate, respond and adapt to the changing

---

16 See Matthew Arnold's poem, 'Dover Beach' in C. B. Tinker and H. F. Lowry (eds), *Arnold, Political Works*, London: Oxford University Press, 1950, pp. 210–12.

17 O'Neill, *A Question of Trust*, p. 49.

needs of consumers. Third, markets presuppose a degree of economic free-dom which is an important element of political freedom.

The traditional case for the market economy as presented by Adam Smith and Friedrich Hayek was built on an explicit anthropology: namely, the human person as enterprising, creative, possessing moral sentiments. By contrast, a reductionist view of the person as the rational, evaluative, maximizing, individual, 'economic man', constantly weighing up an eco-nomic calculus for each decision, leads to a distorted view of economic and social life. Economic values predominate, few limits are placed on the scope of markets and market outcomes are placed beyond any moral critique. In making the case that markets contribute to the common good, the assumption one makes regarding anthropology is fundamental.

Successful markets would not exist without a foundation of trust, which in turn depends on the honesty, integrity and reliability of market partici-pants. Markets cannot function without values and the primary source of values is not within markets, but outside.

Markets succeed but they also fail. When they fail, politicians are imme-diately placed under pressure to strengthen regulation in order to be seen to be doing something. In certain cases this will be the right course of action. Swift action was needed to shore up financial markets follow-ing the 2008 financial crisis. Regulation can also fail as happened in the run-up to the financial crisis of 2008. In the years leading up to the crisis it was not as if there were no regulation in place. One reason regulation may not succeed is because of unintended consequences. Another is that fresh regulation will be sought by powerful groups to protect vested inter-ests. However, regulation is necessary to ensure competitive markets. For markets to contribute to the common good, regulatory authorities must be vigilant in ensuring there is freedom of entry for new entrants into the industry they regulate.

Finally, markets need boundaries. Certain goods and services are suit-able for trade in markets. Others are not. A market economy can serve the common good. When a market economy becomes a market society it can undermine the common good because of a bias to individualism, the lack of a moral framework and the inference of a materialist philosophy of life. Markets are easily judged by the culture in which they are embedded. In view of the changes which have taken place in our culture over the past half-century we should be cautious in criticizing markets when the real focus of the criticism should be the culture in which they are embedded.

II

Pluralism and the Common Good in a Market Economy

PHILIP BOOTH

In a market economy, people exchange goods and services for money. This is often done on an impersonal basis in the sense that one person does not know personally those with whom they are exchanging. As is explained in the well-known tale *I Pencil*,[1] a market economy allows long and complex chains of economic activity to develop among people who will never meet each other.

There are, of course, strands of Christian economic thinking that seek to restore a more personalized approach to economic exchange,[2] but the cost, in terms of much lower levels of economic output, of rejecting impersonal exchange in a market economy, would be huge – certainly if impersonal exchange were rejected altogether. Arguably, too, those costs would primarily be suffered by the poor. This is so, first, because the least well off have benefited from goods and services once thought to be luxuries becoming everyday items (refrigerators, freezers, mobile phones, and so on) as a result of complex supply chains and economies of scale and, second, because the least well off in many formerly very poor countries have benefited from supplying goods and services to richer economies. Without the development of global supply chains, the unprecedented reduction in global poverty since 1980 would not have been possible. Indeed, it is worth noting that many of the more recent Christian attempts to try to bring what some might regard as a more human touch to the market economy have involved accepting the concept of the extended market order but developing within that order specific institutions such as Fairtrade[3] and other ethical trading labels which relate especially to the needs of groups regarded as especially vulnerable.

---

1 L. Read, *I Pencil*, New York: Foundation for Economic Education, 1958.

2 Most notably, 'distributists' such as G. K. Chesterton and Hilaire Belloc. For an introduction, see *The Distributist Review* (http://distributistreview.com/mag/).

3 I have doubts about Fairtrade (see P. M. Booth and L. Whetstone, 'Half a Cheer for Fair

The Catholic Church has not generally opposed a business economy or globalization, even if it has criticized certain manifestations of both. For example, in *Centesimus annus*, Pope John Paul II asked the rhetorical question whether capitalism is the system to be adopted after the decline of the Soviet system. The answer is quite direct:

> If by 'capitalism' is meant an economic system which recognizes the fundamental and positive role of business, the market, private property and the resulting responsibility for the means of production, as well as free human creativity in the economic sector, then the answer is certainly in the affirmative, even though it would perhaps be more appropriate to speak of a 'business economy', 'market economy' or simply 'free economy'.[4]

The reason John Paul II gave for this answer was not especially related to the importance of providing goods and services efficiently but because it allowed the acting, reasoning human person to exercise their free will to choose the good rather than be part of a system which required them to be a small cog in a large system.

> The fundamental error of socialism is anthropological in nature. Socialism considers the individual person simply as an element, a molecule within the social organism ... Socialism likewise maintains that the good of the individual can be realized without reference to his free choice, to the unique and exclusive responsibility which he exercises in the face of good or evil.[5]

Thus, the common good cannot be realized – either in terms of meeting basic human needs or in terms of ensuring that the human person can act as a reasoning person to choose what is good in the economic sphere – without a reasonably free economy, though whether the common good is promoted is, of course, dependent on how people act within a free economy.

The importance of trust

A market economy is often caricatured by Catholic writers on the left, and sometimes in Catholic documents, as something that its believers see as

---

Trade', *Economic Affairs* 27:2 (2007), pp. 29–36) but those relate to the practical benefits of that particular set of schemes and not to the general concept.

4 John Paul II, *Centesimus annus*, 1991, 42. Hereafter *CA*.
5 *CA*, 13.

necessarily self-correcting and autonomous. However, the whole point of a market economy is that it involves free human decisions and those decisions are taken by reasoning human persons capable of choosing either right or wrong.

The absence of personal relationships in an extended market economy makes trust and a healthy ethical culture especially important. This was an issue discussed in *Caritas in veritate* in which Pope Benedict XVI said: '*Without internal forms of solidarity and mutual trust, the market cannot completely fulfil its proper economic function.*'[6] It should not be thought that, if trust has broken down in the economy, regulation and government action can be an adequate replacement. The flawed nature of the human person acting within a market economy means that the outcomes will be that much less desirable than we would hope. However, the impact of poor moral behaviour is at least somewhat attenuated within a market economy because market transactions require the agreement of all parties involved. Furthermore, within a market economy institutions that promote trust are often developed. For example, the stock exchange (an entirely private institution that was more or less the sole regulator of securities markets transactions until 1986 in the UK), after over two centuries of developing mechanisms by which those who did not keep the written and unwritten rules of the exchange were brought to heel, adopted as its motto, in 1923, 'my word is my bond'.

On the other hand, where an economy is strongly controlled by government and there is a breakdown in trust and unethical behaviour, the arbitrary power that can be wielded by people who do not exhibit self-restraint will often lead to far worse results than those arising from a poorly functioning market economy. Furthermore, regulation by government cannot be an effective replacement for virtue. As the Catholic Bishops of England and Wales put it in their paper, 'Choosing the Common Good', published before the 2010 election: 'In place of virtue we have seen an expansion of regulation. A society that is held together just by compliance to rules is inherently fragile, open to further abuses which will be met by a further expansion of regulation.'[7]

Indeed, markets are often criticized for being 'amoral'. When people use this term, however, all it is intended to mean is that the outcome within a market economy will depend on the moral disposition of the individuals concerned: the market itself does not have outcomes independent of those

---

6 Benedict XVI, *Caritas in veritate*, 2009, 35, emphasis in original. Hereafter *CV*.

7 Bishops' Conference of England and Wales, *Choosing the Common Good*, Stoke on Trent: Alive Publishing, 2010, p. 12.

who take moral decisions within its structures. As Pope Benedict wrote in relation to the financial crash:

> Economy and finance, as instruments, can be used badly when those at the helm are motivated by purely selfish ends. Instruments that are good in themselves can thereby be transformed into harmful ones. But it is man's darkened reason that produces these consequences, not the instrument *per se*. Therefore it is not the instrument that must be called to account, but individuals, their moral conscience and their personal and social responsibility.[8]

In the same way as a market is 'amoral', a village is 'amoral' – it is simply a community of men and women living together. The morality of the outcomes will depend on the free decisions in both social and economic life that those men and women take.

Of course, there are important issues to be discussed. For example, does a market economy encourage greed and other forms of sinfulness and therefore make it more difficult for people to choose what is good simply because it produces goods in abundance? And the *Catechism of the Catholic Church* states (quoting from *Centesimus annus* 42) that the market economy must be undergirded by a juridical framework that is ethical and religious at its core.[9] This point is not exceptional, uniquely Catholic or especially interventionist. Nearly all economists who are supporters of a market economy – from Smith to Hayek – would accept the need for a juridical framework: there are relatively few anarchists among supporters of a market economy, though there are some.[10]

Though it may be true that a market economy can provide opportunities for various forms of sinfulness, such as greed, it is not self-evident that opportunities for such forms of sinfulness are any less apparent under alternative economic models in which resources are allocated by government officials. Self-interest operates when economic resources are allocated either by government or by the free interplay of individuals and organizations in a market economy and, in either case, self-interest can be disordered and become destructive greed – though, as noted, in a market economy, the constraints on abuse tend to be more effective because

---

8 *CV*, 36.

9 *The Catechism of the Catholic Church*, London: Geoffrey Chapman, 1994, 2431, quoting *CA* 48.

10 Examples would include Peter Leeson of George Mason University. The Catholic academic Gerard Casey has made what he describes as the 'anti-anti-anarchy case': see G. Casey, 'Meddling in Other Men's Affairs: the case for anarchy', *Economic Affairs* 27:4 (2007), pp. 46–51.

market transactions require the agreement of all parties and institutions involved.[11] However, few would disagree that the common good is more easily promoted when trust and other virtues are at the heart of economic activity. This not only ensures that the economy is more effective; it also improves the personal relationships that are at the heart of economic life.

Economic action and economic motives

As noted above, human action in a market economy can have a variety of motivations. This, in itself, leads to a range of institutions within a market economy which can have different objectives. Cristo Rey schools,[12] for example, operate entirely within a market economy but do not have profit-maximizing (or even profit-making) objectives. They buy food, buildings and textbooks and hire teachers, and so on within a market economy which brings together willing participants with different motives to exchange economic resources. They charge fees and even send their students out to work in commercial organizations (indeed, this is one of the distinctive features of the model: a 14-year-old may well find himself working part-time for Goldman Sachs). However, Cristo Rey schools explicitly exist to serve disadvantaged students and fund part of their work through charity. Other schools, to a greater or lesser extent, will combine in different combinations the various motives among those who support them, use them or work for them.

The same principle applies to a huge range of other institutions that form the rich tapestry of a market economy: supermarkets, the organic movement, fair trade, mutual savings institutions, friendly societies in the days before health provision became dominated by the state,[13] trade unions (which were known in the early twentieth century for their welfare functions as well as for bargaining to improve pay and conditions). In their different ways, such institutions contribute to the common good

---

11 Of course, there are problems of abuse of market power to be considered and these raise moral questions too. They also raise questions of political economy as such abuses are often most prominent where government is not fulfilling its basic functions properly or is doing so corruptly – South American examples come to mind. However, debates such as how to deal with monopolies (where a single provider controls the market); cartels (where a few providers work together to control the market); monopsonies (where a single purchaser controls the market); and so on, are perfectly legitimate among supporters of a market economy.

12 The Cristo Rey Network comprises 28 Catholic secondary schools for under-represented urban youth in the United States (see, www.cristoreynetwork.org/).

13 It could be argued that recent reforms to healthcare provision will allow what will be described as 'commissioners' to commission care from private institutions but the whole structure is still basically a state-organized structure.

by providing for direct economic needs, but also combining economic exchange with socialization, reciprocity and charity to bring both social and economic development to members of society.

Just as action in the economic and social sphere can follow various different motives when the economy and social institutions are free from government control, social and economic action can also follow various motives – good or bad – when the state is involved in the provision of social services or the direction of economic activity. This was perhaps most obvious in former Communist countries where, as a matter of ideology, education systems tended to promote the party and state and, otherwise, to follow relatively utilitarian objectives. However, this is also true in our own context.

In the UK healthcare system, for example, many of the objectives followed are utilitarian in nature. For example, the 'quality adjusted life year' (QALY) has often been used to determine which treatments are funded and which are not.[14] The National Institute for Health and Clinical Excellence uses QALYs as one of the determining factors for deciding whether treatments are to be funded.[15] The NHS funds the abortions of around one in six of all pregnancies in the UK, decisions which, according to the legal grounds, can be taken on the basis of whether the mother's mental or physical health is impaired or whether the baby will suffer serious mental or physical disability.[16] Disabled babies can be aborted until birth because of their supposed inferior quality of life. Of course, individuals caring for patients within the system will often have very different motivations from those expressed by the system as a whole.

A similar situation exists with regard to education. Many Christian schools would claim that they exist to educate the whole person. However, government regulation tends to put subjects in silos to limit the extent to which this is possible and prescribe the content of the subjects through

---

14 For a methodological critique of QALYs, see the European Guidelines for conducting Cost Effectiveness Analyses (2013) prepared by the European Consortium in Healthcare Outcomes and Cost-Benefit Research (ECHOUTCOME) which recommend that QALY assessment for healthcare decision making should be abandoned (see, www.echoutcome.eu).

15 See, www.nice.org.uk/media/default/About/what-we-do/Research-and-development/Social-Value-Judgements-principles-for-the-development-of-NICE-guidance.pdf. Other criteria are used as well. However, whatever criteria are used are subjective and may not accord with a Christian – certainly a Catholic – view of an ethical approach to healthcare.

16 See, for example, www.homehealth-uk.com/medical/abortion.htm. This is not the place to address the ethical issues relating to abortion. However, it is worth noting that, even if it is not accepted that the unborn baby has a right to life if the mother does not wish it, potentially disabled unborn babies are treated as having less worth than others. It should be noted that the NHS is only carrying out what is permitted by law and there are many private providers of abortion too.

a national curriculum. At the same time, the government tends to focus extra subsidies on science, technology and engineering subjects which are believed to have greater economic utility than arts subjects. Furthermore, religious education has been excluded from the government's core subject areas which make up the English Baccalaureate. State schools also often have the facility to provide on-site contraceptive advice and so-called 'emergency contraceptive' advice and, sometimes, provide abortion advice without the knowledge of parents.[17]

The implication should not be taken that healthcare or education provided privately, charitably, through mutual or profit-making organizations, necessarily tends to follow higher motives than state-provided healthcare. However, we should not automatically assume the opposite. A service which is free at the point of use provided by the state may indeed have philosophical foundations with which Christians are comfortable. However, this need not be so. Whatever the means of provision of a particular service, the values underlying the service will depend on the values and courage of those responsible for taking decisions. It is an advantage of more decentralized systems which follow the principle of subsidiarity that people will be more likely to be able to obtain a service that is in accord with their own conscience. However, this will not prevent the development of institutions that have a morally relativist or utilitarian conception of the world. But, unless those who are motivated by higher values are able to obtain services and found institutions motivated by those values, the common good cannot be realized.

Markets, society and the state in welfare provision

Though Christians may differ with regard to the extent that they believe economic activity should be regulated, most people would accept that the sort of consumer goods and services we buy in everyday life should be produced within an extended market economy. However, the big change in recent decades is in the way, across a wide range of countries, the state has taken over functions such as the provision, finance and regulation of education, healthcare, forms of social insurance and the like. In many countries, these services have traditionally been provided by the Church or by a range of civil society institutions. The institutions were allowed to operate freely but they had a variety of corporate forms and objectives.

---

17 See, www.rcn.org.uk/__data/assets/pdf_file/0005/78665/Emergency_contraception_position_statement_Final.pdf. The phrase 'so-called' is used because emergency 'contraception' may prevent implantation rather than conception.

Some would have been charitable, others profit-making, some fee-charging but not profit-making, and so on. In this respect, many of the institutions that provided health, education and social insurance fulfilled the criteria discussed in *Caritas in veritate* for a more 'civil' economy. Although the primary focus of *Caritas in veritate* was not the welfare state, it pointed out that:

> Alongside profit-oriented private enterprise and the various types of public enterprise, there must be room for commercial entities based on mutualist principles and pursuing social ends to take root and express themselves. It is from their reciprocal encounter in the marketplace that one may expect hybrid forms of commercial behaviour to emerge, and hence an attentiveness to ways of *civilizing the economy*.[18]

In Victorian times, the middle class donated around 10 per cent of their incomes to charity, whereas today the figure is less than 1 per cent.[19] But the bounty of charity was perhaps not the most important feature of Victorian and early twentieth-century society. Perhaps more important were the societies for mutual aid. Societies, including friendly societies, were voluntary, commercial and fraternal to varying degrees and in varying combinations.

In early twentieth-century Britain, mutual organizations providing social insurance functions thrived. As well as providing insurance services, they were fraternal organizations. In 1910, between 6.3 and 9.5 million people were members of friendly societies. This figure excludes members of mutual insurance organizations that were not registered as friendly societies. The Manchester Unity of Oddfellows alone had over one million members.[20]

These institutions were part of the market economy even though they were not necessarily profit-maximizing businesses. Although such organizations still exist in the field of health care and education today – especially in health and social care in, for example, Germany[21] – they do tend to be controlled to a greater degree by the state rather than being products of a free economy. Unemployment insurance, health, pensions, and so on –

---

18 CV, 38.

19 See, J. Bartholomew, *The Welfare State We're In*, London: Politico's, 2006, p. 42. Bartholomew relies for his information about the Victorian Age on *The Times* survey of middle-class donations in late nineteenth-century Britain; for modern times, on the National Council for Voluntary Organisations and *Social Trends*.

20 See www.history.org.uk/resources/student_resource_7082_107.html.

21 One prominent example is *Diakonie Deutschland*, the social welfare organization of Germany's Protestant churches (www.diakonie.de/).

can be provided by a rich tapestry of commercial, mutual and charitable organizations. In the tradition of Catholic Social Teaching, it is not the role of the state to displace these initiatives but to *support* them.

Before World War Two, charitable hospitals (the same names we know today: Great Ormond Street, St Bartholomew's, and so on) took in 60 per cent of all patients requiring acute care, and local government provided places for many others. About 19 million people had health insurance and most of the rest of the population were members of friendly societies or made direct payments for their medical costs. Less than 15 per cent relied on free services provided charitably, through the goodwill of doctors or funded by government. In the demands for reform it was that 15 per cent about which there was most concern.[22]

Rather than supporting the development of such institutions, along the lines of the principle of subsidiarity, and perhaps trying to fill in the gaps in provision, British policy took quite a different route. In the creation of the national insurance system in 1910, reformers copied the evolving German socialist system. In the case of the creation of the National Health Service in 1948, Bevan, though not other supporters of reform, again looked to centralized state socialist models. It is worth noting in passing that, when the NHS was created, the then Catholic Archbishop of Westminster, Cardinal Bernard Griffin, fought for and obtained exemptions from nationalization for the small number of Catholic hospitals. He argued that it would be a 'sad day for England when charity becomes the affair of the state'.[23]

The division of economic activity between market and state – thus bypassing civil society – has been decried by people on both the left and right of the philosophical spectrum. Indeed, H. B. Acton (a Protestant philosopher) argued that the market economy appears much shallower than it really is, or should be, because of the expansion of the activity of the state into those areas where the provisions of goods and services is undertaken on a more human level, leaving the market to be concerned with the production of goods for conspicuous consumption.[24]

The role of society – as distinct from the state – in the context of a free economy has long been admired in Catholic Social Teaching. In *Rerum novarum*, for example, Pope Leo XIII made clear that the state should be the last resort when it came to welfare. He spoke admiringly of welfare associations and the importance of their freedom:

---

22 See Bartholomew, *The Welfare State We're In*.

23 D. Kynaston, *Austerity Britain 1945–1951*, London: Bloomsbury, 2007, p. 282.

24 H. B. Acton, *The Morals of Markets and Related Essays*, Indianapolis, IN: Liberty Fund, 1993.

And there are not wanting Catholics blessed with affluence, who have, as it were, cast in their lot with the wage-earners, and who have spent large sums in founding and widely spreading benefit and insurance societies, by means of which the working man may without difficulty acquire through his labour not only many present advantages, but also the certainty of honorable support in days to come ... The State should watch over these societies of citizens banded together in accordance with their rights, but it should not thrust itself into their peculiar concerns and their organization, for things move and live by the spirit inspiring them, and may be killed by the rough grasp of a hand from without.[25]

And Pope John Paul II made clear the problems that had arisen from the state overreaching in these areas and distinguished clearly between 'society' and 'state'.

Malfunctions and defects in the Social Assistance State are the result of an inadequate understanding of the tasks proper to the State. Here again *the principle of subsidiarity* must be respected ... By intervening directly and depriving society of its responsibility, the Social Assistance State leads to a loss of human energies and an inordinate increase of public agencies, which are dominated more by bureaucratic ways of thinking than by concern for serving their clients, and which are accompanied by an enormous increase in spending. In fact, it would appear that needs are best understood and satisfied by people who are closest to them and who act as neighbours to those in need.[26]

Pluralism, the common good, religious freedom and education

Independent institutions for the provision of welfare are important for promoting the common good because they enrich society by 'civilizing' the economy and provide vital goods and services, often combined with opportunities for socialization and fraternity. However, they also allow individuals to take decisions with regard to the provision of services such as health and education in accordance with their own consciences. A denial

---

25 Leo XIII, *Rerum novarum*, 1891, 55.

26 *CA*, 48. The principle of subsidiarity is defined in the following way: 'a community of a higher order should not interfere in the internal life of a community of a lower order, depriving the latter of its functions, but rather should support it in case of need and help to coordinate its activity with the activities of the rest of society, always with a view to the common good'. It should be noted that there are papal documents, including *Caritas in veritate*, which have praised some of the outcomes of the welfare state.

of this freedom, especially if state systems do not provide opportunities to obtain health care and education according to Christian principles, cannot possibly allow the common good to be achieved. Though these institutions are important in a wide field of social and economic activity, the rest of this chapter will focus on education as a field in which truly independent institutions can serve the common good.

The publication in 1965 of *Dignitatis humanae*, the Declaration on Religious Freedom from the Second Vatican Council, marked an important development in Catholic teaching. The importance of religious freedom was made clear and the understanding of the separation of Church and state was clarified. The Declaration states that 'government is to see to it that equality of citizens before the law, which is itself an element of the common good, is never violated, whether openly or covertly, for religious reasons. Nor is there to be discrimination among citizens.'[27] The document did, though, make clear that there was an obligation on all to seek the truth – freedom not to respond to God's calling does not make the truth any less true. It should also be noted that, despite the argument developed below in relation to the importance of free institutions in a peaceful and harmonious society, the common good is surely not realized unless all come to know the truth about God. Freedom involves freedom to seek the truth, not freedom to do as we please.

Dignitatis humanae argued that not only is freedom of religion important but that this implies freedom to evangelize. In particular: 'the social nature of man and the very nature of religion afford the foundation of the right of men freely to hold meetings and to establish educational, cultural, charitable and social organizations, under the impulse of their own religious sense'.[28]

In a very important way, freedom in education is part of freedom of conscience and freedom to evangelize, and is important for promoting the common good. Catholic Social Teaching has made clear these principles in many contexts over the years.[29] Indeed, *Dignitatis humanae* states that parents have a right to determine the religious education their children receive, that a single system of education from which religious education is excluded should not be imposed on all, and that parents must be genuinely free to choose schools and other forms of education.

In the Vatican II document *Gaudium et spes*, it was pointed out that, in order to live in dignity and for the promotion of the common good,

---

27 Vatican II, *Dignitatis humanae*, 1965, 6.

28 *Dignitatis humanae*, 4.

29 See, for example, *Divini illius magistri*, 1939 and Vatican II, *Gravissimum educationis*, 1965. Hereafter *GE*.

all must have education.[30] If other forms of finance are insufficient for all to have an education, it is suggested that the state may step in. But, then there is the question of how the state should step in. The principle of subsidiarity demands that the state does not undertake functions which can be undertaken by families and other institutions in society. Freedom of action in education is one especially important area for the exercise of the principle of subsidiarity.

It has been suggested that the principle of subsidiarity is less important than other principles of Catholic Social Teaching such as solidarity because it 'can by no means claim to be directly deduced from one of the two great commandments'.[31] However, the principle is simply an application of the Church's teaching on human dignity, the promotion of the common good and the natural rights that all have to act in accordance with their conscience. The state is there to ensure that all can flourish – not to make provision for all. And this is especially clear in Catholic Social Teaching on education. The Catholic Church has promoted the concept of parental freedom in education as part of her social teaching, from well before *Dignitatis humanae*.

Education and public policy

In general, in a free economy, economic resources are allocated by agreement, peacefully. I buy something from a retailer and the retailer sells the products to me. We both benefit from the transaction but we are not in competition and conflict. The ends of the business are served by meeting the ends of the consumer. That does not mean that there will not be tensions, possible conflicts and sometimes disruptive change as customers change their preferences between different products and services and production techniques change. However, the market economy is a forum for social cooperation, and this is a further way in which it promotes the common good.

When a fixed set of economic resources is distributed by the state there is likely to be conflict. In fact, it was partly this issue of conflict in a planned economy that motivated F. A. Hayek's *The Road to Serfdom*. He argued that, philosophically, it might be widely agreed that an economy should be centrally planned, but different people would want different plans –

---

30 Vatican II, *Gaudium et spes*, 1965, 26. Hereafter *GS*.

31 See Clifford Longley, 'Government and the Common Good', in N. Spencer and J. Chaplin (eds), *God and Government*, London: SPCK, 2009, p. 163. The notion of 'subsidiarity' was introduced in 1931 in *Quadragesimo anno*, 79, though the term was not used.

and there can be only one plan.[32] This problem is particularly evident in education, with the frequently expressed concerns over admissions processes that allocate a fixed number of places at better state schools to the children of competing parents. It is also illustrated by the way in which different groups may try to control and change school curricula.[33] Centralized decision-making may be tolerably peaceful in a society with a very high degree of consensus such as post-war Christian Democrat, continental European societies, but Christian values are no longer sufficiently widely shared for the democratic system to be effective in allocating economic resources without conflict.

Within the British system, religious schools (especially, though not only, Catholic and Anglican schools) are prominent among the Academies which have greater freedom over their budget than schools supported by the local authority and there are also a limited number of Free Schools which have a high degree of independence from both central and local government control. Ever since the 1944 Education Act, there has also been a large number of Catholic and Anglican voluntary aided schools, together with a few Jewish voluntary aided schools. These schools have a degree of autonomy – especially over admissions – but are funded by the state. However, the settlement in relation to religious schools is fragile because it is seen to provide privileges to religious schools. There are many in politics who would like to end the state funding of religious schools completely. This has generally been the official position of the Liberal Democrat Party. It is also the strongly held view of the British Humanist Association and other atheists prominent in public life.

Such people argue that the state should not use taxpayers' money to provide religious education and that all children should be taught at secular schools. It is, of course, worth noting that Christians are, in fact, taxpayers – they are simply being given some freedom within a system which

---

32 F. A. Hayek, *The Road to Serfdom*, London: Routledge and Kegan Paul, 1944. This particular point was illustrated by the cartoon strip which appeared in *Look* magazine reproduced at www.iea.org.uk/sites/default/files/publications/files/upldbook351pdf.pdf. An important point being made is that planning can work in war time because the whole nation shares one objective. In normal times, families have different objectives, needs and preferences. This is true in general but is especially true in pluralistic societies.

33 Current ongoing battles include whether to make sex education compulsory; whether Christian schools should be allowed to operate with state funding (see below); and the content of the English, history and mathematics syllabi. These things are controlled by the politicians in power on behalf of the whole country. It should be noted in this context that the 'Trojan Horse' scandal in Birmingham, in which it was alleged radical Muslims attempted to take over control of five schools, did not relate to Muslim Free Schools but to four schools with Academy status (i.e. funded directly by the Department for Education) and one, Saltley, still under the control of the local authority.

involves the state taking part of the income of the family in the first place. There is, though, no such thing as a secular school that can somehow teach a neutral curriculum. Christians do not believe that you can educate a person without educating the whole person, including informing the person's conscience and developing the practice of the virtues which are, to Christians, God-given. A secular education may be sought by some religious families who may then supplement it with education from other sources. However, religious and non-religious approaches to education are fundamentally different and to enforce one approach is to deny the other approach.

Thus, the current settlement is unstable. Different groups can compete with each other to try to influence education policy at a national level in a way which satisfies their own particular interests. It happens at the current time that some religious groups tend to want more freedom and secularist groups want less and this also permeates through the regulation of the school curriculum.[34] If radical secularists were to win this battle, the situation would be no more satisfactory than was the complete integration of Church and state in some countries in the nineteenth century, a situation seen as a problem to be addressed by *Dignitatis humanae* in 1965.

There is an alternative to the central control of education, the competition for scarce school places at institutions that are not allowed to expand, and the political competition for the levers of power in education. This is to accept the Catholic view that the parents are the prime educators of children[35] and that it is for the state to assist them, rather than to displace them, in this role. Indeed, Catholic teaching indicates how this should be done. In successive Church documents (for example, *The Catholic School on the Threshold of the Third Millennium, The Catechism of the Catholic Church* and *Gravissimum educationis*)[36] it has been made clear that parents must have genuine freedom in their choice of school and that non-state schools should not be discriminated against in terms of how they are financed. Indeed, it is argued that a state school monopoly offends justice.[37]

---

34 There is currently much discussion, for example, about whether compulsory attendance at sex education lessons should be extended.

35 Cf. *GS*, 48: 'Graced with the dignity and office of fatherhood and motherhood, parents will energetically acquit themselves of a duty *which devolves primarily on them*, namely education and especially religious education.' (My emphasis.) Cf. *GE*, 3.

36 The Congregation for Catholic Education, *The Catholic School on the Threshold of the Third Millennium*, 1997; *The Catechism of the Catholic Church* 2229; *GE*, 6.

37 See *Divini illius magistri*, 48.

It is worth noting that, in many senses, Catholic Social Teaching in this area separates the issue of funding schools from the issue of provision – something that economists also tend to do.[38] No judgement is made in this chapter about the extent to which, and for which groups, the state should fund schooling. However, it is argued that the mechanism of funding should be neutral between providers of schools independent of whether schools are government-run, local-government-run, Christian schools, schools controlled by other religious groups, or schools controlled by secular foundations or even profit-making companies. In a sense, such a system might look like a 'voucher' system which funded parents to obtain an education for their children rather than funded institutions themselves.

Catholic teaching does not argue that freedom in education is a right only for Catholics. All parents should have the right to educate their children. This means that humanists would have the same rights to establish schools funded in the same way as any other school. Catholics wish to give to humanists freedoms that some humanists would deny to Catholics. This may never be explicit in Catholic teaching, because Catholic teaching on education has normally been articulated with the needs of the Church's own flock in mind. However, it is strongly implicit. Freedom of conscience and freedom to worship, as set out in *Dignitatis humanae*, apply to education and the wishes of parents are paramount. The state is there to assist the family, not to displace it.

Education and social cohesion

There are two major concerns from the widening of freedom in education. The first is that institutional variety and competition is likely to lead to inequalities. The evidence here is quite strong:[39] competition increases quality, but those with special educational needs and those who are least well off benefit most. One reason for this is likely to be the way catchment areas work in uniform state systems: it tends to be the least well off who find it more difficult to ensure that their children are able to attend better

---

38 It should be noted that the Church does not say a great deal that is definitive about how and to what extent education should be funded by the state, though this chapter assumes that education will continue to be funded by the state for all parents who wish to take advantage of state funding.

39 See G. Sahlgren, 'Schooling for Money: Swedish Education Reform and the Role of the Profit Motive', *Economic Affairs* 21:3 (2011), pp. 28–35, and M. R. West and L. Woessmann, '"Every Catholic Child in a Catholic School": Historical Resistance to State Schooling, Contemporary Private Competition and Student Achievement Across Countries', *Economic Journal* 120 (2010), pp. 229–55.

schools. With regard to those with special needs, the advantage of variety stemming from competition is likely to help such people to a greater degree because of the degree of uniformity that tends to pervade a state comprehensive system.[40]

A second problem is that it is feared that freedom in education will promote sectarianism and prevent the absorption of norms that lead to greater social cohesion. There may be concerns about, for example, extremism in Muslim schools or creationism being taught in conservative evangelical schools, even if there is less concern about Catholic/Protestant divisions than there was at one time in most of Britain. However, in a wide variety of schools systems across the world, schoolchildren are separated along religious lines – though very often non-Catholic or non-Christian children will attend Catholic or Christian schools, because the values and virtues taught by the school are sought by their parents. It is difficult to find evidence of problems arising from religious schooling which were not already pre-existing in society. Prohibiting parents from being prime educators of their children – a role they played for thousands of years before formal schooling became the norm around 1880 – seems itself to be an extreme way of dealing with the problem of extremism. As has been noted, the main concern in the UK has been expressed in relation to concern over *secular state* schools being allegedly infiltrated by Muslim extremists.

With regard to the teaching of shared social norms, Catholic Social Teaching addresses this point. *Gravissimum educationis* states that it is reasonable for the state to specify some aspects of the curriculum that should be taught in state-financed schools in order to ensure that children are prepared to fulfil their civic duties.[41] In different legal systems this might have different implications. In the author's view, in the UK common-law context, this might involve some specification in primary law of what is to be expected and what is to be prohibited in schools.[42] Then courts, rather than civil servants, could interpret the law where a school is challenged. It is only recently that the state started to specify in detail what

---

40 This is not to say that there is not some excellent provision currently, but specialization of schools especially for those with special needs (of any type) is very difficult in the UK state system given the scale at which schools tend to have to operate. An interesting development recently has been the development of a free school for children with autism (www.therise school.com/). This was born out of a concern that existing provision includes plenty of resources for individual autistic children without providing an overall structure within which they can flourish.

41 GE, 6.

42 For example, in the first group proficiency in basic subjects, knowledge of legal and political institutions, and so on; in the second group, incitement to violence to achieve religious or political ends.

should be taught in schools and when schools are responsive to parents they tend to naturally want to prepare children as fully as possible for further educational opportunity, for employment and to take their place in society.[43] Many schools would, of course, be part of a wider supportive institutional network such as a Church or ecclesial community.

Conclusion

A free economy allows people to achieve their objectives peacefully, by cooperation and agreement. Catholic Social Teaching argues that parents should have the right to obtain an appropriate education for their children, because this is an extension of freedom of conscience, the right to evangelize and the duties of parents as prime educators. Although, according to Catholic teaching, the common good is not fully realized while people do not know God and fail to practise what is good, this does not mean that non-Christians should not be able to exercise freedom of choice in schooling too.

In the UK context, the implementation of such a policy would mean the state controlling education and schools to a much lesser degree and funding all parents on an equal basis regardless of where they sought an education for their children. Such a system has the additional advantage of depoliticizing education. It would be no longer necessary for secularists to try to prevent the state funding of Christian schools, for moral relativists to try to control the sex education curriculum, for Muslims to try to take over secular schools, or for Christians to try to hold on to what they regard as their privileges. The focus would be on parents exercising their freedom and not on interest groups battling for the levers of political power.

Parents must be able to choose an education for their children that is appropriate for their particular needs if there is to be human flourishing for all. Parents are, in the Catholic view, prime educators because they are chosen by God and know their children better than a state agency could possibly know them. But the promotion of the common good also

---

43 There is much more that could be said about this issue. However, the national curriculum was introduced by Margaret Thatcher in 1988 and, though there were many shortcomings before then and some things have improved, it is certainly not clear that there were huge numbers of schools not teaching key subjects – even without the effect of competition. There is no clear evidence that standards have since improved as a result of the introduction of a national curriculum. Prior to its introduction, the only compulsory subject was religious education.

considers the flourishing of the community. As *Gravissimum educationis* puts it:

> But it [the state] must always keep in mind the principle of subsidiarity so that there is no kind of school monopoly, for this is opposed to the native rights of the human person, to the development and spread of culture, to the peaceful association of citizens and to the pluralism that exists today in ever so many societies.[44]

44 *GE*, 21.

12

Politics, Employment Policies
and the Young Generation[1]

MAURICE GLASMAN

I work from within the British Labour tradition whose indebtedness to its Christian inheritance extends even wider than its undoubted debt to Catholicism. The Labour movement in my country was shaped decisively by the dockers strike of 1889 in which the workers were supported and protected by Cardinal Manning and William Booth, founder of the Salvation Army. A common good was discovered between Catholic and non-established Protestant congregations within the Labour movement itself in divided cities such as London, Glasgow, Liverpool and Manchester on the basis of upholding the dignity of the working person and resisting the domination of a ferocious free market and the Poor Law state. This politics driven by the common good, founded upon the restoration of humanity within the economy, was not the least of Labour's achievements. I am also Jewish, an inheritance which has made its own distinctive contribution to the history of the Labour tradition through its stress on the virtues of family life, education and self-organized community organizations.

I discovered Catholic Social Thought while studying for my doctorate at the European University Institute in Florence.[2] Neither Keynesian nor liberal economic theory could explain the distinctive institutions that characterized the German economy: the vocational system of not only training but labour market entry, the balance of power in its corporate governance between capital and labour, the regional banks that were constrained only to lend in the area within which they were endowed, the co-determination of the pension system – all of these were elusive for analytical models that could not conceptualize any intermediate

---

1 This is an edited version of an address given by Lord Glasman to the *Centesimus Annus* Pro Pontifice Foundation at their 20th Anniversary International Conference 'Rethinking Solidarity for Employment: The Challenges of the Twenty-First Century', Rome, 23 May 2013.

2 Published as Maurice Glasman, *Unnecessary Suffering: Managing Market Utopia*, London/New York: Verso, 1996.

institutions between the individual and the collective, the market and the state. Rational choice theory was tying itself in knots trying to work this one out. The distinctive stress within the German system on labour value, the importance of place and relationships, was practically real but theoretically obscure within the prevailing academic literature. I was also interested in the particular nature of its welfare system which worked through civic institutions and preserved a sense of status, solidarity and subsidiarity. I could not find a theory that could explain the data.

I was discussing my theoretical problems with a fellow student called Kees van Keesbergen. He asked me if I had read any Catholic Social Thought. I had no idea that such a thing existed. It was not a big deal in England when I was growing up. I knew about liberation theology, but this was something very different. The first encyclical that I read was *Laborem exercens* (1981), which was followed quickly by *Centesimus annus* (1991). The insights I discovered concerning the meaning of labour, vocation, virtue and value as economic categories, the balance of power in corporate governance, the constraints on capital and the centralized state within a defence of private property, were not only transformative of my understanding of the German political economy but transformative of my understanding of politics.

This has led to the establishment of Blue Labour, a new formation within the British Labour Party, which places Catholic Social Thought at the centre of its concerns and believes that it offers the basis for a humane and competitive economic system in an environment where both Keynesian and neoliberal theories have failed. Catholic Social Thought offers the possibility of a rationally superior paradigm of economics, precisely because it includes tradition, institutions and labour value as constitutive of an innovative and competitive economy. The crash of 2008 is the defining moment for articulating the limits of both state and market approaches, and it will be suggested here that the most plausible narrative is one based on the concepts and assumptions of Catholic Social Thought.

I am grateful for the opportunity of being able to say thank you for the extraordinary gift of Catholic Social Thought which the Church has given to me and for the friendship and solidarity of the Catholic Church in England in supporting the campaigns over the last 20 years for a living wage and an interest rate cap. Pope Pius XI quoted St Ambrose approvingly in *Quadragesimo anno* (1931), when he wrote that 'there is no duty more urgent than that of returning thanks'.[3] It is a tremendous relief to fulfil that obligation.

---

3 Pius XI, *Quadragesimo anno*, 1931, 16. Hereafter *QA*.

The politics of paradox

In *Centesimus annus*, published 22 years ago, the political challenge is clearly stated by John Paul II:

> It is right to speak of a struggle against an economic system, if the latter is understood as a method of upholding the absolute predominance of capital, the possession of the means of production and of the land, in contrast to the free and personal nature of human work. In the struggle against such a system, what is being proposed as an alternative is not the socialist system, which in fact turns out to be state capitalism, but rather a society of free work, of enterprise and of participation. Such a society is not directed against the market, but demands that the market be appropriately controlled by the forces of society and by the state, so as to guarantee that the basic needs of the whole of society are satisfied.[4]

The political challenge laid down by John Paul II is not being met. One might say that the tragedy of contemporary European politics is that Germany remains misunderstood as exclusively fiscally conservative when this is only one aspect of its economic system. It is also characterized by a vocational economy in which labour market entry is regulated by self-organized institutions which preserve and renew the traditions of a particular craft, by regional banks that are constrained to lend within their region, by the significant representation of the workforce in the corporate governance of firms, and by the co-determination of pensions by capital and labour. In other words, Germany has a competitive economy characterized by the plural governance of non-pecuniary institutions which uphold and embody a virtue that is irreducible to state or market definitions or domination. None of these have been generalized as necessary features of a European economic system which has become increasingly characterized by the free movement of labour and capital within a framework of remote directives.

The economic debate remains polarized in terms of stimulus or austerity, Hayek or Keynes, as if we have learned nothing in the intervening 80 years. Germany has successfully exported its goods but not the virtues of its economic system. For this reason, the European Union appears as a technocratic and administrative system, detached from the civic institutions that give our continent life: our free cities, universities, churches and vocational institutions that embody traditions of self-government

---

4 John Paul II, *Centesimus annus*, 1991, 35. Hereafter *CA*.

over many centuries. It promotes, in contrast and as its highest priority, the free movement of capital and labour within its sphere. The EU thus appears as a force hostile to the particular institutions and coalitions that constitute a politics of the common good and an enforcer of unmediated procedural domination in which any impediment to the free movement of the factors of production is dismissed as populist and reactionary. It is not a mystery, in such an environment, that democratic politics itself is seen as powerless and subordinate and that all manner of morbid systems should emerge, in Italy as well as England.

The paradox of contemporary European politics is that the country with the greatest degree of labour representation in its corporate structure, the most intense system of vocational interference in labour market participation, the greatest degree of constraint on finance capital in its banking system, generates the greatest value and is the most competitive within the international economy. Another way of saying the same thing is that while Catholic Social Thought has been vindicated in its practices of a balance of interest, the importance of place, the preservation of status, solidarity and subsidiarity in the organization of a political economy, it has yet to be articulated or organized as a political force.

Neither economic liberalism nor Keynesianism can conceptualize vocation, virtue or labour value as economic categories, nor can give a primary economic value to intermediate institutions, whether they be the corporate governance of a firm, vocational colleges, regional banks or supporter-owned football clubs. They can only conceptualize the state or the market, and all forms of particular association are viewed as at best 'cultural' or at worst 'obstructive'. They can give no conceptual status to the specificity of place and the necessity of institutions in generating virtue and value within it.

My political duty, therefore, is not exhausted by gratitude to the inheritance of Catholic Social Thought, preserved, renewed and strengthened by the Church for over a century. It is also necessary to take the argument out and present a constructive alternative to the relentless pressure of commodification and centralization, with the resultant sense of powerlessness that is generated by the joint sovereignty of financial markets and the administrative, procedural state. It is necessary to assert and organize around the necessity of tradition, of an inheritance, as a condition of meaningful action, the preservation and renewal of virtue, of good practice within decentralized institutions that function within the economy, and the democratic participation of workers in the governance of the economy which underpins the wellbeing of their families, their colleagues and their neighbours.

The overriding paradox is that a democratic and vocational 'resistance' to modernity, defined as the joint sovereignty of financial markets and public administration, is the most efficient, competitive and sustainable modern position. The tragedy is that such a reasonable political position is unavailable within mainstream European politics; indeed, there are those who argue that it would be illegal and an infringement of EU rules concerning competition.

The political task is to organize estranged interests, in which capital and labour play an important role, around a politics of the common good which upholds virtue, vocation and value as economic categories; subsidiarity, status and solidarity as political categories; and places relationships, reciprocity and responsibility at the heart of both the public and private sectors. This is what Blue Labour is about as a political force within British politics. It asserts the mutual necessity of tradition and innovation, of liberty and solidarity, of cooperation and competition, the necessity of tension for the common good, of honouring the dignity of labour as a condition of competitive success.

One of the themes of the encyclicals is the recurring argument that a proper understanding of things makes the old new and the new old.[5] Through this paradoxical insight we can understand the continuities in circumstance that reveal the old truths concerning the social nature of the person, the need for relationships and the relentless threat of domination. Blue Labour is an attempt to take these paradoxes into the political realm in order to challenge the prevailing orthodoxies of political economy, whether market or state based. For example, blue is not the workers' colour, but that of conservatism, yet the blood and martyrdom of red socialism has a great difficulty in grasping the common good that needs to be built, precisely around the political economy between capital and labour, immigrant and local, secular and faithful, men and women. It still clings to the incommensurability of capital and labour, of faith and reason. The Labour tradition needs to understand the grandeur and profundity of conservatism so that it can renew its radicalism. The common good must involve 'the honest discussion of differences founded in a desire for justice'.[6] That political space of honest discussion, of difference bound by a common commitment to justice, is precisely the space that Catholic Social Thought allows to be formed. It is not a neutral space but a mutual space. The reconciliation of estranged interests through a paradoxical politics of the common good by actively resisting commodification and state domination is the meaning of Blue Labour.

---

5 John Paul II, *Laborem exercens*, 1981, 11. Hereafter *LE*.
6 *QA*, 114.

Undominated diversity bound by a commitment to the common good between institutions, regions, vocations and disciplines, is what Blue Labour is trying to craft so that, for example, people of faith can be heard in the public square and workers in the boardroom. We are as much an enemy of aggressive secularism as we are of belligerent religiosity in which one faith seeks to dominate others and not work through reason, love and persuasion. The Labour movement in the UK has been arrogant in relation to faith in general and careless in its recognition of its Christian inheritance and in order to renew itself as a tradition, it must recognize that no one is innocent.

The common good that will be fashioned will not be around the culture wars of polarized opposition between progressive and religious forces, but around those areas which also pertain to human dignity and the possibilities of the person for love and grace that relate to their working lives, to the ferocious energy of capital and the deathly embrace of the administrative state and how best to resist their domination. People will find in the politics of the common good their necessary and active dependence on each other to fulfil their needs and secure their life and livelihoods. Politics, as a vocation, will flourish 'by the moderation and equal distribution of public burdens', whereby there is a sharing of responsibility and a mutuality of sacrifice.[7]

Employment policies: virtue, vocation and value

The politics of the common good is what is lacking and what is required. We will have to rediscover the old in order to refashion the new. And this leads to the second part of this chapter, which follows from the politics, and is about employment policy. When I was invited to speak at the *Centesimus Annus* Pro Pontifice Foundation Conference, I was surprised to be asked to reflect in these terms because employment is a neutral and technical term that refers to a job and wages. The tradition of Catholic Social Thought usually prefers to talk in terms of work, labour and a vocation in the conceptualization of what constitutes employment. Joining 'employment' with the concept of 'policy' does not help. The subordination of politics to technocratic policy is part of the problem. It conceives of politics in terms of remedies devised by the state and considered rationally on the basis of evidence. It does not conceive of the creation of new institutions, of a politics that is driven by interests and their reconciliation in the common good.

---

7 Leo XIII, *Rerum Novarum*, 1891, 26. Hereafter *RN*.

I think it is more faithful to the tradition as well as more insightful to conceive of employment and the policies required to change its degradation and absence through the concepts of 'labour' and 'vocation' and the role of new institutions established within the economic sphere that can act as generators of value and virtue. In the same way that labour is given priority over capital because it is the human element, so it is that politics should be given priority over policy, and the representation of estranged interests in positions of power within shared institutions is necessary for that.

Labour has value in itself and is constitutive of the person and of the species.[8] It is a cruel paradox that it should also be the site of domination and exploitation. According to the Catholic theory of labour value, reason is not found exclusively in management but also in the act of work, which draws upon an inheritance of good practice and tradition and is a realization of the reason and creativity of the person.[9] Capital is also a paradoxical force, capable of creativity and destruction, innovation and exploitation.[10] In its pursuit of the maximum immediate return on investment, however, capital views labour merely as a factor of production and not as the bearer of reason and virtue and this can lead to exploitation unless it is 'curbed strongly and ruled with prudence'.[11] The principle means of curbing its domination, its tendency to short-term rationality over a more substantive reason, is through the presence of countervailing institutions in the economic realm that uphold labour power and the preservation of tradition through their practices. Universities, vocational colleges, regional banks and unions are examples of these. Their function is to constrain capital and hold it to account.

The fundamental problem that we confront is that finance capital, severed from its origins in labour and traditions that generate value, is by its nature promiscuous. It is constantly seeking new partners, higher returns on investment, more bang for its buck, trying to break free of old entanglements and relationships and hook up with new and younger partners that offer less resistance to its will and easier returns. Outside all relationships, it acts as Aristotle said that anyone would act who was outside constraint and relationships, 'like a beast or a god'.[12] Capital in this form tries to commodify, to turn something that was not produced for

---

8 'Man is born to labour as the bird to fly', *QA*, 61.

9 *LE*, 6.

10 *LE*, 11.

11 *QA*, 88.

12 Aristotle, *The Politics*, Loeb Classical Library, trans. H. Rackham, Cambridge, Mass/London: Harvard University Press, revd edn 1944, I, 1253a, p. 13 (translation adapted).

sale, such as human beings and nature, into a commodity for sale on the market.[13] It leads to the exhaustion of the person and their environment.

The constructive political alternative is to be found within the tradition of Catholic Social Thought. The idea of worker representation in corporate governance was already present in *Rerum novarum* as a practice that would promote the balance of interests needed for the necessary reconciliation between capital and labour.[14] Corporate governance representation for labour addresses the necessity of a form of accountability that does not claim all advantage for one side, and can restrain cheating, greed and avarice in the working life. The specific technique developed within Catholic Social Thought was a form of relational accountability, in which the real physical presence of the workforce on boards required a sharing of information regarding the firm and the sector, a negotiation of modernizing strategy which was not conducted exclusively on terms beneficial to capital.[15]

It is the absence of relational accountability, the lack of internal constraint on capital, and the absence of the labour interest, that provides the fundamental explanation of the crash of 2008. The financial crisis was generated by the concentration of capital, a lack of accountability so that money managers could lie, cheat and exaggerate without any specialist scrutiny, based on knowledge of the internal working of the firm, that could challenge them. We learned that accountability is too important to be left to accountants. It was a crisis of accountability, of a lack of virtue, and 'incentives to vice' in the form of bankers' bonuses and unilateral self-remuneration. It was also a result of the disentangling of capital from its origins to such an extent that it was unconstrained and exerted relentless demands for higher rates of returns. These turned out to be speculative and fantastical. There was no vocation or virtue in the governance of the financial sector and the key to its remedy lies in the expertise and interests of labour, who through their representation in the firm could hold the un-virtuous elites to account and bring about the necessary cultural change required to break out of the present malaise. Responsibility and power needs to be shared in order to be effectively exerted.

Central to this is the concept of a vocation, and vocational institutions, which were preserved within the Catholic tradition when modernity seemed to demand transferrable skills or a stress on a career. Vocation includes within itself a calling, or something that is appropriate for the person that comes from within, to work that is authentically your own

---

13 *CA*, 4.
14 *RN*, 34.
15 See *QA*, 132.

and not defined exclusively by its external rewards or demands but characterized too by internal goods that are rooted in a tradition of practice. A vocation requires discipline and judgement, 'good doing', and constrains vice through the concept of good practice, institutionally enforced. Honour, skill, loyalty and dedication are necessary for the preservation and renewal of value, which is judged by other practitioners and not exclusively by the price system.[16] What academics call Peer Group Review is built into the vocational system. It allows for an inheritance to be received, renewed and passed on. It places work, not exclusively as the immediate fulfilment of a task but as something that is received from the past and oriented towards the future. Vocational institutions valorize labour, constrain capital and promote virtue. The internal goods preserved by vocational institutions are a direct threat to the domination of capital but necessary for its successful reproduction.

Regional banks that are constrained to lend within a particular area are a necessary part of the institutional ecology in that they resist the centralizing power of capital, allow a more stable access to credit for regional and smaller businesses, and encourage relationships and reciprocity to constrain the demand for higher rates of return that have decimated the mutual bank sector in Britain. They also offer an alternative to usurious lending, one of the great growth areas in our economy.

The inheritance of Catholic Social Thought is practised in five fundamental ways within the German economy:

1 The representation of the labour interest in the various forms of co-determination typical of German corporate governance of which the 'equalization of the burdens', established in 1952, is characteristic.
2 The regulation of labour market entry by vocational institutions that are democratically self-organized and enforce training and ethical practice within the sector, with the power of expulsion. The rules that apply to doctors, lawyers and accountants in other countries apply in Germany to workers.
3 The co-determination of the pension fund between capital and labour so that they share an interest in the future and the health of the sector that is mutual. This is a good example of the 'incentives to virtue' that are required to resist commodification and the domination of one interest alone and its ability to maximize its power.
4 The power to form unions that promote and protect the labour interest as self-organized democratic institutions.

16 CA, 32; LE, 18.

5 The endowment of regional and sectoral banks constrained to lend within their area and specialist sphere.

Any serious reflection on 'employment policies' must confront the central-ization of capital and the state. It must seek to constrain both through the endowment of decentralized regional and sectoral institutions that stand against centralization and preserve and renew traditions of virtue within the economy through resisting the commodification of human beings, nature and knowledge which is demanded by the maximum return on investment. It must allow initiative and enterprise to be oriented towards the future.

Not a policy, but a radical redistribution of power and responsibility based around a common good within and between institutions, is the generator of value and employment. That is the task of statecraft.

The younger generation: rethinking solidarity

This leads directly to the consideration of the younger generation. It would be hostile to the entire tradition to view the young in isolation from other generations, and it would be entirely consistent to reconcile the excluded poles of young and old. The breakdown of familial obligation and the enforcement of retirement rules, combined with a general fetishism for all things young that characterizes totalitarian ideologies, has led to an increasing abandonment of old people. There is a general recognition that life should be characterized by 'lifelong learning'. What is less often acknowledged is that there is a role for 'lifelong teaching'.

Vocational institutions are a crucial way of brokering intergenerational solidarity. By honouring the wisdom and experience of the old and bring-ing them into a relationship of teaching and mentoring with the young, by passing on their skills and their stories, they build the character and expertise of the young. Intermediate institutions sustain a human scale of engagement, make demands on people as members, encourage the virtues of self-government indispensible to a good life.[17] Solidarity is not gener-ated by collectivism. The building up of trust and mutual interests that is generated by common action and shared institutions which allow for participation by their members transforms a fate into a destiny that can be shaped through democratic action. In *Centesimus annus* this is stated clearly:

---

17 CA, 49.

The individual today is often suffocated between two poles represented by the state and the marketplace. At times it seems as though he exists only as a producer and a consumer of goods, or as an object of state administration. People lose sight of the fact that life in society has neither the market or the state as its final purpose, since life itself has a unique value which the state and the market must serve. Man remains above all a being who seeks truth and strives to live in that truth, deepening his understanding of it through a dialogue which involves past and future generations.[18]

Through labour and the renewal of vocation and virtue, what is estranged can be reconciled – and this needs to be applied to the young and the old. The solution to the problems confronting the young is not to isolate them and treat them as a specific category, as modern marketing is seeking to do. It is to bring them into a necessary and mutual relationship with older people, to reconstitute intergenerational solidarity by giving incentives for them to meet and care for older people and to learn from and be nourished by them. This indicates both a form of a more relational welfare system and another way in which we make the new old and the old new.

Conclusion

It is not always clear within the tradition where it is necessary to start. In asserting the priority of labour, of the primacy of persons before things, the integrity of family life, and the superiority of work to welfare, it is necessary for all people of good will to champion the living wage, so that each worker can feed their loved ones and fulfil their duties as human beings as an inheritor of the dignity of labour.[19] It is also necessary to limit the power of money, particularly in relation to debt and usury, so that the rich do not prey upon the misfortunes of the poor. A living wage and an interest rate cap are the floor and ceiling of the new European home but they need to be complemented by a new kind of statecraft that cherishes and strengthens civic institutions which treasure and protect their internal practices and judgements and allow virtue and vocation to flourish without the domination of the market or the state.[20]

---

18 *CA*, 49.

19 For the Living Wage, see *RN*, 10, 34; *QA*, 71; *LE*, 19; *CA*, 8, 15:'The wage paid to the workingman should be sufficient for the support of himself and his family.' For the constraint on usury, see *RN*, 2, 33.

20 See *QA*, 73–4.

John Paul II described politics, following in a long Aristotelian tradition, as 'a prudent concern for the common good'.[21] A common good between young and old, capital and labour, immigrants and locals, Christians and Muslims, city and countryside, faithful and secular: this is how solidarity needs to be rethought. Its appropriate vehicle is a politics of the common good that is built upon resisting the domination of capital and the state by local and decentralized democratic politics. The common good is discovered between people and returns their agency. Such a politics is a vocation, it has all the characteristics of labour, it is definitive of our humanity and can cause great suffering, frustration and tension. In all its forms, however, it is better than the politics we have now.

---

21 *LE*, 20.

13

Market Economics, Catholic Social Teaching and the Common Good

CLIFFORD LONGLEY

Something went very astray in the world of economic theory two or three decades ago. In place of the idea that national economies should be managed by governments so they served the public interest, it became fashionable to say they should be left to their own devices – and the public interest would look after itself. This theory, generally now known as neo-liberalism or by its critics as market fundamentalism, became the standard orthodoxy not just in the world of economic and political science, but gradually – partly through the influence of business schools – in the financial sector such as banking, and then in business generally.

What helped it enormously was that people wanted to believe it. Free market economics fitted neatly into a general libertarian framework, where governments were the enemy. They should be made to interfere as little as possible in the personal choices of individuals. Freedom was the only good – freedom to pursue one's self-interest. Neoliberal theory absolved business of any responsibility for the consequences of their actions, or as Milton Friedman, neoliberal guru of the Chicago School, put it, 'the business of business is business' – business alone.

So, the duty of company directors was to shareholders, no one else, and that duty was fulfilled by maximizing the value of their shareholding. In order that directors should know and feel that they were unambiguously on the side of shareholders, it became standard practice for directors to be shareholders too. In maximizing shareholder value they were also maximizing their own wealth. And in order that they didn't need to ask themselves whether their activities were harmful to society, they were assured that that benefit was automatic. A rising tide lifts all boats, they were told; wealth trickles down from the top and eventually helps everyone.

The political and economics commentator Will Hutton called free market fundamentalism 'the biggest intellectual mistake this generation has ever witnessed, arguably the world has ever witnessed'.[1] There is much talk of 'remoralizing' economics, arguing that 2008 would not have happened if people had behaved better, been less greedy. But this hardly scratches the surface. The core problem is ideological, and bankers behaving better won't solve it. The ideology asserts, with a profound, quasi-religious conviction, that markets always self-correct, market forces are sovereign. What it completely ignores, therefore, is the common good. Market fundamentalists have no room for such a concept.

The Governor of the Bank of England, Mark Carney, told a conference on Inclusive Capitalism in London in 2014:

> My core point is that, just as any revolution eats its children, unchecked market fundamentalism can devour the social capital essential for the long-term dynamism of capitalism itself. To counteract this tendency, individuals and their firms must have a sense of their responsibilities for the broader system. All ideologies are prone to extremes. Capitalism loses its sense of moderation when the belief in the power of the market enters the realm of faith. In the decades prior to the crisis, such radicalism came to dominate economic ideas and became a pattern of social behaviour. Market fundamentalism – in the form of light-touch regulation, the belief that bubbles cannot be identified and that markets always clear – contributed directly to the financial crisis and the associated erosion of social capital.[2]

As Pope Francis said recently:

> Some people continue to defend trickle-down theories which assume that economic growth, encouraged by a free market, will inevitably succeed in bringing about greater justice and inclusiveness in the world. This opinion, which has never been confirmed by the facts, expresses a crude and naïve trust in the goodness of those wielding economic power and in the sacralized workings of the prevailing economic system. Meanwhile, the excluded are still waiting. To sustain a lifestyle which excludes others, or to sustain enthusiasm for that selfish ideal, a globalization of indifference has developed. Almost without being aware of it, we end up being incapable of feeling compassion at the outcry of the poor, or weeping for other people's pain.[3]

---

1 Will Hutton, 'Thanks to the credit crunch all bets are off', *Guardian*, 27 February 2009, www.theguardian.com/commentisfree/video/2009/feb/27/will-hutton-capitalism-crisis.

2 Mark Carney, 'Inclusive Capitalism: Creating a sense of the Systemic', http://www.bankofengland.co.uk/publications/Pages/speeches/2014/731.aspx.

3 Francis, Apostolic Exhortation, *Evangelii gaudium*, 2013, 54.

Yet, these doubts about free market theory rarely communicate themselves to politicians and political commentators, who continue to act as if there were an agreed and unassailable body of doctrine called 'economics' whose truth could no more be denied than the fact that the earth goes round the sun.

One undeniable change, which makes life much more difficult post-2008, is the decline of trust – trust in those with whom one does business, but also trust in the reliability of the whole economic process. This is what Carney means by the 'devouring of social capital' that market fundamentalism can be blamed for. Through this decline in trust, risk assessment has become more difficult. This is one of the fundamental reasons why medium and small businesses have found it so hard to get credit. Lending institutions have lost confidence in their ability to work out who is credit-worthy. They no longer trust their computers to know best. In the wine bars of the City of London, where 'my word is my bond' was once a solemn and sacred oath one banker swore to another, repetition of the phrase now triggers nothing but scornful laughter.

So far, efforts to rebuild the free market system on a more secure basis have made slow progress. What holds them back is the lack of an alternative economic theory to replace neoliberalism, which continues to exercise a hold over the imaginations of many economists because of its elegant simplicity and promise of mathematical certainty – not to mention an abundance of wealth for themselves.

The most obvious challenge to these free market assumptions is that they do not correspond to how people actually behave in real life, beyond the wall or outside the cocoon within which economics operates. Indeed, it has been pointed out that many of the people who spend time behind the wall or within the cocoon do return to real life, for instance when they go home to their families every evening and when they engage in all the activities that make life satisfying and fulfilled. There, values are different. They live, in short, divided lives.

One major study to identify and name this phenomenon came about as a collaboration between the Vatican and the John A. Ryan Institute for Catholic Social Thought of the Center for Catholic Studies at the University of St Thomas, Minnesota. Prepared with the aid of business people, *The Vocation of a Business Leader* struck a chord in many business and professional circles. It stated that:

Obstacles to serving the common good come in many forms – lack of rule of law, corruption, tendencies towards greed, poor stewardship of resources – but the most significant for a business leader on a personal level is leading a 'divided' life.[4]

The phenomenon is easily observed and commonly experienced. It was mentioned by Mark Carney in the speech already referred to when he said 'Financiers, like all of us, need to avoid compartmentalization – the division of our lives into different realms, each with its own set of rules. Home is distinct from work; ethics from law; the individual from the system.'

The description of the divided life proposes as an antithesis – as the presumed opposite of the rational self-interest of *Homo Economicus* – the principle of the common good. This clearly goes beyond saying that economics and finance cannot function without moral values. It is more subversive of standard economic doctrine than that, raising fundamental questions, for example, about the philosophical and cultural underpinning of modern economics, whether mainstream (or neoliberal) or opposed to mainstream theory.

Both sides of that argument concentrate on the word 'rational' in the phrase 'rational self-interest', and on the word 'interest'. The premise behind the word rational is 'unmoved by emotion or any other irrational influence, including morality'. The assumptions behind 'interest' are to do with personal advantage, over and against advantage to others. The touchstone often cited is a phrase from Adam Smith's *The Wealth of Nations*:

It is not from the benevolence of the butcher, the brewer, or the baker, that we can expect our dinner, but from their regard to their own interest. We address ourselves, not to their humanity but to their self love.[5]

Smith's belief in the benefits of pursuing self-interest is expressed in his famous reference to the 'invisible hand', which has become almost the foundational text of modern economics. Writing of a hypothetical businessman who exercises a preference for home grown produce, he says:

By preferring the support of domestic to that of foreign industry, he intends only his own security; and by directing that industry in such a manner as its produce may be of the greatest value, he intends only his own gain; and he is in this, as in many other cases, led by an invisible

---

4 Pontifical Council for Justice and Peace, *Vocation of a Business Leader: a Reflection* (2012); www.hightail.com/download/M3BrToNUY1NGRoVFSzhUQw.

5 Adam Smith, *The Wealth of Nations*, ed. Andrew Skinner, 2 vols, London: Penguin, 1970, Vol. I, p. 119.

hand to promote an end which was no part of his intention. Nor is it always the worse for the society that it was no part of it. By pursuing his own interest, he frequently promotes that of the society more effectually than when he really intends to promote it.[6]

The notion of the invisible hand has been used to elevate free market economics to an almost mystical level, hinting that a benevolent Providence watches over market forces to ensure an outcome which is always to the general benefit. But the invisible hand hypothesis also acquits those engaged in economic processes of having any responsibility towards the common good beyond that of making a profit.

The principle of the common good challenges Smith's utilitarian theory of rational self-interest most radically at the level not of 'rationality' or 'interest' but at the level of 'self'. Smith was a leading member of the Scottish Enlightenment, a philosophical school that helped to give birth to the modern notion of the 'self' as an autonomous unit of consciousness. This self knows of its own existence not because it is loved and can love, for example in relationship, but because it can think rationally, that is enclosed in its own mental space, as in Descartes' *cogito ergo sum*. This idea of the self as an unencumbered individual became the dominant idea of modern secular liberal democracy, an individualism that Western culture to a large extent takes for granted as normal, indeed normative. And when such an individual engages in finance or trade or economics, he or she is pleased to note that social obligations are not part of their responsibility, and they become, of course, the autonomous rational creature, *Homo Economicus*.

The Enlightenment itself was much more complex than this, but its emphasis on the autonomous self was a logical corollary of its rejection of any moral philosophy based on Aristotle such as that of Thomas Aquinas. So central to liberal individualism is this idea of the individual self, that some have seen it as a threat to the very idea of the common good – and vice versa.

Catholic Social Teaching offers a definition of the common good, given in the document *Gaudium et spes* of Vatican II as 'the sum total of social conditions which allow people, either as groups or as individuals, to reach their fulfilment more fully and more easily'. Other documents within this tradition describe 'fulfilment' as 'integral human development': integral, meaning relating to the whole person in every aspect, which includes educational, emotional, physical, cultural, psychological and spiritual factors

---

6 Smith, *Wealth*, Vol. 2, p. 32.

but acting together rather than in isolation; human, embracing all that the word means, especially human dignity but also in mutual relationships that are beneficial and fruitful; development, meaning growth in health and wellbeing and the realization of all that a person has been given in his or her talents and capacities, or 'capabilities'.[7] It has been described as 'becoming whom one is meant to be' (which does, however, raise the theological question – the question of *telos* – of 'meant by whom?').

Take Laura and Emma, hypothetical teenage schoolfriends. As well as progressing in their general education and wellbeing, Laura loves playing hockey, while Emma is learning the violin. Emma likes watching Laura play; while Laura likes listening to Emma practise. They both want to be good at what they do, and they both want each other to be good at what they do too. Their gradual progress towards excellence in each field is not only satisfying and pleasurable to both of them, but is of real benefit to both of them, to their 'integral human development'. It forms their character.

They share, therefore, a 'good' – their progress towards excellence in their particular skill – even though it is in different fields. We can call that a shared good, a common good. The idea can readily be extended to the whole class, the whole school or college, and the whole community outside. Indeed, the very existence of a school in which Laura and Emma can progress in their different ways is an expression of an attitude on the part of the community – and more than an attitude, a commitment – to the integral human development, by the full realization of their capabilities, of all the children in that community. It represents also a political decision by the community, that that is the sort of society they want to live in, just as Laura wants to live in a society where Emma's talents are developed, and Emma wants to live in a society where Laura's talents are developed.

It is a product of the emphasis on the individual self in modern Western culture that choices such as these are not understood according to a calculus of the common good, but in terms of a polarized choice between selfishness and altruism. These two are construed as zero-sum, which is to say that the more selfish one is, the less altruistic, and vice versa. Laura's delight in Emma's progress is seen as unselfish, and no doubt praiseworthy for that reason – but there is more to it than that. There is much cultural baggage attached to both these ends of the spectrum. Selfishness may be seen as less admirable, but it is also seen as a basic human characteristic, maybe the most basic of all. There is a residual trace here of a Protestant ethic which sees human nature as fundamentally corrupt, or 'totally

---

7 See, Vatican II, *Gaudium et spes* (*The Pastoral Constitution on the Church in the Modern World*, 1965) 26.

depraved' as the sixteenth-century Reformers put it. So is it 'natural' for a human being to be selfish, more natural than being altruistic? Human nature may be fashioned from warped timber, but Thomas Hobbes' description in his *Leviathan* of everyone being perpetually engaged in a 'war of every man against his neighbour', is fortunately much more the exception than the rule. Nevertheless, even if selfishness has to prevail because it characterizes human nature, much ingenuity has gone into trying to harness it for better purposes, such as providing a public benefit.

The seventeenth-century-Anglo-Dutch writer Bernard Mandeville described this as the trick of turning 'private vices' into 'public virtues'. This is the beauty of Adam Smith's proposition concerning the effect of an 'invisible hand'. Modern mainstream economics has taken to heart the notion that, though an individual may be operating in pursuit of self-interest in a free market economy, social benefits will arrive unbidden. Thus has what might otherwise have been seen as a human flaw been turned to good use. This kind of judgement stands at the heart of virtually all defences of free market economics on moral grounds: that it has the alchemy to turn bad into good, dross into gold.

The principle of the common good makes this assumed polarization between selfish and altruistic choices redundant. Emma does not have to choose her own interests over and against Laura's, because she benefits from Laura's growth and development. And Laura reciprocates, to Emma's benefit. But they can also pursue their own good, for the benefit of themselves, of each other and of the wider whole. They participate and advance in a common good they share. However, so well established is the idea that individuals are basically selfish and reluctant to contribute to the good of others, that some people find this notion of a shared common good hard to accept.

They fail to realize that the concept of the free individual self is a social construct of relatively recent origin, and that the identity of the self has no content until it is forged in relationships during the growth of the child. However much they may eventually emerge as individuals, human beings start life as social animals who must depend on others long before they can depend on themselves, and they are shaped by others long before they can take charge of their own destiny. Indeed, they can only learn how to do this from others. It is parents and teachers who show children how to stand on their own feet.

The notion of a common good was once so familiar that it didn't even need a name. Indeed, what makes the language of the common good a central necessity to contemporary political and economic theory, rather than a fringe idea of out-of-date philosophers, is neoliberalism and its intentional and specific denial of the common good. The notion that within the 'commons' is an implicit structure of justice – social justice – was ridiculed by Friedrich Hayek, the chief apostle of free market economics before Friedman, as 'absurd' and 'mere superstition'.[8]

The principle of the common good applies par excellence to families, through the mutual support that loving partners, married or otherwise, supply to each other for the benefit of both, and of any children they may have. Nobody reduces that to mere 'altruism' or measures each partner's share according to some index of selfishness: the principle of the common good is the natural and logical ethic of family life.

There are other institutions in British society where the natural ethic is the common good principle. As well as the state school system already mentioned, the National Health Service is one obvious case. Both within the NHS and in the democratic and financial support the whole community gives to it, the NHS represents the principle that the health care interests of everyone are the responsibility of everyone. Few would regard paying tax to support the NHS as altruism or those who use the NHS as being selfish: it is a civic responsibility for a shared benefit – for the common good.

Those who experience a 'divided' life as they pass between their place of work and the rest of their everyday lives are in fact passing between these two modes of moral consciousness – the 'everyday' social self where the culture and ethos of the common good is taken for granted as normative, and a 'workplace' where the culture of neoliberal individualism and ethos of self-interest is imposed by the exigencies of the job. There are signs that such individuals increasingly try to resolve the conflict by taking the values of the workplace into their home and social life – what has been called the 'marketization' of the culture.

It can mean the transfer of faith in an invisible hand – served by the rational pursuit of individual self-interest – from the economic sphere into non-economic affairs, including human relationships. The consequences are invariably unhappy, because this is based on a misreading of human nature. But it is powerfully corrosive of social trust. The view that politicians are 'only in it for themselves' – assiduously fostered by journalists of whom that is manifestly only too true – is easily cultivated. Indeed it becomes a culture in which 'every man for himself' ('and devil take the hindmost') is becoming a universal ethic.

---

8 Friedrich Hayek, *Law, Legislation and Liberty: A new statement of the Liberal Principles of Justice and Political Economy*, revd edn, London: Routledge and Kegan Paul, 1982, pp. 65–7.

At the foundations of Catholic Social Teaching are two related principles, the common good and human dignity. They stand together jointly and equally – with a warning not to separate them nor to let one take precedence over the other. The key documents of this tradition, known as the 'social encyclicals,' have elaborated these principles and explored how they might apply to contemporary circumstances. The most significant and recent document, *Caritas in veritate*[9], was directed at the causes of the 2008 economic and financial crisis. The first, *Rerum novarum*, was published in 1891 and addressed the plight of workers caught up in nineteenth-century industrialization and urbanization.

The common good and human dignity lead directly to a pair of concepts which need to be observed in any social, political or economic system if it is to be stable and sustainable: solidarity and subsidiarity. Solidarity makes the observation that human beings are social beings, connected and dependent on one another, and asserts that therefore all members of society have obligations to one another. 'All are responsible for all', as one encyclical expresses it.[10] This applies across the whole range of human activities. There is no domain – called economics or anything else – where solidarity does not operate.

Solidarity expresses a natural law, a truth about human nature, a basic tribal instinct. Hence any economic theory that also claims to be based on truths about human nature ought to be compatible with it. This does raise serious questions about the neoliberal insistence on competition as a basic law of economic life, which has sometimes taken elements from Darwinism in order to claim that 'survival of the fittest' – which Darwin never actually preached – necessitates a state of perpetual rivalry for scarce resources. Though competition is embedded in Nature, so is cooperation. It is solidarity which rescues human life from being what Thomas Hobbes described as 'life in an unregulated state of nature' – that is to say 'solitary, poor, nasty, brutish, and short'.

But solidarity, left to itself, can exert a pressure towards collectivism – the notion that mutual responsibility can only satisfactorily be organized by joint action, for instance by the state on behalf of the community. It has a centralizing tendency, which is also therefore a disempowering tendency.

Subsidiarity is an equal and countervailing force to solidarity, pushing against centralization and collectivism. It has an empowering effect. It is also based on a truth about human nature in human society: that

---

9 Benedict XVI, *Caritas in veritate*, 2009. Hereafter, *CV*.
10 John Paul II, *Sollicitudo rei socialis*, 1987, 38. Hereafter, *SRS*.

individuals, small units, families, local societies, have a natural inclination towards self-determination and therefore to a degree of self-government.

As Catholic Social Teaching expresses it, this principle of social organization is so important that to obstruct it is morally wrong. It is as relevant to the organization of society as a whole as it is to any sub-division within it, including the institutions we call limited companies or business corporations. And as is the case with solidarity, if it is part of human nature, economic systems which also claim to be based on human nature cannot ignore it.

Catholic Social Teaching identifies several clear threats to the common good arising from the way free markets operate when they are exclusively pursuing short-term profit. The 2008 crisis brought them to the fore and allowed them to be examined critically in a way that had not been possible before. It drew attention, for instance, to the way economic pressures distort and shrink civil society, which becomes squeezed between the two pincers of the market and the state. *Caritas in veritate* declares: 'The exclusively binary model of market-plus-State is corrosive of society, while economic forms based on solidarity, which find their natural home in civil society without being restricted to it, build up society.'[11]

Instead of this binary model, Catholic Social Teaching proposes a triangle of forces: state, market and civil society. In fact, civil society comes first – it is the *polis* analysed by Aristotle and Plato and almost every philosopher since. A state's boundaries may move, transferring a city or town from one jurisdiction to another while its life continues; economic systems, likewise, may come and go. But the *polis* must continue. If civil society is the source of something essential to the functioning of the economy, such as the social capital present in networks of people who trust each other, then the diminishment of civil society necessarily means the decline of trust within the economy.

In the inner detailed working of the financial crisis which developed in the course of 2007–8, there is no trace of civil society having any positive influence, but plenty of it itself being influenced negatively. Networks of trust, which are the hallmark of civil society, would have enabled financial institutions to assure themselves that the business they were doing was sound, because they knew the people they were dealing with were honest and reliable. But the bank managers – the local custodians of social capital – had all been made redundant. Their many civic virtues were deemed old fashioned and inefficient.

---

11 CV, 39.

Neoliberal economists felt they had removed the need for trust, both in principle because untrustworthy operators would be eliminated through the 'natural' working of the market; and more practically, by the use of devices which allowed the risks of untrustworthy behaviour to be absorbed, mainly through insurance and what was called 'securitization'. Because neoliberalism thinks of itself as a closed and self-sufficient system not in need of moral input from outside itself, the elimination of trust was a breakthrough. It also meant that the vice or virtue of a particular operator was neither here nor there. If he was a bad apple those he had affected could claim on their insurance.

In place of neoliberal economics, Catholic Social Teaching advocates a return to the ethical basis of classical economics that would have been familiar to Adam Smith and Edmund Burke – who took trust for granted as a basic value underlying the whole system. *Caritas in veritate* states:

> Finance, therefore – through the renewed structures and operating methods that have to be designed, after its misuse which wreaked such havoc on the real economy – now needs to go back to being an instrument directed towards improved wealth creation and development. Insofar as they are instruments, the entire economy and finance, not just certain sectors, must be used in an ethical way so as to create suitable conditions for human development and for the development of peoples.[12]

And where are these genuinely ethical foundations to be rediscovered? In civil society, of which subsidiarity is the fundamental principle. Subsidiarity, often regarded as one of the more right-wing or individualistic aspects of Catholic Social Teaching (certainly when compared with solidarity), therefore presents in this respect a strong case against neoliberal ideology.

Caritas in veritate also identifies another factor which, beyond a certain degree, constitutes a threat to civil society as an indirect consequence of market forces left to run free without regard for the common good – that is to say, growing inequality. But it is not just the wealth of elites and oligarchs per se that the encyclical sees as a threat to the social order, but the undermining of social capital. Democracy rests on the consent of the governed. That consent requires at least a minimum of trust that the promise of mass prosperity will be fulfilled. Catholic Social Teaching has in principle accepted a degree of social and economic inequality, unless it has these damaging side effects. In the UK today, inequality has clearly

---

12 CV, 65.

passed the point beyond which it should not go. Over the past 30 years, overall wage inequality in Britain has reached the point where the top fifth of earners now earn 14 times as much as the bottom fifth. The graph of inequality over that timescale follows a similar pattern to the graph of the decline of trust, strongly suggesting one is causing the other. *Caritas in veritate* declares:

> Through the systemic increase of social inequality, both within a single country and between the populations of different countries (i.e. the massive increase in relative poverty), not only does social cohesion suffer, thereby placing democracy at risk, but so too does the economy, through the progressive erosion of social capital.[13]

At the same conference as Mark Carney, Christine Lagarde of the IMF, also a Catholic, quoted Pope Francis, saying he

> recently put this in stark terms when he called increasing inequality the root of social evil. It is therefore not surprising that IMF research – which looked at 173 countries over the last 50 years – found that more unequal countries tend to have lower and less durable economic growth.[14]

Social capital, trust and virtue are a cluster of related concepts which are very important to Catholic Social Teaching. Where do they come from? As well as biblical sources already mentioned, a fundamental influence in this area of moral philosophy and theology has been exercised by classic Greek philosophers, notably Aristotle. His influence waned at the end of the classical period but was revived, indeed rediscovered, through the impact of Islamic philosophers in medieval Spain – who had kept the Aristotelian spirit alive along with many other areas of Greek learning such as mathematics and medicine.

In philosophy their impact was greatest on Christian thinkers like Thomas Aquinas. What Aristotle brought to the debate via Aquinas was the development of the concept of 'the good' as the realization of human potential – of becoming what one was meant to be – and of 'virtue', behaving as one ought to behave if one was actually to advance 'the good' of oneself and others. By practising the virtues one strove after 'excellence,' which was good in itself. It is fair to note that other philosophical schools are sceptical of such concepts. But in ordinary speech, both the idea of

---

13 *CV*, 32.

14 Christine Lagarde, *Economic Inclusion and Financial Integrity*, www.imf.org/external/np/speeches/2014/052714.htm (2014).

'virtue' – in essence, a judgement of a person's moral character – and 'the good', are still very familiar and well understood, as are their opposites.

The virtue of solidarity – essentially 'loving your neighbour as yourself' – is closely related in Catholic Social Teaching to the common good. The 1987 encyclical *Sollicitudo rei socialis* of Pope John Paul II describes solidarity as the acceptance of the moral obligations which arise from fully recognizing the interdependence of all human life.

> This then is not a feeling of vague compassion or shallow distress at the misfortunes of so many people, both near and far. On the contrary, it is a firm and persevering determination to commit oneself to the common good; that is to say to the good of all and of each individual, because we are all really responsible for all.[15]

Solidarity in this treatment is extremely political. It requires a commitment to the common good that is 'based on the solid conviction that what is hindering full development is that desire for profit and that thirst for power already mentioned' – referring to an earlier passage where the encyclical speaks of 'on the one hand, the all-consuming desire for profit, and on the other, the thirst for power, with the intention of imposing one's will upon others'.[16]

It goes on to invoke the powerful concept of 'structures of sin' – internal structural frameworks and systems within institutions which cause injustice and oppression – which can only be overcome

> by a diametrically opposed attitude: a commitment to the good of one's neighbour with the readiness, in the Gospel sense, to 'lose oneself' for the sake of the other instead of exploiting him, and to 'serve him' instead of oppressing him for one's own advantage.[17]

The value of the 'structure of sin' concept is that it shows how a political or economic institution can act sinfully, without personal responsibility for that sin necessarily falling wholly on any one individual. What many commentators on the run-up to the 2008 crisis may have missed is the way financial institutions can give great leverage to small acts of individual self-interest, amplifying their harmful effects far beyond what the actor intended.

---

15 *SRS*, 38.
16 *SRS*, 38, 37.
17 *SRS*, 38.

An important corollary of the principle of the common good is that persons and communities who are economic actors are also moral actors. Hence all economic choices, whether as consumers, business leaders, bankers, or policy-makers, inescapably have a moral dimension – often far greater than an individual may have bargained for. The concept of 'structures of sin' explains how a small mistake or moral slip in the world of finance can do much harm to many people. This explains why the loss of trust is so destructive: it spreads like a cancer through the entire economic process. Would anybody be so foolish, knowing what we now know about the misselling of payment protection insurance policies by banks, as to buy such a policy in the future simply on the basis that they trust the good faith of the bankers trying to sell it to them? Surveys tell us that bankers are the least trusted of all classes of business persons. Yet bankers are at the very heart of our economy.

Caritas in veritate points out that,

> if the market is governed solely by the principle of the equivalence in value of exchanged goods, it cannot produce the social cohesion that it requires in order to function well. Without internal forms of solidarity and mutual trust, the market cannot completely fulfil its proper economic function. And today it is this trust which has ceased to exist, and the loss of trust is a grave loss.[18]

Thus Catholic Social Teaching is clearly relevant to the perceived need for the better underpinning of economic activity by ethical principle. Thanks to its basis in Aristotelian and Thomistic philosophy, it has a coherence and even an elegance that gives it intellectual rigour and frees it from self-righteous judgmentalism, emotionalism, subjectivism and political prejudice. Its fundamental focus is not on money and how to make more of it, but on the person as a moral agent in a market which *at the same time* serves both the individual and the common good.

---

18 CV, 35.

Select Bibliography

Aquinas, Thomas, *Summa Theologiae*, Blackfriars edition, 60 vols, London: Eyre and Spottiswood/New York: McGraw-Hill, 1964–81.

Archbishop of Canterbury's Commission on Urban Priority Areas, *Faith in the City: A Call for Action by Church and Nation*, London: Church House Publishing, 1985.

Arendt, Hannah, *The Human Condition*, Chicago/London: University of Chicago Press, 1958.

Aristotle, *The Politics*, Loeb Classical Library, trans. H. Rackham, Cambridge, Mass: Harvard University Press, revd edn, 1934.

Armando, Salvatore and Eickelman Dale F. (eds), *Public Islam and the Common Good*, Leiden/Boston: Brill, 2004.

Pope Benedict XVI, *Caritas in veritate*, 2009.*

Beveridge, William, *Social Insurance and Allied Services* (The Beveridge Report), London: HMSO, 1942.

Booth, P. (ed.), *Catholic Social Teaching and the Market Economy*, 2nd revd edn, London: St Pauls Publishing, 2014.

Bretherton, Luke, *Christianity and Contemporary Politics*, Oxford: Blackwell, 2010.

Brown, Malcolm (ed.), *Anglican Social Theology: Renewing the Vision Today*, London: Church House Publishing, 2014.

Brueggemann, W., *Theology of the Old Testament: Testimony, Dispute, Advocacy*, Minneapolis: Fortress Press, 1997.

—— *Journey to the Common Good*, Louisville, Kentucky: Westminster John Knox Press, 2010.

Burke, Edmund, *Reflections on the Revolution in France* [1790], ed. L. G. Mitchell, Oxford: Oxford University Press, 2009, first issued as an Oxford World Classics paperback (1999).

Catholic Bishops' Conference of England and Wales, *The Common Good and the Catholic Church's Social Teaching*, Manchester: Gabriel Communications, 1996.

—— *Choosing the Common Good*, Stoke on Trent: Alive Publishing, 2010.

—— *The Catechism of the Catholic Church*, London: Geoffrey Chapman, 1994, especially paras 1905–12.

Christian Aid, *Tax for the Common Good: A Study of Tax and Morality*, London: Christian Aid, 2014.

Council of Churches for Britain and Ireland, *Unemployment and the Future of Work*, London: CCBI, 1997.

Figgis, John Neville, *Studies of Political Thought from Gerson to Grotius, 1414–1625* [1907], 2nd edn, Cambridge: Cambridge University Press, 1916.

Finnis, John, *Natural Law and Natural Rights*, Oxford: Clarendon Press, 1980.

—— *Human Rights and Common Good, Collected Essays*, Vol. III, Oxford: Oxford University Press, 2011.

Pope Francis, Apostolic Exhortation, *Evangelii gaudium*, 2013.*

Glasman, Maurice, *Unnecessary Suffering: Managing Market Utopia*, London/New York: Verso, 1996.

Gorringe, Timothy, *The Common Good and the Global Emergency: God and the Built Environment*, Cambridge: Cambridge University Press, 2011.

Gregg, Samuel and James, Harold (eds), *Natural Law, Economics and the Common Good*, Exeter: Imprint Academic, 2005.

Hayek, F. A., *The Fatal Conceit*, London: Routledge, 1988.

Hollenbach, David, *The Common Good and Christian Ethics*, Cambridge: Cambridge University Press, 2002.

Insole, Christopher and Dwan, David (eds), *The Cambridge Companion to Edmund Burke*, Cambridge: Cambridge University Press, 2012.

Ipgrave, M. (ed.), *Building a Better Bridge: Muslims, Christians and the Common Good*, Washington, DC: Georgetown University Press, 2008.

Pope John XXIII, *Mater et magistra*, 1961.*

Pope John Paul II, *Laborem exercens*, 1981.*

—— *Sollicitudo rei socialis*, 1987.*

—— *Centesimus annus*, 1991.*

Kohn, Marek, *Trust, Self-Interest and the Common Good*, Oxford: Oxford University Press, 2008.

Pope Leo XIII, *Rerum novarum*, 1891.*

Longley, Clifford, *Just Money: How Catholic Social Teaching can Redeem Capitalism*, London: Theos, 2014.

MacIntyre, A., *After Virtue*, revd edn, London: Duckworth, 1985.

—— 'Politics, Philosophy and the Common Good', reprinted in *The MacIntyre Reader*, ed. Kelvin Knight, Cambridge: Polity Press, 1998.

Maritain, Jacques, *The Person and the Common Good*, London: Geoffrey Bles, 1948.

Marquand, D, *Mammon's Kingdom: An Essay on Britain, Now*, London: Allen Lane, 2014.

Marx, Karl, *The Communist Manifesto: A Modern Edition* [1848, this translation 1888], London: Verso, 1998.

Miller, Patrick and McCann, Dennis P. (eds), *In Search of the Common Good*, London/New York: T & T Clark, 2005.

Nussbaum, Martha, 'Aristotelian Social Democracy', in R. Bruce Douglass et al. (eds), *Liberalism and the Good*, New York/London: Routledge, 1990, pp. 203–52.

O'Brien, David J. and Shannon, Thomas A. (eds), *Catholic Social Thought: The Documentary Heritage*, Maryknoll, NY: Orbis Books, 2005.
O'Neill, Onora, *A Question of Trust*, Cambridge: Cambridge University Press, 2002.

Pally, Marcia, *The New Evangelicals: Expanding the Vision of the Common Good*, Grand Rapids, MI: Eerdmans, 2011.
Pope Pius XI, *Quadragesimo anno*, 1931.*
Plant, Raymond, *Politics, Theology and History*, Cambridge: Cambridge University Press, 2001.
Pontifical Council for Justice and Peace, *Compendium of the Social Doctrine of the Church*, 2004.*

Rawls, John, *A Theory of Justice*, revd edn, Oxford/New York: Oxford University Press, 1999.
—— *Political Liberalism*, New York: Columbia University Press, 1993.
Riordan, Patrick SJ, *A Politics of the Common Good*, Dublin: Institute of Public Administration, 1996.
—— *A Grammar of the Common Good: Speaking of Globalization*, London: Continuum, 2008.
—— *Global Ethics and Global Common Goods*, London: Bloomsbury, 2014.

Sacks, Jonathan, *The Politics of Hope*, London: Jonathan Cape, 1997.
—— *The Dignity of Difference: How to Avoid the Clash of Civilisations* [2002], revd edn, London: Continuum, 2003.
Sagovsky, Nicholas, *Christian Tradition and the Practice of Justice*, London: SPCK, 2008.
Sandel, Michael, *What Money Can't Buy: The Moral Limits of Markets*, London: Allen Lane, 2012.
Sheppard, David, *Built as a City: God and the Urban World Today*, London: Hodder and Stoughton, 1974.
—— *Bias to the Poor*, London: Hodder and Stoughton, 1983.
Sheppard, David and Worlock, Derek, *Better Together: Christian Partnership in a Hurt City*, London: Hodder and Stoughton, 1988.
Skidelsky, Robert and Skidelsky, Edward, *How Much is Enough? The Love of Money and the Case for the Good Life*, London: Allen Lane, 2012.
Smith, Adam, *The Wealth of Nations*, ed. Andrew Skinner, 2 vols, London: Penguin, 1970.
Spencer, N. and Chaplin, J. (eds), *God and Government*, London: SPCK, 2009.
Stanlis, Peter, *Edmund Burke and the Natural Law*, Lafayette: Huntington House, 1986.

Tawney, R. H., *The Acquisitive Society* [1921], London/Glasgow: Fontana, 1961.
—— *Equality* [1931], 4th edn, revised, London: George Allen, 1964.

Temple, William, *Christianity and Social Order* [1942], London: Shepheard-Walwyn and SPCK, 1976.

Vallely, Paul (ed.), *The New Politics: Catholic Social Teaching for the Twenty-First Century*, London: SCM Press, 1998.

Vatican II, *Gaudium et spes (The Pastoral Constitution on the Church in the Modern World)*, 1965.*

Volf, Miroslav, *A Public Faith: How Followers of Christ should serve the Common Good*, Grand Rapids, MI: Eerdmans, 2011.

Wallis, Jim, *On God's Side: What Religion Forgets and Politics Hasn't Learned about Serving the Common Good*, Oxford Lion/ Grand Rapids, MI: Brazos, 2013.

Wilkinson, Richard and Pickett, Kate, *The Spirit Level, Why More Equal Societies Almost Always do Better*, London: Allen Lane, 2009.

Williams, Rowan, *Faith in the Public Square*, London: Bloomsbury, 2012.

*All texts of official Roman Catholic documents are available on the Vatican website: www.vatican.va/offices/papal_docs_list.html, or classified according to the issuing Pope: http://w2.vatican.va/content/vatican/en.html.

Name and Subject Index